Hiking Maryland and Delaware

A Guide to the States' Greatest Hiking Adventures

Fourth Edition

Terry Cummings

FALCONGUIDES

ESSEX, CONNECTICUT

To my father, my friends, and all the trail managers and
volunteers without whom none of this would have been possible.

FALCONGUIDES®

An imprint of Globe Pequot, the trade division of
The Rowman & Littlefield Publishing Group, Inc.
4501 Forbes Blvd., Ste. 200
Lanham, MD 20706
www.rowman.com

Falcon and FalconGuides are registered trademarks and Make Adventure Your Story is a trademark of
The Rowman & Littlefield Publishing Group, Inc

Distributed by NATIONAL BOOK NETWORK

Copyright © 2024 The Rowman & Littlefield Publishing Group, Inc.
Maps by Melissa Baker and The Rowman & Littlefield Publishing Group, Inc.

British Library Cataloguing in Publication Information available

Library of Congress Cataloging-in-Publication Data

Names: Cummings, Terry, author.
Title: Hiking Maryland and Delaware : a guide to the states' greatest hiking adventures / Terry Cummings.
Description: Fourth edition. | Essex, Connecticut : FalconGuides, [2024] | Series: A Falcon guide |
   "Maps by Melissa Baker and The Rowman & Littlefield Publishing Group, Inc."—Copyright page. | Includes
   bibliographical references and index. | Summary: "Hiking Maryland and Delaware explores
   56 easy-to-follow and easy-to-get-to hikes from rugged mountains and old-growth hardwood forests
   to salt-marsh wildlife preserves and Piedmont stream valleys"—Provided by publisher.
Identifiers: LCCN 2023050720 (print) | LCCN 2023050721 (ebook) | ISBN
   9781493076451 (paperback : acid-free paper) | ISBN 9781493076468 (epub)
Subjects: LCSH: Hiking—Maryland—Guidebooks. | Hiking—Delaware—Guidebooks. |
   Walking—Maryland—Guidebooks. | Walking—Delaware—Guidebooks. | Maryland—Guidebooks. |
   Delaware—Guidebooks.
Classification: LCC GV199.42.M3 L55 2024 (print) | LCC GV199.42.M3
   (ebook) | DDC 796.5109752—dc23/eng/20231227
LC record available at https://lccn.loc.gov/2023050720
LC ebook record available at https://lccn.loc.gov/2023050721

∞™ The paper used in this publication meets the minimum requirements of American National Standard
for Information Sciences—Permanence of Paper for Printed Library Materials, ANSI/NISO Z39.48-1992.

Contents

The Hikes

HELP US KEEP THIS GUIDE UP TO DATE

Every effort has been made by the author and editors to make this guide as accurate and useful as possible. However, many things can change after a guide is published—trails are rerouted, regulations change, facilities come under new management, and so forth.

We would love to hear from you concerning your experiences with this guide and how you feel it could be improved and kept up to date. While we may not be able to respond to all comments and suggestions, we'll take them to heart, and we'll also make certain to share them with the author. Please send your comments and suggestions to the following address:

Falcon Guides
Reader Response/Editorial Department
Falconeditorial@rowman.com

Thanks for your input, and happy trails!

Overview

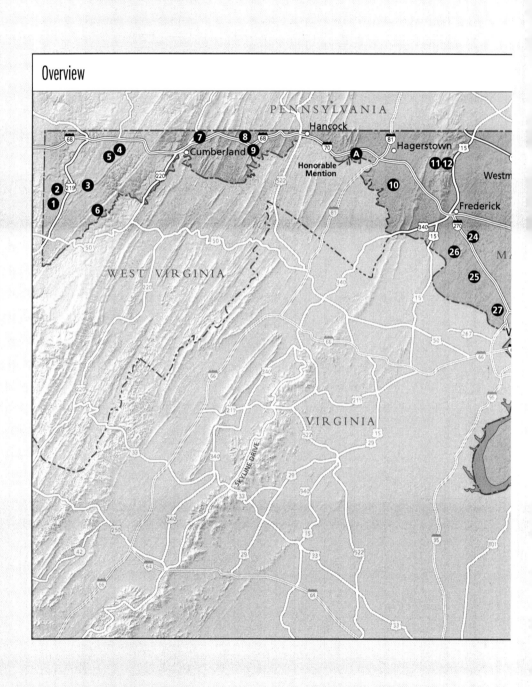

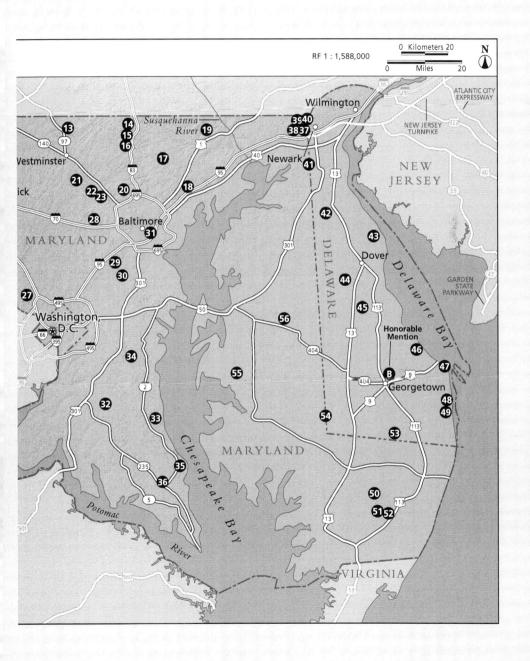

RF 1 : 1,588,000

0   Kilometers   20

0   Miles   20

N

Acknowledgments

As in the third edition, I thank David Lillard, author of the first two editions, for his trust that I could step in for him and build upon his vision.

Thank you to the many agency staffers and land managers in Delaware and Maryland who took the time to help ensure the accuracy of information contained in the guide. These courteous folks are truly dedicated public servants, doing their work under considerable budget constraints with joy and a deep appreciation and respect for the lands they manage. With their help, these hikes engender a feeling of outdoor adventure.

In addition, the trail managers and land trusts rely on many volunteers and under-paid interns in their efforts to preserve the wild, which is quietly but quickly disappearing. Thank them if you see them on the trail or in the office.

Introduction

You would not think it could be such a secret to residents, but here it is: Delaware and Maryland are wonderful day-hiking states. It is true that remote backpacking experiences are rare in both states, with the rugged mountains of western Maryland offering the only real places to disappear into the landscape for a few days. But if you are looking to spend a day wandering through hardwood forests, along meandering creeks, or through the mixed scent of salt water and beach pines, both states have plenty to offer.

Although housing development exploded in the Washington, D.C., to Wilmington, Delaware, corridor in the past thirty years, both states have invested heavily in conserving land for outdoor recreation. Two examples illustrate the types of hiking lands found most often in both states: White Clay Creek State Park, in Delaware's New Castle County, offers hikers several thousand acres of woodland rambles, despite its proximity to tens of thousands of homes. Remarkably, White Clay Creek still supports a wild brook trout population. Likewise, the Gunpowder Falls State Park system in Maryland, connected by the riverway, preserves the wild feeling of "fall zone" and piedmont stream valleys. It too boasts of some of the best trout fishing in the state. These valleys attracted settlers to the region more than three centuries ago. Now they are within minutes of one of America's largest cities—and yet, you can escape the bustle for a few hours.

Most of the hiking trails in these states are only a few miles in length, with the average being 3 to 5 miles long. For many hikers, a hike of that length does not make

Huge ant mound in Little Bennett Regional Park.

a destination in and of itself. The truth is, few out-of-staters travel to either of these states just for the hiking, except those hiking the Appalachian Trail, the Chesapeake & Ohio Canal Towpath, or the Allegheny Mountains in Allegany (yes, they are spelled differently) and Garrett Counties of Maryland. Thankfully, there is a lot to see and experience that offers a perfect complement to hiking.

Often it is a small town or crossroads near the trail that rounds out the hiking day. For example, it is hard to think about hiking Snavely Ford Trail in Antietam National Battlefield without considering the ice cream that follows in Sharpsburg.

Many of the trails in both states are managed to accommodate bicycles and horses as well as human feet. Sometimes this can put a damper on the attempt to find solitude, especially when you have hiked several miles into a lonely wood only to have a bicycle whiz past. However, relations among so-called user groups in these states are good for the most part, in no small part due to the education efforts of mountain-bicycling groups in the area. Both states do restrict bicycle and horse traffic on a portion of their trails, allowing hikers to find the narrow, quiet footpaths they crave.

The Hiking Regions

This book is divided into three hiking regions: West from Catoctin, West of the Chesapeake Bay and Susquehanna River, and Land between the Bays.

West from Catoctin. Just west of Frederick, Maryland, the rolling piedmont gives way to a series of northeast-leading ridges. Catoctin Mountain is home to a national park, three state parks, and a municipal forest—all strung together to provide plentiful day-hiking opportunities. The Catoctin Trail, a pathway winding along the length of the mountain, makes possible a short but sweet backpacking trip.

Although the border between Maryland's western, mountainous counties lies atop South Mountain, Catoctin Mountain actually serves as the mental demarcation line between mountain hiking in Maryland and everything to the east. The farther west you go, the taller and more remote the mountains you will find. Green Ridge State Forest, at more than 40,000 acres, and Savage River State Forest, at 53,000 acres, are the two largest land areas devoted to recreation. The backpacking options are there but limited, yet there are plenty of trails to take you into the woods where you can find a quiet place to spend a night. In addition, there are "primitive" campsites along the back roads throughout these forests that provide for a reasonably secluded base camp.

In this West from Catoctin region, you will find the mountainous terrain, waterfalls, and tumbling streams beneath hemlock groves that capture the spirit of any hiker. Unfortunately, in many of the western forests, the great stands of hemlocks are succumbing to the hemlock woolly adelgid, an invasive species from Asia. In the near future, much of western Maryland may be devoid of this climax species.

A NOTE ABOUT INVADERS AND A STORM

Since the last edition of this guide was published, the region continues to see noticeable changes in its flora and fauna. In our parks and woodlands, and indeed along many of our roadways, invasives have overwhelmed much of the natural fauna. Multiflora rose, mile-a-minute, kudzu and vines of all sorts, and English ivy are a few of the concerning species. The *Bay Journal* describes invasives as "nonnative (species) that cause or are likely to cause economic or environmental harm." They are easy to spot as they crowd out the native species. By contrast, you will invariably see sections of trails where you cannot see through the under-story and those sections that are clear of invasives allowing you to see through the forest.

It is a sad and alarming commentary on the human footprint. For example: The Asian invader the hemlock woolly adelgid has destroyed much of the ancient hemlock forests in west-ern Virginia and is moving north into Maryland. The hemlocks are the East Coast's version of California's giant redwoods, with some living to 400 years old. But they are disappearing. The Maryland Department of Natural Resources is working to prevent a devastating loss of these ancient giants, and you will see rectangular aluminum strips on some hemlocks indicating that they have been treated, but it's difficult to inoculate thousands of acres of state forest.

You can learn more about forest invaders through the Maryland Department of Natural Resources at https://dnr.maryland.gov/forests/Pages/programapps/pests.aspx.

And then there was the storm that devastated Maryland. In 2012, a derecho, a term most of us had never heard before, came through at 35 miles per hour with winds of 65 to 85 mph, cracking limbs, shearing off tops of trees, and blowing down hundreds of long-standing giants. It was something not seen in a long while, if ever. It devastated almost every hiking area in Maryland detailed in this book. You would see pines literally snapped off 30 feet from the ground; Swallow Falls lost many trees this way. Huge oak and tulip poplar were blown over like toys. Trees crashing down took others with them, creating a tangled mess of branches, trunks, and 10-foot-high root balls. It was an amazing site given the force that it wielded; the roar of the wind and snapping of timber must have been terrifying. Today, more than a decade later, the forests have recovered, and the damage is hardly noticeable but for the rotting hulks of oak and poplar. In part, thanks to the resource managers, the forest renewed itself and maybe even flourished in places, but the multiflora rose is today's scourge. I commend the trail managers, their agencies, the nonprofits, and the many volunteers who endeavor to keep these places wild, open, and free of the invaders.

West of the Chesapeake Bay and Susquehanna River. The content of this section—covering trails east of Frederick, Maryland, and west of the Susquehanna-Chesapeake waterscapes—is grouped together here as much for its proximity to Baltimore, Washington, D.C., and Annapolis as for any topographic or geologic similarities. From the almost lunar surface of the serpentine grasslands in Soldiers Delight to the rolling agricultural lands of Baltimore and Carroll Counties, to the brackish still-water creeks of the Chesapeake's western shore, this region has all the physiographic complexity of a small country. There are few trailheads in this region that cannot be reached within 2 hours on a weekend morning, and the region happens to be home to some of the most overlooked hiking trails in the east. Residents of the Baltimore-Washington metropolis will be amazed at how much hiking there is so close to home, even in Baltimore city.

Most remarkable about hiking in this region are the surprises in store on every hike, such as the lovely river walk along the Torrey C. Brown Rail Trail and the old carriage road that follows a narrow ridge above Big Pipe Creek in Carroll County. When you watch a blue heron grab a fish dinner out of the ponds at Patuxent River Wildlife Area, you have to remind yourself you are hiking in the epicenter of 7 million people.

Land between the Bays. This region encompasses two distinct areas essentially east of the Chesapeake Bay and the Susquehanna River. First is Cecil County, Maryland, and northern New Castle County, Delaware—two counties that were transformed from mostly rural to mostly suburban in twenty short years beginning in the 1970s. But for residents, even the workaday routine need not be an impediment to hiking. With Lums Pond, White Clay Creek State Park, and Brandywine Creek State Park nearby, you can stow a pair of boots in the trunk and hit the trail whenever the gift of an extra 2 hours presents itself.

Below the Chesapeake & Delaware Canal is the Delmarva Peninsula. Here, hiking opportunities are found in the salt marsh wildlife preserves, the pine-covered state forests, and the shores of inland bays. Mountain snobs, who believe the quality of the hiking experience is directly proportional to the elevation above sea level, will be amazed to lose themselves amid the tall shore grasses and backwaters. One winter hike in Delmarva, with its abundance of migrating waterfowl, is all it will take to turn any hiker into a cool-weather lowlander.

How to Use This Guide

Hikes in this book were selected with two guiding principles: Are they easy to find and easy to follow, and would I recommend them to a friend? Few things are more frustrating than spending an hour trying to find a trailhead to a 2-hour hike or spending half your time trying to match the trail before you to a map in your hand. Secondly, the trails must be worthy of telling your friends about when you get home.

We have selected not only the best day hikes in Delaware and Maryland but also ones that even novice hikers can navigate. Unless otherwise noted, all hikes in this guide have minimal elevation gain. This book is for hikers of all abilities and interests. If you have never hiked before, this book will put you on the trail in safe, beautiful settings. For seasoned hikers, this book will help you discover new destinations.

To put this book to work for you, start with the overview map on pages vi and vii. Each hike is numbered, and its location is represented on the map by its number. Then go to the Trail Finder (pages 14–17) to find a hike that matches your plans for the day—for example, a hike for kids, a walk along the water, a snowshoe hike. Then find your hike listed by number in the table of contents. Go to that hike's pages and read about what you will see.

Be sure to read the entire entry for a hike before you go (and make a copy to take with you) in case there is anything special you need to know to enhance your enjoyment of or safety for the trip. For example, the trails in Herrington Manor and Swallow Falls State Parks are groomed for cross-country skiing. In other hikes, under the "Special considerations" heading, you are told which trails pass through lands managed for hunting in autumn and winter. That is important to know! *Read the entire hike description before you leave.*

To really make use of this guidebook and discover the best trails in Maryland and Delaware, keep a copy of this book in your car, right next to that extra pair of boots or running shoes in the trunk. Delaware's moniker as the "Small Wonder" holds true for hiking trails in both states. There are many, many fine short hikes that you may never make a destination of but will be glad you visited when you had a chance.

The Appalachian Trail: Long-Distance Hiking and Backpacking

There are only a handful of truly worthy backpacking trips in Maryland and none in Delaware. By worthy, we mean hikes that will keep you on the trail for more than 25 miles and longer than a couple of days—and that do not include a great deal of road walking. Those few hikes are adequately documented in other sources and are therefore not the subject of this book. Contact information for those sources is available in the appendices of this guide.

Among the most notable backpacking trips in Maryland are the 40-plus miles of the Appalachian Trail in the Old Line State. The majority of those miles traverse South Mountain from the Potomac to the Pennsylvania line. While there are many opportunities for day hikes along the AT, most involve either a two-car shuttle or hiking in and hiking out. Because of the narrow corridor preserved for the trail by the State of Maryland, the number of loop hikes utilizing the AT and side trails does not compare to, for example, the Virginia sections of the trail.

Like most of the trails in the United States, the AT is maintained by volunteers. The Appalachian Trail Conservancy (https://appalachiantrail.org) in Harpers Ferry, West Virginia, is a nonprofit organization charged with overall management responsibility of the "longest national park," under a unique partnership arrangement with the National Park Service. The volunteers of the Potomac Appalachian Trail Club (PATC) perform the on-the-ground work that keeps the trail open and safe in Maryland. The PATC also maintains some of the trails in this guide. If you would like to help and become a volunteer, contact them at www.patc.net.

The longest trail in Maryland is the 184-mile Chesapeake & Ohio Canal National Historical Park. Begun in 1828 as a transportation route between the commercial centers in the East and the frontier resources of the West, the C&O Canal stretches along the Potomac River from Georgetown in Washington, D.C., to Cumberland, Maryland. Remnant canal locks, lockhouses, and other historical features interpret the past along the waterway known as the "Nation's River." The trail is the former towpath followed by the mules that pulled cargo barges downriver. It also provides incredible up-close contact with the Potomac for many miles while traveling through woodlands and small towns.

It is a wonderful trail, but like the AT in Maryland, there are limited opportunities for loop hikes. Most of the day hikes on the C&O Canal are "in-and-out" walks, and all but one of the backpacking trips along it require a shuttle or two cars. This edition of the guide eliminated the Paw Paw tunnel loop as the tunnel is being renovated. The trail is managed by the National Park Service and is supported by the nonprofit C&O Canal Association.

Three other backpacking trips bear noting. A 25-mile loop created from trails in Maryland's Savage River State Forest and New Germany State Park requires a longish stretch of road walking but is otherwise an enjoyable and very popular hike. The Green Ridge Hiking Trail covers some 19 miles as it climbs from the Potomac River and winds its way north to Pennsylvania, where it connects with Pennsylvania's Mid State Trail to make a hike of more than 200 miles. It is a lovely hike but also one requiring a shuttle arrangement. Finally, one loop utilizes portions of the C&O Canal Towpath and the Green Ridge Hiking Trail to assemble a very nice 50-plus-mile hike. To obtain information on these hikes, contact the Potomac Appalachian Trail Club.

That is the best of it for backpacking. But again, that does not mean that other "day hikes" in this book do not offer splendid spots for an overnight in the woods, even if you are hiking only several miles.

Being Prepared: Safety and Hazards

Here are a few basic planning strategies and precautions to keep you safe on the trail. For a thorough understanding of backcountry travel and safety, consult the Falcon-Guides *Wilderness First Aid* and Will Harmon's excellent *Wild Country Companion*.

Planning and Preparation
The two easiest ways to stay safe when hiking the trails in this book are to plan ahead and to stay on the trail. When you head out for a hike, especially to a backcountry location that is new to you, take a few precautions. Pack a little extra food, warm clothing, rain gear, and anything else you may need if you are forced to rough it for

the night. We are not talking about packing a tent and sleeping bag every time you go out for a day hike. But when you're hiking in the "West from Catoctin" region, it is a good idea to know what you need to survive for a night, even uncomfortably, if you are forced to do so.

A second precaution is to always tell someone where you are going, your basic itinerary, and when you plan to return. If you have told a spouse or roommate that you will be home by noon on Sunday, then you know someone will be looking for you if you do not come home. This is especially important when hiking in western Maryland, where the woods are wonderfully deep. Remember, most tragedies start out simply. All it takes is an unexpected slip on a rock to twist or break an ankle. If you have not left word about where you are, no one will be looking for you.

Although Maryland and Delaware are not known as states with vast wilderness areas, anyone can get lost in the woods by straying from the trail. Experienced hikers can and do get lost. If you do unwittingly leave the trail you are supposed to be on, follow your footsteps back until you find the place where you went astray.

If you are totally lost and you have taken the precautions outlined above, the worst that will happen is that you will spend an uncomfortable night in the woods. Stay put, eat your extra food, find shelter, and wait until morning. If you have left word with someone of your whereabouts, someone will be searching for you soon. Whatever you do, do not go scrambling around in the darkness; that is an easy way to get hurt.

An essential precaution is to carry a first-aid kit. The Hiker's Checklist in appendix D lists some of the items every hiker should carry. Your personalized first-aid kit should contain a couple of days' worth of any prescription medications you take, a bee-sting kit if you have a known allergy, your eyeglasses if you are hiking in contact lenses, and other similar items. When hiking in the "West from Catoctin" region of this guide, a snakebite kit is also recommended.

Blowdowns caused by storms can be dangerous. Watch for broken-off, overhanging branches that can be dislodged by an unexpected wind gust. Trail managers call these "widow-makers" as they can be deadly. Avoid walking under dangling branches. Contact the trail office for the latest information on trail closures.

Your Feet and Footwear

The proper footwear is arguably the most important consideration of all when it comes to being comfortable, dry, and pain-free. You will see lots of different footwear, from sandals and sneakers to hiking shoes and boots on the trail. My advice is to avoid the former and stick with the latter. Hiking footwear is designed to support your feet (and ankles) on trails full of roots, rocks, and wetness. (Sneakers aren't.) When buying hiking shoes, look for ones with a stiff sole to protect the bottoms of your feet from the constant pounding over broken rocks or roots. Hiking boots help support your ankles and are preferred when backpacking. Today many hiking shoes and boots are waterproof, a serious bonus in the rain or wet terrain.

Make sure you have room in the toe box but not so much as to allow your foot to slide into the toe when descending a steep slope. Be sure your heel doesn't rise out of the shoe cavity. And trim your toenails and be sure to carry moleskin for hotspots that will turn to blisters if not addressed promptly.

And lastly, try to avoid sprained ankles by not stepping on roots that run parallel to the trail. Rather, step on roots perpendicular to the trail to avoid sliding off and twisting an ankle. And avoid loose rocks that could shift with your weight and turn an ankle.

Under Your Feet

Most of us walk with our heads down to watch where we are going; it's only natural. This is especially true when you are hiking. So, when you're watching your step, keep an eye open for what's on the trail. You may see a 4-inch millipede or a tawny toad, or scat from vole to fox to coyote, or even owl pellets and bones. There may be animal tracks, especially in wet areas. Fallen leaves, seeds, nuts, and "pine cones" indicate what's over your head, and flowers adorn the trail borders. Its all a sign of the life in the woods or fields you are passing through.

About Cell Phones

The first thing is to charge it. The second thing is to have additional battery power or a solar recharger. Third thing is to have a good app if that's what you're relying on, but really, you won't be because you are reading this. And remember you may be in a remote area where coverage is spotty at best. Bring it with you but turn it off and follow the paths and directions laid out in this book.

Animals and Critters

When hiking in the mountains of western Maryland, if you are very lucky, you will see a black bear or a rattlesnake. There is no need to be afraid of either if you keep your distance. In general, black bears stay clear of humans, but if cornered or hungry, their behavior can be unpredictable. If you happen upon a bear, make sure you leave it an escape route so that it will not feel threatened. Back away slowly and it will go about its business. For an excellent, short book on bear behavior, read FalconGuide's *Bear Aware*.

Rattlesnakes and/or copperheads are most often seen sunning themselves on rocks or stretched out across a trail where the sun is poking through the trees. Give the snake plenty of room when you walk by. When hiking in the mountains, make a habit of stepping onto rocks or logs and then over them. Do not stretch to put your foot down just beyond the rock or log where you cannot see the ground. The two most common snakebite incidents involve reaching around a rock or tree or stepping into rocky crevices where you cannot see. Watch your step. Rather than describe every critter, hazard, and remedy in this book, again we refer you to two comprehensive resources: *Wild Country Companion* and *Wilderness First Aid*. Carry the latter in your daypack.

A Word about Water

Your best bet is to assume that no stream or spring you encounter is safe to drink from without treatment, with the exception of protected springs emerging from the ground or pipe before your eyes. In both the "West of the Chesapeake Bay and Susquehanna River" and the "Land between the Bays" regions, agricultural runoff and suburban nonpoint-source pollution compromise water safety. In the more rural areas, the problem is a parasite called *Giardia lamblia*, a protozoan that when ingested can cause "backpacker's diarrhea," a mild name for the intense abdominal cramps brought on by the illness. Additionally, it may be dangerous to swim in or allow dogs to swim in or drink water where there are harmful algae blooms. Check with the park manager if there's a concern.

In the "West from Catoctin" region, in addition to the giardia from farm and wild animals, streams in the Allegheny Mountains suffer from the presence of heavy metals leaching into the waterways from mining operations.

Because this book consists primarily of day hikes, let us assume that you will either bring your water with you or get it at the trailhead. In the introduction to each hike, there is a heading called "Trailhead facilities." If water is available at the trailhead, it is noted there.

Now a word about how much to drink. Without getting too technical, drink a lot, especially in summer. In the heat and humidity of Maryland and Delaware summers, plan for about a quart for every 90 minutes you will be on the trail—assuming you have downed at least that much just before hitting the trail. *Wild Country Companion* will give you the precise details about figuring your body's need for water at various altitudes and temperatures, but here is an easy guideline for the day hikes in this book.

1. Hydrate the day before your hike and the day of. Do not make coffee the only beverage you consume before starting out on a summer hike. The best way to avoid thirst-related problems is to drink before your body is crying for it.
2. Pack at least one full quart-size water bottle.
3. Have an extra quart bottle or more in the car for your return.
4. On longer hikes, invest in a simple water-purification system, and carry it with you just in case. A bottle of iodine tablets stowed in your daypack will usually get you through a one-day water emergency.

Trail Etiquette

Courtesy on the trail is contagious. Here are some guidelines.

- Go gently. Observe the Zero-Impact Hiking guidelines outlined later in this section.
- Go courteously. Because most of the trails in Maryland and Delaware are used by hikers and bicyclists—and many by equestrians as well—a few rules of the trails help ensure enjoyment by everyone. Hikers should yield to horses. Yes, horses are big and their dung is dropped right on the trail, but they have to deal with you, too. Bicyclists are supposed to yield to hikers, but there are times when it is easier

for hikers to step aside. Work it out courteously. In Maryland, most of the trails open only to hikers are designated as such because of a wildlands designation or the fragility of the ecology. Report trail-use violations to park officials.

- Avoid "citizen trails": those shortcuts not on the map nor sanctioned by the trail managers. They can pose safety issues and cause serious erosion problems.

- Being courteous also means not hogging the scenery. If you have made it to the top and there is limited space from which to enjoy the view, do not bring a crowd to spend a day in the way of everyone else trying to get a look. Get there, savor it, and then let others enjoy it. It is annoying to hike a few miles to a popular feature and then be made to feel like you are an intruder.

- Go quietly. If you can be heard from more than a few feet away when hiking, you are talking too loudly. Not only are you destroying the quiet for other hikers, but you are scaring off the deer, the foxes, and all the other wildlife that are seen only by those who go quietly.

Seasons and Weather

Bug Season

If you live in Delaware or east of Allegany County, Maryland, you know that summer means heat and humidity. It also means mosquitoes in the woods and marshlands. In the section that introduces each hike in this guide, there is an entry called "Best season." You will notice that a number of hikes omit summertime from their season. In general, this is an effort to spare you the misery of mosquitoes. If you are prepared for the annoyance or have a high tolerance for these pests, take the necessary precautions (use repellent) and hike away.

By far the most treacherous creature on Delaware or Maryland trails is the deer tick. The best precaution against ticks is to hike in long pants with the cuffs tucked in. A pair of polyester-nylon blend pants will protect you from the elements without making you uncomfortably hot. After the hike be sure to check your legs, torso, and head for these little arachnids.

Unfortunately for naturalists, nothing else is as effective for repelling mosquitoes and ticks as the chemical compound DEET, found in most insect repellants. Never put DEET directly on your skin, and never put it on the skin of a child. If you use a DEET-based product, apply it to your clothing, especially around the ankles and wrists. Some hikers spray a little on the outside of their hats.

There are now many products on the market that contain no DEET. Instead they contain everything from citronella oil to complex concoctions of other organic compounds. These are the ones to use on your skin.

Stormy Weather

Another summer phenomenon in most of the United States is the afternoon thunderstorm. Always check local weather forecasts before heading out, and think twice about starting a hike when electrical storms are forecast. If you are caught in an electrical storm, here are a few basic precautions:

- Find shelter in a low-lying area, preferably amid the shorter trees and shrubs in the area. If you are hiking on a ridge when the storm hits, move off the ridge into a hollow. If possible, move to the side of the ridge opposite the side from which the storm is approaching.
- Do not run for cover under tall trees—they act as huge lightning rods. The lightning that strikes any tree in the area causes a charge known as ground current that momentarily electrifies the very ground where you are standing. In fact, most people who are killed by lightning are not actually struck by lightning— they are electrocuted by ground current.
- If you are carrying a pack constructed with a metal frame, ditch it at least 50 yards away and seek low ground. Avoid standing water or getting too close to a water source. In short, do not be on high ground and do not be in the water. Just hunker down. Thankfully, most afternoon storms do not last long. And if you can find adequate shelter, a storm on the trail can be beautiful.

Let It Snow

Western Maryland is blessed with snowy winters. This is great for hikers. Because the Maryland mountains are not prone to avalanches and the trails covered in this book travel fairly moderate terrain, snow time is a great time for hiking on snowshoes.

Snowshoe hiking is one of the fastest-growing outdoor pursuits, and for good reason. Hiking in snowshoes can take you into winter wonderlands you have never been able to access. The popularity of snowshoeing, along with several technological advances in the materials used in the construction of snowshoes, has resulted in much lower prices for the gear.

However, one note of caution: Snowshoes are not magical antigravity devices. Walking on a narrow snow-packed ledge on a trail you are not intimately familiar with should be left to the experts. A good guideline for beginner snowshoe hikers is to snowshoe on trails you have already hiked in snow-free months. In the Trail Finder there is a heading for hikes where snowshoes can provide winter access without traversing questionable terrain. For example, the hike through Green Ridge Forest's Fifteen Mile Creek Canyon may be suitable for experienced snowshoe hikers, but the terrain will present special challenges to novice snowshoers. Therefore, it is not a highlighted snowshoe hike in this book.

A few hikes in this book are on trails managed for cross-country skiing or snowmobiling. Those are noted in each hike under the "Special considerations" heading.

Backcountry Essentials

Many of the hiking areas in Maryland and Delaware are managed primarily for day use. For these areas, the only permit requirement may be an entrance fee payable at a contact station. However, some of the state parks do provide developed campsites for tent camping and recreational vehicles. The fees and facilities vary widely. Check with the appropriate managing agency listed in appendix C.

Most of the hikes in the "West from Catoctin" region allow backcountry camping. They are listed as day hikes in this guide because they are short enough to be hiked in a day. Camping is permitted in Maryland state forests, provided a backcountry permit is received from the area's managing agency. Information on these agencies can be found in appendix A.

Zero-Impact Hiking

The increased popularity of hiking has put added pressure on the natural resources that draw us to the trail. Many new hikers, bicyclists, and others have taken to the trail without learning how to protect the natural environment. You can help protect trails and become a knowledgeable steward of the land. To begin, here are eight basic steps. These are only an introduction, however. Consult the FalconGuide *Leave No Trace* for further information.

1. Plan ahead, prepare well, and prevent problems before they occur.
2. Keep noise to a minimum, and strive to be inconspicuous.
3. Pack it in, pack it out.
4. Properly dispose of anything that cannot be packed out.
5. Leave the land as you found it.
6. In popular places, concentrate use.
7. Avoid places that are lightly worn or just beginning to show signs of use.
8. Avoid "citizen trails." These are unofficial trails created by hikers as shortcuts around loops, to watercourses, overviews, or other places of interest. Citizen trails are discouraged because of their deleterious impact on natural resources. Trail managers strive to protect the very forests or wildlands you're enjoying (not to mention your safety) by directing hikers to stay on a specific path. So please stay on the designated trail and off citizen trails.

If you can become an evangelist for only one example that encapsulates the zero-impact ethic, perhaps it should be the care with which you hike along streams, marshes, and shorelines. Everyone loves a water feature. We want to get as close as we can, to dip our hot feet into cool waters, to see the shorebirds dancing and feeding their chicks. Responsible hikers always resist the urge to get too close.

The trees along these streams play an important role in the health of a stream, not the least of which is to prevent erosion of the fragile stream banks that are the habitat for riparian life. The forest cover over the Maryland and Delaware streams began to disappear long ago when the landscape was cleared for farming and timber. Unwitting hikers can do more damage by stomping down the vegetation around streams and ponds. In the marshlands in southern Maryland and Delaware, shorebirds and aquatic animals mate and inhabit these riparian zones. Stand clear and observe from a distance.

Hiking with Children

Courtesy of the gentle terrain over the two eastern regions covered by this guide, Delaware and Maryland are wonderful places for hiking with children. Kids enjoy the world differently than adults do. Many adults expect their kids to like the same things about hiking that they do. You may enjoy getting to the wide-open view of a valley. Well, that may be your mission, but it may not be your kids'. Young hikers are often more smitten with the idea of lingering to play in creeks and springs, watching the antics of insects, finding treasures on the trail, or just hanging out. Take along a hand lens so that they can see things up close, and a picture book that identifies the plants, trees, or bugs they'll see.

If you are planning a 3-hour hike, pack a light blanket or sleeping bag so that you can all enjoy a post-lunch siesta. Also, there are a number of quality "kid packs" on the market that enable you to carry a child in a special backpack. For your own enjoyment, when you first start hiking with kids, start with short outings and work up to longer day hikes.

Trail Finder

Use the following table for a quick glance at the special features of each hike.

Water features: A waterfall, significant contact with creeks and streams, or nice views of water.

Open vistas: Either an open view from a summit or hill or a broad open view of the landscape—not just a view across a field.

Primitive camping: Allows you to find a place to camp along the trail.

Campground or cabin: Developed campsites, car camping, or cabins available for rent; may require you to drive from trailhead to campground.

Snowshoeing: Annual snowfall is above average for the region and snowshoe hiking is permitted and safe for novices. Nearly every hike in both the "West of the Chesapeake Bay and Susquehanna River" and the "Land between the Bays" regions is open to, and safe for, snowshoe hiking; however, snowfalls here tend to be only a few inches at a time.

Suggested for kids: Short to moderate distance, with a minimal degree of difficulty.

Autumn colors: Nice views of deciduous trees displaying foliage, even if the views are across a field; more than just a quick glance from one place.

No car sounds: Sounds of cars do not intrude on a quarter or more of the hike, except at the beginning, where the trail may be near a roadway, or when crossing a road.

Trail Finder

	Water Features	Open Vistas	Primitive Camping	Campground or Cabin	Snowshoeing	Suggested for Kids	Autumn Colors	No Car Sounds
1. Herrington Manor SP Loop	•	•		•	•	•	•	•
2. Swallow Falls SP Loop	•	•			•	•	•	•
3. Deep Creek Vista, Deep Creek Lake SP	•	•		•	•	•	•	
4. Poplar Lick Run, New Germany SP	•			•	•	•	•	
5. Monroe Run Trail, Savage River SF	•		•		•		•	•
6. Lostland Run Loop, Potomac SF	•			•	•		•	•
7. Rocky Gap Canyon to Evitts Summit, Rocky Gap SP		•		•	•		•	
8. Twin Oaks Trail, Green Ridge SF	•	•	•		•		•	•
9. Fifteen Mile Creek, Green Ridge SF	•		•		•		•	
10. Snavely Ford Trail, Antietam National Battlefield	•	•	•	•	•	•	•	•
11. Hog Rock–Blue Ridge Summit, Catoctin Mountain Park	•	•		•	•	•	•	
12. Wolf Rock–Chimney Rock Loop, Catoctin Mountain Park	•	•	•	•	•		•	
13. Hashawha Loop, Hashawha Environmental Appreciation Area		•				•	•	•
14. BeeTree Preserve		•				•	•	•

	Water Features	Open Vistas	Primitive Camping	Campground or Cabin	Snowshoeing	Suggested for Kids	Autumn Colors	No Car Sounds
15. Torrey C. Brown Rail Trail	●	●				●	●	●
16. Lefty Kreh Fishing Trail and Gunpowder Falls North Loop, Gunpowder Falls SP	●					●	●	●
17. Sweet Air Loop, Gunpowder Falls SP	●	●				●	●	●
18. Wildlands Loop, Gunpowder Falls SP	●	●					●	
19. Susquehanna SP Loop	●	●		●			●	
20. Oregon Ridge Park Loop		●				●	●	●
21. Morgan Run Natural Environment Area	●	●			●	●	●	●
22. Soldiers Delight East Loop, Soldiers Delight Natural Environment Area	●					●		●
23. Soldiers Delight Serpentine Trail Loop, Soldiers Delight Natural Environment Area		●				●		●
24. Little Bennett Loop, Little Bennett RP	●	●		●		●	●	●
25. Schaeffer Farm Trail, Seneca Creek SP						●	●	
26. Northern Peaks Trail, Sugarloaf Mountain	●	●					●	●
27. Billy Goat Trail, Great Falls	●	●					●	●
28. Sawmill Branch Trail, Patapsco Valley SP, Hilton Area	●			●			●	●
29. Wincopin–Quarry Run Loop, Savage Park	●	●				●		

	Water Features	Open Vistas	Primitive Camping	Campground or Cabin	Snowshoeing	Suggested for Kids	Autumn Colors	No Car Sounds
30. Cash Lake Loop, Patuxent Research Refuge	•					•	•	
31. Druid Hill Loop, Jones Falls Trail, Baltimore		•				•	•	
32. Cedarville State Forest Loop	•	•				•	•	•
33. Parkers Creek Loop, American Chestnut Land Trust	•	•				•	•	•
34. Jug Bay Blue Loop, Patuxent River Park	•	•				•	•	•
35. Calvert Cliffs SP	•			•		•	•	•
36. Greenwell SP	•	•				•		•
37. Chestnut Hill Trail, Judge Morris Estate, White Clay Creek SP	•					•	•	
38. Middle Run Valley Loop, Middle Run Valley Natural Area	•				•		•	•
39. White Clay Creek Preserve Loop, White Clay Creek SP	•	•				•	•	
40. Twin Valley Trail, White Clay Creek SP	•					•	•	•
41. Swamp Forest Trail, Lums Pond SP	•	•	•	•			•	•
42. Blackbird State Forest Loop, Tybout Tract						•	•	•
43. Bombay Hook National Wildlife Refuge Loop	•	•	•					

	Water Features	Open Vistas	Primitive Camping	Campground or Cabin	Snowshoeing	Suggested for Kids	Autumn Colors	No Car Sounds
44. Norman G. Wilder Wildlife Area Loop								●
45. Killens Pondside Nature Trail, Killens Pond SP	●	●				●	●	●
46. Prime Hook National Wildlife Refuge Loop	●	●				●	●	●
47. Gordons Pond Trail, Cape Henlopen SP	●	●		●		●		●
48. Burton Island Loop, Delaware Seashore SP	●	●	●			●	●	●
49. Sea Hawk/Seahorse Trail, Holts Landing SP	●	●	●	●		●	●	●
50. Paul Leifer Nature Trail, Furnace Town Historic Site						●	●	●
51. Pocomoke State Forest Trail				●		●	●	●
52. Bald Cypress Nature Trail, Milburn Landing SP	●			●		●	●	●
53. Bob Trail, Trap Pond SP	●	●	●	●		●	●	●
54. Nanticoke Wildlife Area Loop		●				●	●	●
55. Old Schoolhouse—Holly Tree Loop, Wye Island	●	●		●		●	●	●
56. Tuckahoe Creek Loop, Tuckahoe SP	●			●		●		●

Map Legend

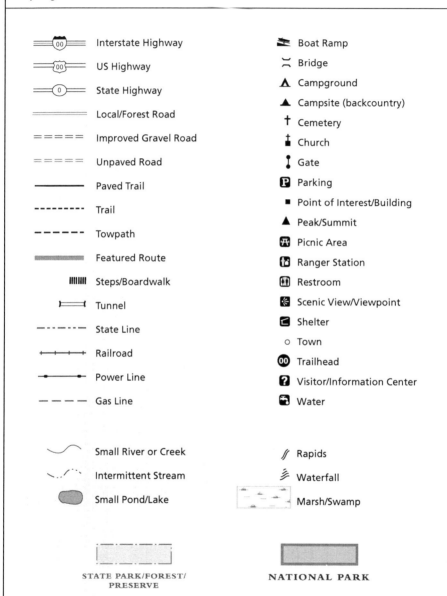

Interstate Highway	Boat Ramp
US Highway	Bridge
State Highway	Campground
Local/Forest Road	Campsite (backcountry)
Improved Gravel Road	Cemetery
Unpaved Road	Church
Paved Trail	Gate
Trail	Parking
Towpath	Point of Interest/Building
Featured Route	Peak/Summit
Steps/Boardwalk	Picnic Area
Tunnel	Ranger Station
State Line	Restroom
Railroad	Scenic View/Viewpoint
Power Line	Shelter
Gas Line	Town
	Trailhead
	Visitor/Information Center
	Water
Small River or Creek	Rapids
Intermittent Stream	Waterfall
Small Pond/Lake	Marsh/Swamp

STATE PARK/FOREST/
PRESERVE

NATIONAL PARK

West from Catoctin

Use caution and good sense at the Swallow Falls swimming hole.

1 Herrington Manor State Park Loop

A woodland stroll leads through a pine grove, a forgotten cemetery, and the mixed hardwood forest surrounding Herrington Lake. This is a wonderful, easy hike for a family with young children. The path is wide and mostly grassy, with beautiful stands of American cherry and a variety of lush ferns. The hike finishes at the lake's beach.

Start: The hike begins at the trailhead sign to Swallow Falls at the far end of the parking area.
Distance: 4.2-mile loop
Hiking time: About 1.5 hours
Difficulty: Moderate
Elevation gain: Minimal
Trail surface: Mostly grass
Best season: Year-round
Schedule: 8 a.m. to sunset
Other trail users: Mountain bikers
Canine compatibility: Leashed dogs permitted on trails
Land status: Herrington Manor State Park; Garrett County, Maryland, near the West Virginia border, about 200 miles west of Washington, D.C.
Nearest town: Oakland

Fees and permits: A per-person entrance fee is charged from Memorial Day to Labor Day. For the rest of year, the fee is per car.
Camping: Cabins are available for a fee with advance registration.
Trailhead facilities: Snack bar (seasonal), water, restrooms
Maps: USGS Oakland MD
Trail contact: Herrington Manor State Park, 222 Herrington Lane, Oakland, MD; (301) 334-9180; herringtonmanor.statepark @maryland.gov; https://dnr.maryland.gov/ publiclands/Pages/western/herrington.aspx
Special considerations: When snow is on the ground, plan to visit these trails only on skis. The hike passes through areas managed for hunting; inquire at the park office.

Finding the trailhead: From I-68, take exit 14A and drive 19 miles south on US 219, passing Deep Creek Lake, and turn right onto Mayhew Inn Road. Drive 4.3 miles north, and then turn left onto Sang Run Road. In 0.25 mile turn right onto Swallow Falls Road, which becomes Herrington Manor Road and leads west to the park entrance in 8.7 miles (4 miles past the entrance to Swallow Falls State Park). Follow signs to trails and the parking lot. (This is also the trailhead for the trail to Swallow Falls.) GPS: N39 27.207' / W79 27.037'

The Hike

This leisurely walk follows ski trails near Herrington Lake. The beach, concession, and kayak rentals make the park an ideal spot to spend the day hiking and enjoying the lake.

Start the hike by walking back up the park road 0.3 mile. The trailhead is not well marked, but you will see a yellow blaze on a post to your left. This is a loop trail to an old cemetery, and it circles around a large grove of planted pines. The path is identifiable largely by mowing. Enter the woods, and go right at the fork near a giant oak.

Begin circling the pine grove at 0.4 mile. The straight, evenly spaced trunks here are wonderfully reminiscent of Ansel Adams's photography. Enter a clearing at an old

Look for jack-in-the-pulpits along the trail.

family cemetery at 0.7 mile. Of particular interest is a series of markers for Uphold, the spelling of which is modified over three successive generations and illustrated by adjacent headstones.

To continue, return to the point at which you first entered the cemetery clearing and go right, following the yellow blazes around the grove. Through the grove, especially where hemlocks are clustered to the east, there is the strong scent of conifers. In May and June, bluets carpet the pathway in places, shimmering all around. Ferns cover the open understory under the pines. At the junction go right to retrace your steps to the park road; cross the road and follow the yellow blazes.

Stay with the yellow blazes past the rental cabins to your left. As of this writing the trail turns briefly into a dirt road. Follow the road a short distance until it turns back into the yellow trail and heads into the woods. Presently you will come to a T intersection with the green trail. Go right and walk below black oak and blue spruce with an understory of American hornbeam. This is a very pretty green and open forest following the wide, well-manicured path. Look for jack-in-the-pulpits in the early summer, but be aware of ticks in the tall grass along the trail. Continue straight at the clearing, where a sign marks the beginning of the managed hunting area.

NOT TO SCALE

N

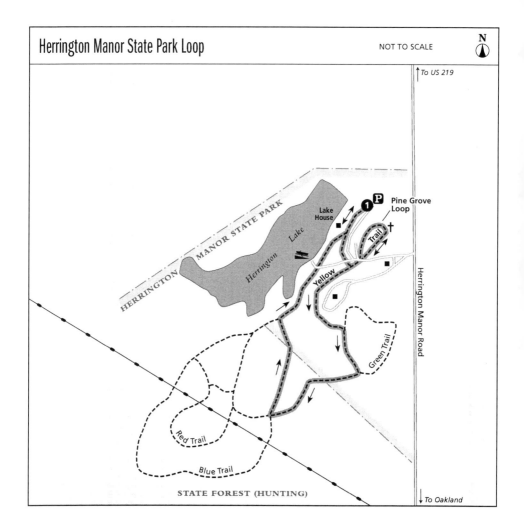

To US 219

HERRINGTON MANOR STATE PARK

Lake House

Herrington Lake

Pine Grove Loop

Trail

Yellow

Green Trail

Red Trail

Blue Trail

Herrington Manor Road

STATE FOREST (HUNTING)

To Oakland

At 2 miles you will come to a four-way intersection of trails. Here the trail signs and the trail map are confused. The trail signs label "connector" trails in black, but the map has them in various colors depending on where they lead. The signs point to the red, blue, and green trails. Take the blue-blazed trail to the right and follow it downhill to the lake.

At 3.5 miles emerge from the woods at the boat launch; follow the paths beside the lake back to the trailhead.

The trail signs are well placed and detail specific distances for the red, blue, and green loop trails, should you want a longer hike.

Herrington Manor Loop—the kids will enjoy romping along this wide, lovely trail.

Miles and Directions

0.0 Start at trailhead.

0.4 Begin circling a pine grove.

0.7 Enter the clearing at the old cemetery.

2.0 Reach the four-way intersection. Go right on the blue-blazed trail.

3.5 Emerge from the woods at Herrington Lake boat launch. Follow lakeside path toward trailhead.

4.2 Arrive back at the trailhead.

Options: Herrington Manor is a favorite for cross-country skiing, and the trails have been designed, in part, for that activity. Take a winter break, rent a cabin, and experience the wonder of woods in winter.

2 Swallow Falls State Park Loop

This easy circuit hike in Swallow Falls State Park passes through a 40-acre, 300-year-old hemlock forest, one of the last stands of mature hemlock in the mid-Atlantic region. The circuit includes four waterfalls, each more spectacular than the last, until you reach Maryland's highest waterfall. Bring a picnic lunch. You may swim in the Youghiogheny River below the second sets of falls, but swimming is not recommended.

Start: Begin at the far end of the parking area.

Distance: 1.2-mile loop

Hiking time: About 2 hours

Difficulty: Moderate due to steps and stairs, rocky sections

Elevation gain: Minimal

Trail surface: Natural packed dirt/stone; rocky, in upland forest

Trailhead elevation: 2,300 feet

Best season: Year-round

Schedule: 8 a.m. to sunset

Other trail users: None

Canine compatibility: Pets permitted in off-season only (Labor Day to Memorial Day)

Land status: Swallow Falls State Park; Garrett County, Maryland, near Deep Creek Lake, about 200 miles west of Baltimore

Nearest town: Oakland

Fees and permits: A fee is charged per person in season and per car in the off-season.

Camping: The park has 64 wooded campsites with bathhouses; 3 with RV hookups. Permits and information are available from the park office. For reservations call Maryland's statewide reservations line for state parks and forests: (888) 432-2267.

Trailhead facilities: Restrooms, water fountain, soft drink vending machine, picnic pavilions and tables

Maps: USGS Sang Run, Oakland, MD–WV

Trail contact: Swallow Falls State Park, c/o Herrington Manor State Park, 222 Herrington Lane, Oakland, MD; (301) 387-6938 (summer), (301) 334-9180 (Nov–Mar), (410) 260-8835 (TDD); https://dnr.maryland.gov/publiclands/pages/western/swallowfalls.aspx. Physical address: 2470 Maple Glade Rd., Oakland, MD.

Special considerations: Swallow Falls was hit hard by Hurricane Sandy in 2012; not all areas of the park or the trails may be accessible. For your safety, adhere to signs indicating what areas are open and do not go beyond posted signs.

Finding the trailhead: From I-68, take exit 14A and drive 19 miles south on US 219, passing Deep Creek Lake. Turn right onto Mayhew Inn Road. Drive 4.3 miles north, and then turn left onto Sang Run Road. In 0.25 mile turn right onto Swallow Falls Road (CR 20), which leads west to the park entrance in 4.7 miles. GPS: N39 29.95' / W 79 25.12'

The Hike

This delightful short hike packs into a small package some of the outstanding features of hiking the Allegheny Front, including a stretch along one of the eastern United States' most notable whitewater rivers, the Youghiogheny. It is also a perfect hike for getting an outdoor fix when traveling with small children or with friends or family who take the outdoors in small doses. There are picnic tables and a pavilion, so a pre-hike picnic makes for a real kid-pleaser.

The trailhead is just beyond the comfort station and kiosk at the north end of the parking area. Traveling southeast (right) from the kiosk, you'll immediately find yourself in a stand of huge, ancient hemlocks and white pines. To protect these 300-year-old trees and their ecosystem, the 40-acre grove is designated a sensitive management area, which means the grove is managed as a wilderness. Trees are allowed to fall or burn as nature wills; only trees blocking trail access are cleared.

At 0.4 mile descend east to the first of four waterfalls on the hike, Toliver Falls on Toliver Run. Here the hemlock boughs slant nearly into the run, creating a dense shade over a low cascade—a nice spot to spend time splashing about in the ripples 100 yards above Toliver Run's confluence with the north-flowing Youghiogheny or, as it is known to whitewater runners everywhere, the "Yough."

Scampering over wet boulders to the mossy Canyon Trail, heading north along the Yough, you will be just out of earshot of Toliver Falls when Swallow Falls appears on your right—the second falls on the hike. The hemlock and pine are accompanied by mountain laurel and rhododendron, and the granite outcrops in and near the water call out for further exploration. As a point of Leave No Trace ethics, follow the established passages to the river. So many enthusiastic hikers have trammeled new paths to the water that in places the bank is losing its protective trees. The trees keep the waters clean and cool enough for trout and other cold water–loving fish.

Another 200 yards downriver is Swallow Rock and the Lower Falls, popular spots to capture this scenic hike on camera. Below the falls, boulders strewn into the river provide access for getting a great angle on the cascade from the middle of the river.

At 0.7-mile Muddy Creek drops into the Yough to create a rare type of river confluence. Muddy Creek flows southeast, anticipating a wash into a south-flowing river. But with the Yough flowing north, Muddy Creek seems to be headed in the wrong direction when it spills into the river. Instead of a smooth junction, the clash creates quite a stir of water and mist.

Just beyond the confluence is Muddy Creek Falls, at 53 feet the highest waterfall in Maryland. To the left, steps lead to the top of the falls; you will want to take plenty of time to explore it from every angle. Prime photography opportunities are at midday, when the sun is high.

From the top of the falls, follow Muddy Creek to a junction with a footpath leading over the creek and into the forest. For an additional ramble of less than 0.5 mile through dense rhododendron, go right at the junction and over the footbridge. On the other side of the creek, the trail makes a circuit.

From the junction with the short circuit trail, it is 0.2 mile back to the car. A wheelchair-accessible trail provides greater access to Muddy Creek Falls. Be sure to stop at the overlook and historical marker commemorating a camping trip of four notable Americans: Henry Ford, Thomas Edison, John Burrows, and Harvey Firestone.

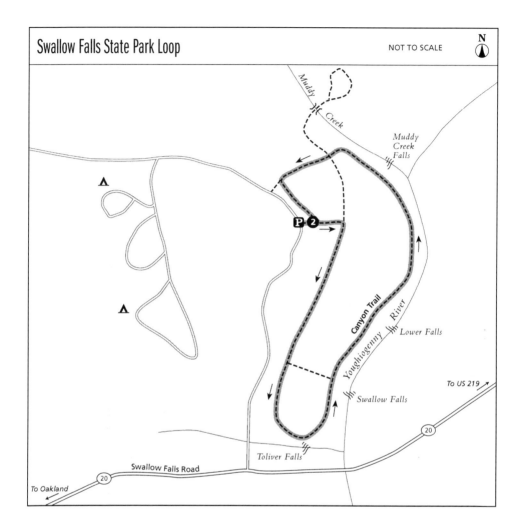

Swallow Falls State Park Loop

NOT TO SCALE

N

Muddy Creek

Muddy Creek Falls

Canyon Trail

Youghiogeny River

Lower Falls

To US 219

Swallow Falls

Toliver Falls

Swallow Falls Road

To Oakland

Miles and Directions

0.0 Start at the trailhead just beyond the comfort station.

0.4 Descend to Toliver Falls on Toliver Run.

0.6 Catch views of Swallow Falls, then arrive at Swallow Rock and Lower Falls.

0.7 Arrive at Muddy Creek Falls.

0.8 Reach the bridge and the junction with the short loop trail.

0.9 Pass the historical marker.

1.2 Arrive back at the trailhead.

Option: This is a terrific winter hike in snowshoes.

3 Deep Creek Vista, Deep Creek Lake State Park

The trail climbs to the flattop ridge of Meadow Mountain for a stunning view of Deep Creek Lake. On the way down, stop at an abandoned mine site for an insight into mountain cultural history.

Start: The trailhead is past the entrance station on the right.
Distance: 3.1 miles out and back
Hiking time: About 2 hours
Difficulty: Moderate
Elevation gain: 500 feet
Trail surface: Natural packed dirt in wooded upland, rocky
Best season: Year-round but best when leaves are off the trees
Schedule: 8 a.m. to sunset; main gate closed during snowmobile season (Dec 15–Mar 15)
Other trail users: Mountain bikers
Canine compatibility: Dogs allowed on trails
Land status: Deep Creek Lake State Park; Garrett County in western Maryland, 175 miles northwest of Washington, D.C.

Nearest town: Oakland
Fees and permits: There is a small entrance fee.
Camping: Developed campsites are available in the park; registration and a fee are required.
Trailhead facilities: Water and privy inside park
Maps: USGS McHenry MD; state park map
Trail contact: Deep Creek Lake State Park, 898 State Park Rd., Swanton, MD; (301) 387-5563; deepcreek.statepark@maryland.gov; https://dnr.maryland.gov/publiclands/pages/western/deepcreek.aspx
Special considerations: For those seeking quiet enjoyment of the natural setting, this hike should be avoided between Memorial Day and Labor Day. The continuous sounds of outboard motors on the lake may be a distraction. Views are best in the fall, winter, and early spring.

Finding the trailhead: From Frederick, Maryland, drive west on I-70 to I-68 West in Hancock. Go 69 miles on I-68 and then exit south on US 219 to Deep Creek Lake. After crossing the lake on US 219, pass through the Thayerville commercial area and turn left onto Glendale Road. After crossing the next bridge, take an immediate left onto State Park Road. Cross a small bridge and turn left at the T junction, pass the Discovery Center, and take your next left on Waterfront Way to the beach area. Follow signs for overflow parking; the trailhead is at the far end of the overflow lot next to the kiosk. GPS: N39 30.902' / W79 18.462'

The Hike

Most of the people who hike in the park never get a good view of Deep Creek Lake—they content themselves with a terribly obstructed peep from the fire tower. Too bad. The view from the wooden platform specially constructed for the purpose is the main objective of this hike.

From the parking area, cross State Park Road and take the Beckman Trail (red) for 0.1 mile to the Meadow Mountain Trail junction. Proceed straight following the white-blazed MMT, an 11-mile trail that follows the ridgeline. Hiking west in a slow ascent, you'll see the striped maple saplings that dot the understory, easily identifiable

Bear trap display.

by the dark-green stripes on their smooth, olive-green bark. Thankfully, there are no invasives to clutter the forest floor, and you have an open view through the maples, hickory, and oaks. You are walking parallel to the road and the lake beyond, so throughout the hike you will hear cars and boats below you.

At 0.7 mile pass the red-blazed Beckmans Trail and continue the ascent. Switchback east for a steep climb of 200 feet over 0.25 mile. Just as the climb becomes a chore, the trail levels off at the top and crosses the Indian Turnip Trail at 0.95 mile. Here it is apparent why this ridge is called Meadow Mountain. Its flat, wide top holds water like a rimmed plate. The ground is carpeted in ferns and mushrooms. Wildflowers typically found in bottomlands flourish in small pockets. Make a right on the orange Indian Turnip Trail downhill.

At 1.3 miles go straight on the blue Overlook Trail/Lookout Trail to the viewing platform; a sign marks the way. After a short climb, reach the overlook at 1.7 miles. When the leaves have fallen, the platform provides a dramatic view south over the lake and into the West Virginia Alleghenies. In summer the sound of motorboats makes its way to the top of Meadow Mountain, so you might want to save this hike for late September. With the leaves already fallen from the ridgeline trees, the lower reaches will be ablaze in color.

Deep Creek Vista, Deep Creek Lake State Park

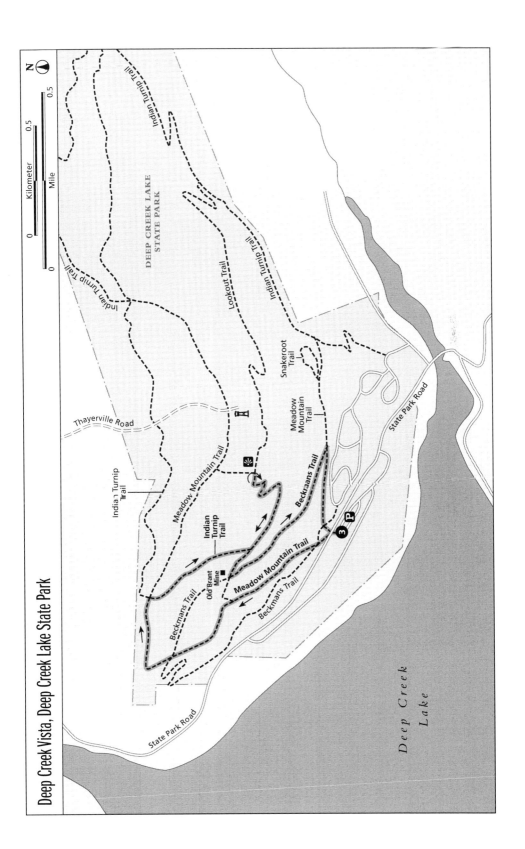

Return to Meadow Mountain Trail by retracing your steps on the blue trail. Make a hairpin left at the junction with the red Beckman Trail at 2.3 miles. If you continue straight on the blue trail, you will quickly reach an abandoned coal mine, the Old Brant Mine, on the right. If you visit the site, take some time to examine the fine reconstructed camp there. The coal mine operated for only a few years in the 1920s, when Garrett County was practically still a frontier. Unfortunately for the mine's owners, both contracted illnesses caused by their work and were forced to abandon the mine.

Moving on downhill from the blue and red junction, reach the white trail and make another sharp right going past the campsites and to the bear-trap display. Then go left to the parking area at 3.1 miles.

Miles and Directions

0.0 Start at the trailhead across State Park Road from the overflow parking lot.

0.1 Take Meadow Mountain Trail (white).

0.7 Reach the junction Beckmans Trail (red). Again, stay on the Meadow Mountain Trail.

0.95 Junction with Indian Turnip Trail (orange); go right.

1.3 Go straight on Overlook/Lookout Trail (blue) to the overlook; start back by retracing your steps.

2.3 At the junction with the red trail, turn left.

3.1 Arrive back at the trailhead.

Option: For a loop of 5 miles, stay east on Meadow Mountain Trail. In 0.9 mile, or 2.4 miles from the trailhead, take the orange Indian Turnip Trail at 3.2 miles and follow it back past the MMT, down the mountain to the next junction with the MMT/white trail, following that back to the parking area.

4 Poplar Lick Run, New Germany State Park

Following wide, color-coded cross-country ski trails, this pleasant walk leads along Poplar Lick Run, a babbling stream offering many opportunities to stop and enjoy the large stand of stately hemlocks throughout the walk. Look for trout from the bridges over Poplar Lick. The trail climbs 300 feet to the top of Red Ridge, where you will enjoy a cool pine grove.

Start: Find the trailhead at the far end of Lot 5, behind the information board.
Distance: 4.2-mile lollipop
Hiking time: About 2.5 hours
Difficulty: Moderate
Elevation gain: 300 feet
Trail surface: Mostly dirt path, some grassy stretches; rolling hills
Best season: Year-round
Schedule: 8 a.m. to sunset
Other trail users: None
Canine compatibility: Leashed pets permitted
Land status: New Germany State Park; Garrett County, 180 miles west of Washington, D.C.
Nearest town: Grantsville
Fees and permits: A per-person entrance fee is charged on weekends from June–Aug.
Camping: Cabins are available within the park; advance registration and a fee are required. In the forest surrounding the park, there are developed sites and backpacking opportunities. Registration is required for both; there is a fee for the developed sites. For reservations, call Maryland's statewide reservations line for state parks and forests: (888) 432-2267.
Trailhead facilities: Water is available from a spigot used by campers, located just past the turnoff to Lot 5. There are restrooms at the park meeting facility, which is walking distance from the trailhead.
Maps: USGS Bittinger MD, Barton MD, Frostburg MD, Grantsville MD; state park map
Trail contact: New Germany State Park, 349 Headquarters Lane, Grantsville, MD; (301) 895-5453; cabin reservations (888) 432-2267; https://dnr.maryland.gov/publiclands/pages/western/newgermany.aspx; newgermany. statepark@maryland.gov
Special considerations: Trails are designated for cross-country skiing when snow is present.

Finding the trailhead: From Frederick, Maryland, drive west on I-70 to Hancock. Then go 65 miles west on I-68 to Grantsville, Maryland. Take exit 22 and go left (south) onto Chestnut Ridge Road, which will end in 2 miles at New Germany Road. Turn left. In 2 miles proceed past the Savage River Complex headquarters on the right. Just beyond, turn left into New Germany State Park. Proceed to Parking Lot 5. The trailhead is at the far end of the lot behind the information board. GPS: N39 37.849' / W79 07.350'

The Hike

Hemlocks, mountain laurel, azaleas, and the sound of tumbling water await you on this woodland hike. From the information board, follow the green blazes on the park road into the woods and adjacent to Poplar Lick. This is called the Turnpike Trail, but it is labeled "Green Trail" on the map. Rhododendrons and ferns form the understory beneath the great hemlocks shading the stream on your right. This is a surprisingly

Hiking along the Poplar Lick among the hemlocks.

healthy stand of hemlocks, which have been devastated in areas just to the west by the hemlock woolly adelgid, a nonnative parasite. Although the parasite is in the area, the land managers have been successfully inoculating the hemlocks. You can see where by the aluminum bands marking the inoculations on the tree trunks.

Pass through an old picnic area and by the water treatment facility on the right. The trail crosses Poplar Lick four times on sturdy bridges. Peer into the shaded pools below the bridges, which teem with fingerling trout and crawfish that will hypnotize young hikers.

Along the pathway, hikers will witness a variety of ferns including sensitive, Christmas, common wood, cinnamon, and lady ferns, while walking through an out-standing forest of healthy hemlocks. Rhododendron bushes flank the creek with their waxy green leaves and white flowers. This is one of the most serene trail segments in the book.

Follow the Poplar Lick green trail along the creek for about 1 mile, passing a number of junctions, to the intersection with the Dynamite Shack Loop (purple) Trail. Just before the intersection, you will notice what appears to be the remnant of a cabin foundation just across the creek; a giant hemlock stands before you. Go straight

Poplar Lick Run, New Germany State Park

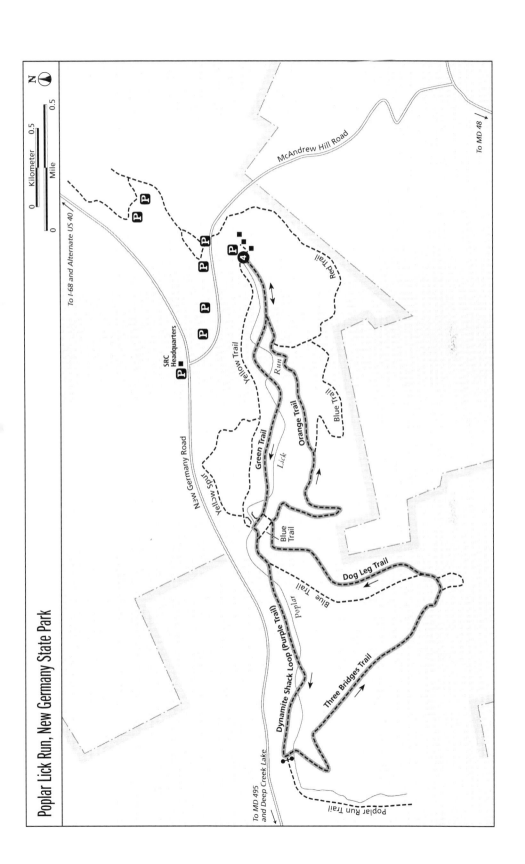

on the purple trail. As the trail nears the park boundary, car traffic can be heard on New Germany Road.

At 2 miles the trail bends sharply left, leaves Poplar Lick, and climbs almost 300 feet over the next 0.5 mile up Red Ridge. It is a long climb, but take a moment to pause and look behind you to Meadow Mountain. These are the only open views on the hike. In early June, blooming mountain laurel walls the trail, with tiger swallowtail butterflies gathering nectar from the flowers.

Reaching a stand of hemlock and cedar on your left at 2.6 miles (elevation 2,690 feet, the highest point on the hike), watch for the purple blazes leading right just as the trail reaches the top of the hill. Here you have a choice: The pine grove loop is a short detour into a dark, swampy world. It offers a striking difference from the lush vegetation only 0.5 mile back. There is almost no ground cover or understory—only straight, fragrant conifers living in a soupy soil created by the small bowl at the top of this knoll. Or you can go left on the purple trail and downhill a few hundred feet to the intersection with the orange Dog Leg Trail less than 0.2 mile ahead at 2.8 miles.

Either trail leads back to Poplar Lick and where you started; but take the longer, more secluded Dog Leg Trail to the right. It is blazed orange.

Almost immediately, you pass through a splendid thicket of mountain laurel bordering the trail, and then you descend back into the hemlocks. It is lush and cool even on a hot day. Notice the small marble-sized seed cones from the hemlocks. Similar to the redwood tree, they are remarkably small for such large trees.

Descend to a junction with the green trail at 3.3 miles, just above the stream. If you go left, you will be back on the green trail where you first started. Go right and up the hill on the orange trail, continuing to follow the Dog Leg Trail. In about 0.25 mile the trail again bisects. Go left and continue to the next intersection with the blue trail. Follow the blue trail to the green trail and back to the parking lot at 4.2 miles.

Miles and Directions

0.0 Start at the trailhead at the information board.

1.0 Pass first intersection with purple trail.

2.0 Reach the end of the trail along the creek and head left up Red Ridge.

2.6 Reach pine grove loop option.

2.8 Junction with Dog Leg Trail (orange); go right.

3.3 Reach the green trail again; go right, then left on the blue trail.

4.2 Arrive back at the trailhead.

Options: The color-coded trails offer many options for shorter and longer hikes through the woods.

5 Monroe Run Trail, Savage River State Forest

A creek-side hike leads into a very remote, wild, stream valley covered by a canopy of hardwoods and hemlocks. There are many stream crossings, some on bridges, many by rock-hopping. On an autumn weekday in late afternoon, you are as likely to see a black bear as you are another person.

Start: The trail begins at the trailhead parking on New Germany Road.

Distance: 4.6 miles one-way (shuttle) or 9.2 miles out and back

Hiking time: About 2 hours one-way

Difficulty: Moderate due to stream crossings; 1,100-foot descent

Elevation gain: 976 feet

Trail surface: Heavily forested

Best season: Apr–Nov; in winter on snowshoes

Schedule: This trail is available for camping, therefore there are no actual hours.

Other trail users: Hunters, fishermen, bird-watchers

Canine compatibility: Leashed dogs permitted

Land status: Savage River State Forest; Garrett County, Maryland, about 185 miles west of Washington, D.C. The trail begins in the state forest and ends in Big Run State Park.

Nearest town: Grantsville

Fees and permits: No fees for day hiking. There is a camping fee.

Camping: Camping is permitted (fee required). Campers must register at the Savage River

Headquarters or any of the bulletin board areas.

Trailhead facilities: Parking

Maps: USGS Bittinger MD; state map

Trail contact: Savage River State Forest, 127 Headquarters Lane, Grantsville, MD; (301) 895-5759; https://dnr.maryland.gov/forests/ Pages/savageguide.aspx; https://dnr.maryland .gov/wildlife/Pages/NaturalAreas/Western/ Monroe-Run.aspx

Special considerations: This trail has many stream crossings that are subject to flooding, and there are no constructed bridges (just a few simple log bridges). Most of the time all the crossings can be managed with only an occasional wet boot. In high water, especially in spring, a few crossings may require wading in shallow water. Fast-moving water, even knee deep, should be crossed only by or with the assistance of experienced hikers. You can also hike this in the reverse direction, but if you do, park in the designated parking area at Big Run and not in the camping area.

Finding the trailhead: From Frederick, Maryland, drive west on I-70 to Hancock. Then go 57.8 miles west on I-68 toward Grantsville, Maryland, and take exit 22. Go 0.6 mile on the exit ramp and turn left at the stop sign onto Chestnut Ridge Road. Travel south 2.6 miles on Chestnut Ridge Road. At the stop sign, turn left on New Germany Road. Travel south on New Germany Road for 5 miles to the Monroe Run Overlook and trailhead on the left. GPS: N39 34.250' / W79 12.101'

The Hike

With the casual terrain of the trail, this hike can be covered in a couple of hours of walking. To truly enjoy it, however, plan on at least twice that long. This is one of

Morning mist rises from a stream valley in western Maryland. MARYLAND DNR

the wildest stream canyons in Maryland and one of the quietest. Because the trail descends into the canyon, there is no intrusion of noise from outside activity.

This hike is especially suited for an overnight trip, either by creating a loop (see "Options," below) or by hiking in to a favorite spot along the stream and then heading out the same way. Before hiking, take a few minutes to gaze at the canyon from the overlook.

Begin by descending on a wide path, remnants of an old road built by the Civilian Conservation Corps (CCC) in the 1930s as a connector between camps atop and below Meadow Mountain. The wooden guardrails on the downhill side at sharp turns were placed by the CCC crews. There are a few openings in the canopy near the top of the route, with views west up the mountain and south toward Savage River Reservoir.

The terrain eases as the trail approaches Monroe Run; at 1.1 miles you come to the first of more than twenty crossings (the precise number depends on the weather). Several good campsites are near the stream at this point, back under tall oaks and tulip poplars. The understory is dense with rhododendron, at times so thick that even on sunny days it is nearly nighttime on the ground.

At 2 miles reach a large hemlock grove. The temperature here seems to drop by several degrees. In fact, the cooling effect of hemlock groves staves off evaporation on headwater streams like Monroe Run. Scientists are battling a blight that threatens to destroy the hemlocks of the southern Appalachians—the hemlock woolly adelgid—a potentially calamitous event that would alter the entire ecosystem of these mountains.

Several stream crossings farther on, beginning at about 2.6 miles, a series of secluded campsites can be found. If you plan to camp along Monroe Run, use one of

Monroe Run Trail, Savage River State Forest

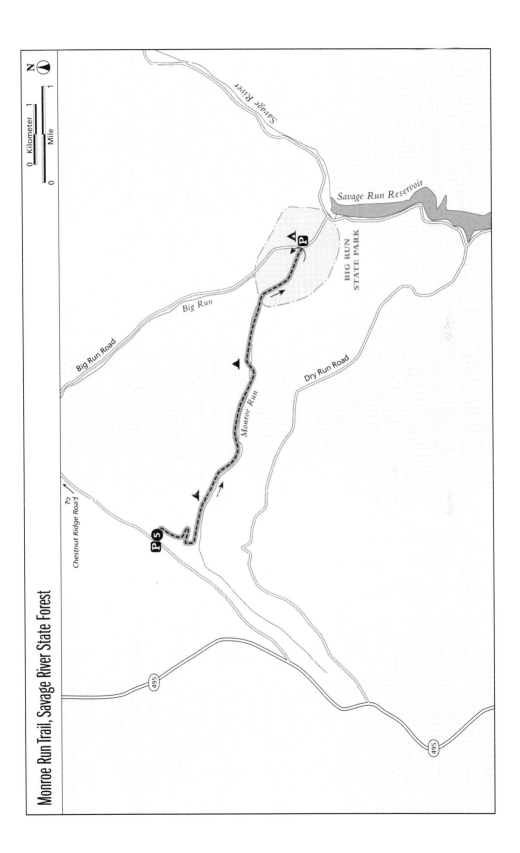

the sites that has already been tended. There are enough sites along the run to provide solitude, but any more such sites would threaten the wild experience of the canyon. If forced to camp in a new site, be sure to exercise Leave No Trace camping by eliminating any sign of your presence before leaving.

The canyon narrows to barely wider than Monroe Run at 3.2 miles and stays that way for about 0.5 mile. Then, in a wider flatland, the run divides into two—at times three—streams, creating small isolated islands. In rainy periods these areas form a washed-out delta of alternately fast-moving and stalled water. Take great care if crossing in these conditions.

The final crossing comes at 3.9 miles, where the run reaches wide bottomland. As you approach the bottom, you are more likely to encounter hikers venturing uphill from the developed campsites near Big Run Road. Still, except on weekends in summer, a lonesome, remote feeling dominates the trail.

At 4.6 miles reach Big Run Road. Car camping at the developed sites through this area affords a quiet spot for launching day hikes to the surrounding mountains.

Miles and Directions

0.0   Start at the trailhead after enjoying the view from the overlook.

1.1   Cross Monroe Run for the first time.

2.6   Reach a series of secluded campsites.

3.9   Cross Monroe Run for the last time; there are developed campsites nearby.

4.6   Reach Big Run Road, your shuttle or turnaround point.

Option: You can make a loop by turning left onto Big Run Road at the bottom of the trail and then turning left onto New Germany Road, for a round-trip of 8 miles. Although this is a road walk, it is very scenic and experiences little automobile traffic.

6 Lostland Run Loop, Potomac State Forest

This serene hike through a hemlock–laurel canyon follows Lostland Run across cable bridges constructed by the Maryland Conservation Corps en route to the Potomac. There are a number of stream crossings on footbridges, a waterfall, and opportunities to view wildlife. The hike is in the far reaches of Maryland's western forests and takes time to get to, but this area is as close to wilderness as we get in Maryland.

Start: The trailhead is just across the road from the headquarters parking area.

Distance: 7.4-mile loop

Hiking time: About 4 hours

Difficulty: Moderate

Elevation gain: 650-foot loss; gain it back on the road walk

Trail surface: Packed dirt, muddy at times; dirt road

Best season: Apr–Nov

Schedule: Dawn–dusk

Other trail users: None

Canine compatibility: Leashed dogs permitted

Land status: Potomac State Forest; Garrett County in western Maryland

Nearest town: Oakland

Fees and permits: None

Camping: The gravel Lostland Run Road serves primitive car campsites, which may be reserved for a fee through forest headquarters. Despite the fact that some of the campsites are literally adjacent to the road, the place has a remote wilderness quality. For more on camping, visit https://dnr.maryland.gov/forests/Pages/publiclands/PotomacGarrett/Camping.aspx.

Trailhead facilities: There is parking at the headquarters office and a water spigot behind the office.

Maps: USGS Gorman MD-WV; Deer Park MD; Mount Storm WV; state park map through website

Trail contact: Potomac State Forest, 1701 Potomac Camp Rd., Oakland, MD; (301) 334-2038; https://dnr.maryland.gov/wildlife/Pages/NaturalAreas/Western/Lostland-Run.aspx; customerservice.dnr@maryland.gov

Special considerations: In the first mile of the hike, there are two sections of rough and rocky terrain. They are passable by hikers of most abilities, but they make for slow going for a time. The trail can also be wet and muddy in places.

Finding the trailhead: From Frederick, Maryland, drive west on I-70 to I-68 west in Hancock. Go 69 miles on I-68. Exit south on US 219 toward Deep Creek Lake, and go 26 miles to Oakland, Maryland. Stay on US 219 when it turns left in Oakland; when US 219 turns right outside of town, go straight onto MD 135. In about 2 miles turn right onto MD 560, just outside Mountain Lake Park. In 2 miles turn left onto Bethlehem Road (staying right at the fork). In 1.4 miles turn left onto Combination Road, and in 0.5 mile turn left onto Potomac Camp Road. The forest headquarters is about a mile farther on the left. To find the trailhead from the parking area, cross the road, walk 75 feet back up the road, and look for a wooden marker. GPS: N39 22.742' / W79 16.975'

The Hike

You can lose your cares amid the hemlock and laurel along the Lostland Run and forget the time gazing at Cascade Falls deep in the gorge. The trail crosses the run several times and there are several scenic falls.

There are a few areas of rough and rocky terrain and a couple of places where the trail seems to disappear, but with little effort you will steer the course toward the cliffs of the Potomac River at the bottom of the run. The Potomac is reached at 4 miles, after a hike that is largely downhill. The return to the trailhead is via the gravel Lostland Run Road, which serves the camping areas. It is mostly uphill from the river, but the grade is not overly challenging and is plenty wide enough to walk side by side with a companion.

From the trailhead the path and white blazes are easy to follow, but it can be slippery and muddy in wet weather. Yet the ferns are glorious. Through a grove of sugar maples, you trace the small drainage of a seasonal run on the north side of South Prong Lostland Run (you will follow the South Prong until its confluence with the North Prong at 2.1 miles). The trail is rocky in places and not well maintained but discernable from the blazes.

At 0.6 mile the trail passes close to the creek and the road. The intermittent clanging of steel you hear is a lime dozer; these are installed on several streams in western Maryland to restore the pH balance after the destruction left by mining operations. Watch for the campsite to the left (accessible from the road) and a sign that talks about coal mining in this area and the reclamation work the government has done to restore the acid levels in the stream due to the mining.

The trail flattens out at this point, and there are places to pitch tents—check with the park office. The trail bends through the hemlocks and is traversed by small springs. Even in dry weather, it is damp here, giving rise to lots of colorful mushrooms—even in August. The trail crosses the stream a few times through this stretch; in wet weather it is slippery and wet (you will find a walking stick very useful). About 1.5 miles into the hike, you will see a wonderful swimming hole fed by a small waterfall flowing over sedimentary rock.

The trail then cuts sharply to the right and follows another feeder stream uphill to a T. Turn right, heading up the hill to an overlook 60 feet above the Lostland Run, where you can see upstream and down.

At 1.7 miles cross the South Prong Lostland Run on a nifty swinging bridge constructed in 1994 by the 95th Maryland Conservation Corps, a youth program responsible for many good works in Maryland forests.

Here you will hike under beech, birch, and tulip poplar. Ascend to the ledge above the run, which now enters a steep gorge. Watch for blazes here—the trail bends above the stream and is not always obvious. There is another campsite to the left above, but the trail continues around the bend to the right.

Lostland Run Loop, Potomac State Forest

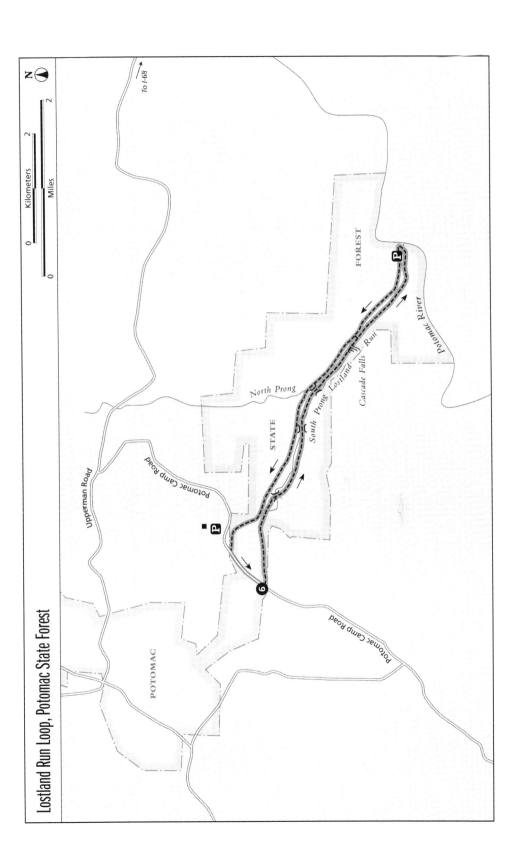

At 2.1 miles the trail breaks left, away from the run, and crosses North Prong Lostland Run just before the confluence of the two prongs. If you miss the break, the path will end at the confluence. From there you will see the bridge 100 feet to the left.

Follow a wide cart path that ascends as the run drops to the right. An eighth of a mile beyond the bridge, watch for a false trail to the right—follow the white blazes to the left. The trail traverses the ridge above the run as it widens to about 50 feet, with numerous feeder streams visible. The next 0.5 mile is a delightful stroll down the gorge, close to the fast-flowing water and shaded by ancient hemlocks. This is prime habitat for black bears and nocturnal hunters such as bobcats and owls. You may see blue blazes along the way and across the run—they are property markers, not trail markers.

Hugging a narrow ledge at stream level, the trail passes under a dense canopy, dark even at midday. At 2.5 miles the trail forks—left goes through two large boulders to a campsite on the road, but right (look for the white blaze on the big hemlock between the boulders) goes around one boulder and down toward Cascade Falls. Be careful here: The blazes are less distinct, but the trail is clearly visible. It crosses several small knobs and then reaches Cascade Falls at 3 miles. A viewing platform provides an excellent prospect. If you are lucky enough to have the falls all to yourself, you will want to linger here.

Climb wooden stairs, following blue blazes that lead to a trailhead serving the falls. At the top of the bluff, follow the white blazes right; the blue blazes continue straight to Lostland Run Road.

The final mile below the falls is the most remote and solitary. The path alternates from ledge walking on the bluffs to close, intimate contact with the stream. Just before the trail emerges at the Potomac River parking area at 4 miles, a footbridge leads across the run.

Before heading up Lostland Run Road for the return walk, follow the path at the end of the parking area to the cliffs above the Potomac and take in the splendid views. Then follow Lostland Run Road uphill back to the parking area.

Miles and Directions

0.0 Start at the trailhead at a wooden marker.

0.6 Pass a lime dozer.

1.7 Cross South Prong Lostland Run on a swinging bridge.

2.1 Cross North Prong Lostland Run on a footbridge.

3.0 Reach Cascade Falls.

4.0 Emerge at the Potomac River parking area. Pick up Lostland Run Road and walk back uphill toward the trailhead.

7.4 Arrive back at the trailhead.

Option: With a second car stashed at the bottom of the trail, you can shorten the hike to 4 miles, eliminating a 3.4-mile walk along the gravel camping road.

7 Rocky Gap Canyon to Evitts Summit, Rocky Gap State Park

This challenging walk through the dark and lush Rocky Gap Canyon is followed by an ascent over an old woods road to a monument marking the Mason-Dixon Line high atop Evitts Mountain, where there are expansive views. Along the way, visit the historic homestead of the first white settler in the rugged Allegheny Mountains.

Start: The trailhead is west of the Rocky Gap lodge, just beyond the Touch of Nature Trail parking lot.
Distance: 6.4 miles out and back
Hiking time: About 3 hours
Difficulty: Moderate due to consistent, steep incline
Elevation gain: 1,050 feet
Trail surface: Packed dirt, sandy in places; wooded highlands
Best season: Year-round
Schedule: Sunrise to sunset
Other trail users: None
Canine compatibility: Leashed pets permitted
Land status: Rocky Gap State Park; Allegany County, Maryland, 6 miles east of Cumberland
Nearest town: Cumberland
Fees and permits: None
Camping: A developed campground is available in the park. For reservations call

Maryland's statewide reservations line for state parks and forests: (888) 432-2267.
Trailhead facilities: Water, restrooms at park headquarters at park entrance, other refreshments at lodge. In early 2013, the park headquarters was relocated to the day-use facility.
Maps: USGS Evitts Creek MD-PA-WV; state park map available through the website
Trail contact: Rocky Gap State Park, 12500 Pleasant Valley Rd., Flintstone, MD; (301) 722-1480; https://dnr.maryland.gov/publiclands/Pages/western/rockygap.aspx; rockygap.statepark@maryland.gov
Special considerations: The wide dirt road of Evitts Mountain Trail makes an especially fine trail for snowshoe hiking. Check with the park office about hunting seasons, as the trail is in a managed hunt area.

Finding the trailhead: From the junction of I-70 and I-68 in Hancock, Maryland, drive 30 miles west on I-68 to exit 50 for Rocky Gap State Park. When you exit the highway, turn left toward the Rocky Gap Casino Resort. Before the entrance to the park, go left. Don't go right into the casino resort but stay straight and continue until the road ends at the Touch of Nature Trail parking lot. Continue on foot along the paved access road. Because the bridge is out, pass Evitts Mountain Trail on your left and go left on the blue connector trail 0.5 mile past the dam. GPS: N39 41.898' / W78 39.844'

The Hike

The bridge across Rocky Gap Run is out, so you must proceed 0.5 mile along the lake, past the dam, and go left on the dark blue "Shortcut Trail." See the notice at the kiosk in the parking area. Hike uphill until you reach the junction with the white-blazed Evitts Mountain Trail.

Fall vista at the Gap. PHOTO COURTESY OF MARYLAND DNR

This hike climbs to the summit of Evitts Mountain, where there are endless views of the Allegheny Mountains and a Mason-Dixon Line marker that is placed, as most were, in the middle of nowhere. You will climb 1,050 feet over 3 miles, but the majority of the ascent is on a wide dirt road that provides a stable surface and plenty of rest spots.

From the Touch of Nature Trail parking area, walk up the paved road (do not follow the gate onto the gravel road at left) and cross the dam, then go left uphill into the woods at 0.5 mile on the blue Shortcut Trail. After climbing about 150 feet in 0.25 mile, reach the white Evitts Mountain Trail and head uphill.

As you begin the ascent, you will immediately forget you are in a resort area, as rhododendron and azalea abound under a dense canopy. The footpath is surrounded by hemlock, table mountain pine, pignut hickory, and scarlet oaks, marked by smooth vertical stripes on the bark.

The pleasant walk under many white oaks, Maryland's state tree, is marred only by the sounds of trucks rising on the wind from the highway a mile away. But as the trail slabs around the hill, you will leave the noise behind. The climb to the top

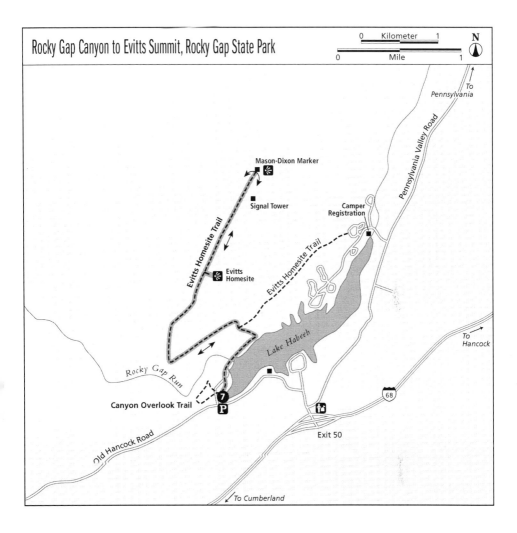

Mason-Dixon Marker

Signal Tower

Camper Registration

Evitts Homesite Trail

Evitts Homesite Trail

Evitts Homesite

Lake Habeeb

Rocky Gap Run

Canyon Overlook Trail

7

To Pennsylvania

Pennsylvania Valley Road

To Hancock

68

Exit 50

Old Hancock Road

To Cumberland

from here is steady but offers plenty of pauses in its bends, where the road is level for short stretches.

A short trail at 2.2 miles leads 75 yards right to the Evitts Homesite. A man whose first name seems forgotten by all, Mr. "Everts" (the spelling varies among local sources) escaped to these rugged mountains in 1801 to live out his life as a hermit. Some accounts cite bad business deals; others, failure at love. Only a stone well and a few stone fences remain.

Back on the trail, climb steadily on the woods road another 0.8 mile to an aviation signal tower. The Mason-Dixon marker is 0.25 mile farther on the left; the views in another 200 feet are farther into Pennsylvania. The wonderful view of the rugged Allegheny Mountains reveals why, to this day, the area remains rather remote, except for the city of Cumberland a short distance west.

Return to the trailhead by retracing your steps. At the bottom, just before the trailhead, a side trip onto the 0.25-mile Canyon Overlook Trail is recommended.

Miles and Directions

0.0   Start at nature trail parking area and walk on the paved road, past the dam.

0.5   Go left on the blue Shortcut Trail after the dam.

0.75 Reach white Evitts Mountain Trail and go right.

2.2   Follow the short trail right to the Evitts Homesite.

2.9   Reach the signal tower.

3.2   Reach the Mason-Dixon Line marker. Enjoy the views before retracing your steps to the trailhead.

6.4   Arrive back at the trailhead.

Option: The Lakeside Loop makes a pleasant but long circle around Lake Habeeb.

8 Twin Oaks Trail, Green Ridge State Forest

This pleasant, sometimes challenging hike features more than a dozen stream crossings, a few rugged ascents through pine forest, and mountain views. A nice day in the woods.

Start: Look for the pink blazes across the road from the parking area.
Distance: 4.4-mile loop; overnight or day hike
Hiking time: About 3 hours
Difficulty: Moderate
Elevation gain: Several steep climbs, none more than 150 feet
Trail surface: Natural packed dirt, stream banks and crossings; forested uplands
Best season: Apr–Nov
Schedule: Dawn to dusk
Other trail users: None
Canine compatibility: Leashed dogs permitted
Land status: Green Ridge State Forest; Allegany County, Maryland, just off I-68, about 140 miles northwest of Washington, D.C.
Nearest town: Cumberland

Fees and permits: None for day use; a registration fee is required if camping.
Camping: Camping is available throughout the area; self-registration is required at the forest office at exit 64 off I-68, where maps are also available.
Trailhead facilities: None
Maps: USGS Artemas MD; state forest map available through the website
Trail contact: Green Ridge State Forest, 28700 Headquarters Dr. NE, Flintstone, MD; (301) 478-3124; https://dnr.maryland.gov/forests/Pages/publiclands/Greenridge/Trails.aspx; customerservice@dnr.state.md.us
Special considerations: During spring, be prepared for muddy conditions along Pine Lick. The area is managed for hunting; check with rangers for season dates.

Finding the trailhead: From the junction of I-68 and I-70 in western Maryland, go west on I-68. Take exit 62 to Fifteen Mile Creek Road/MD 40 and travel northeast. At a fork at 0.5 mile, bear left to follow unpaved Fifteen Mile Creek Road; there is no road sign here, so if you're not paying attention, you could miss it. Proceed 1 mile to Double Pine Road and turn left. Follow this road for 2.5 miles, past several campsites, to the end of the road at Old Cumberland Road. Park here, where Twin Oak Trail crosses. Look for the pink blazes across the road from the parking area. Do not go down the gated road off the parking area that leads southeast. GPS: N39 42.905' / W78 28.171'

The Hike

This is a fine hike for introducing a young person (or even someone not so young) to backpacking. Or you can enjoy it all in a day. The hike offers a blend of streamside rambling, rock-hopping creek crossings, and deep woods walking. Although there are several ascents that will get even a fit hiker gasping for breath, none are sustained for more than a few hundred yards. Nor do they climb more than a couple hundred feet in elevation. At about 49,000 acres, Green Ridge State Forest is Maryland's largest contiguous public land area. It is also a land of incredible biodiversity: There are more species of trees and shrubs in this forest than in all of Europe.

From the trailhead, facing south (away from Old Cumberland Road), turn right to follow the pink-blazed Twin Oaks Trail as it gradually ascends through new pines to the junction with Pine Lick Trail. Turn left, following the blue blazes. Continue a casual climb through hardwood groves mixed with white pines. Pass campsite number 5 on the left at 0.3 mile; if the camp is empty, you can take a break at the picnic site there.

Continue straight on the blue-blazed trail past the picnic area. In the late spring look for blueberries along the trail. In 300 yards the terrain levels as you enter a grassy dale. The unlikely clearing in the forest is a managed "edge," the type of habitat favored by small game and deer. Green Ridge State Forest is managed for multiple use; these small clearings enable managers to concentrate the impacts of game management to specific zones (be sure to check the forest website or with the office for hunting schedules).

Begin a long and sometimes steep descent into the hollow of Pine Lick, a shallow creek that alternates between meandering curves and headlong rushes, toward Fifteen Mile Creek. Following the creek the trail crosses on stepping stones a few times. In dry weather this is easy, but in high water the trip is not one to take with small children, unless they are on your back. In warm weather the worst thing that will happen is your sneakers will get wet—although the whole bottomland can be muddy the day after a big rain. Whatever the weather, Pine Lick Hollow is a kid's paradise, full of wildflowers and tadpoles in vernal pools in spring.

Reach the Pine Lick camping shelter at 1.3 miles, a three-sided primitive outpost facing the creek, and a meadow visited by deer, turkey, and hawks—a nice place to watch the mountains grow dark on a summer evening.

Just beyond the shelter, at 1.5 miles, turn left onto Twin Oaks Nature Trail. Do not follow the old road; rather, look for the pink blazes on the right, and climb steeply through the woods. The trail comes back to the old road and leads to another picnic area. About 200 feet before the picnic site, the trail dodges back into the woods to the right and crosses Double Pine Road at 2.1 miles. Look for the pink blazes across the road, just uphill.

The path on this side of the road is little subtler, but trust the pink blazes as the trail descends into a hollow. Note the many folds and depressions in the land. At the top of the hill, turn left onto an old woods road. After descending, near the bottom of the hill, take a hard left at the T junction at 2.8 miles. There are wonderful views of Green Ridge straight ahead, and the trail is wide enough for kids to run amid the new-growth woodlands. At the bottom of this hill, cross a small stream and turn right, into the woods. After crossing the stream again, ascend on switchbacks for the longest climb of the hike. If you stop for a breath, there are wonderful views behind you.

At the top of the hill, pass through a pine plantation on flat ground, then into a clearing managed for wildlife. About 150 yards beyond the clearing, watch for blazes breaking right—the wide road continues straight, but you will turn right. Continue through dense woods, then descend steeply on switchbacks to cross a bridgeless creek at 3.7 miles. Cross back to the other side 200 yards later and start a long ascent. At the top of the hill is an open forest, lush with ferns and colorful dogwoods, redbud, and mountain azalea in spring. It is a lovely walk to end the hike.

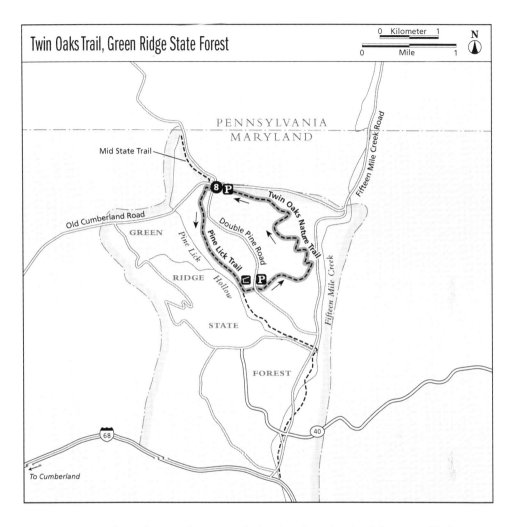

Twin Oaks Trail, Green Ridge State Forest

PENNSYLVANIA
MARYLAND

Mid State Trail

8 P

Twin Oaks Nature Trail

Old Cumberland Road

GREEN

Double Pine Road

Pine Lick

Pine Lick Trail

RIDGE

Hollow

P

STATE

Fifteen Mile Creek

FOREST

Fifteen Mile Creek Road

68

40

To Cumberland

Emerge from the woods on a wide, level path maintained for accessible hunting. Reach Double Pine Road and the end of the hike at 4.4 miles.

Miles and Directions

0.0 Start at the trailhead at the junction of the Twin Oaks Trail and Old Cumberland Road.

1.3 Reach the Pine Lick camping shelter.

2.1 Cross Double Pine Road.

2.8 Turn left at the T junction and enjoy the views of Green Ridge.

3.7 Cross a bridgeless creek.

4.4 Arrive back at the trailhead.

Option: To walk the second half of the loop on a wide, lightly traveled dirt road, turn left onto Double Pine Road at 2.1 miles.

9 Fifteen Mile Creek, Green Ridge State Forest

One of Maryland's best hikes for getting away from it all, this is a challenging hike in and above the remote canyon of Fifteen Mile Creek. There are wonderful campsites along the creek, deep in the woods. Brook trout can be seen in the pools below the trail. Unless you intend to camp, this is an out-and-back hike.

Start: The trailhead, marked with blue blazes, is beside the restrooms in the parking lot.
Distance: 6.2 miles out and back
Hiking time: About 4.5 hours
Difficulty: Moderate to strenuous with some long ascents along a narrow path
Elevation gain: 300 feet
Trail surface: Natural packed dirt; wooded creek valley, rocky in places
Best season: Apr–Nov; best views in spring and fall; wildflowers abundant in May and June
Schedule: Dawn to dusk (unless you are camping)
Other trail users: None
Canine compatibility: Leashed pets permitted
Land status: Green Ridge State Forest; Allegany County, Maryland, 140 miles northwest of Washington, D.C.
Nearest town: Cumberland
Fees and permits: None
Camping: Primitive sites are available along the river; contact the visitor center for information on developed campsites in the forest. This

is an excellent hike for the experienced backpacker, and a great trail to introduce a young person to wilderness camping.
Trailhead facilities: Water, restrooms at comfort station; visitor center has displays
Maps: USGS Artemas MD-PA/WV; state forest map through the website
Trail contact: Green Ridge State Forest, 28700 Headquarters Dr. NE, Flintstone, MD; (301) 478-3124; https://dnr.maryland.gov/forests/Pages/publiclands/western_greenridgeforest.aspx
Special considerations: The forest is open to hunting Nov–Feb; check with the state forest headquarters for details. The trail is not well traveled and in places can be overgrown. In two places the trail follows a narrow ledge that requires careful going. There is no bridge crossing Fifteen Mile Creek so the creek must be waded. A walking stick and sturdy shoes are recommended for this hike. Check with the rangers to learn about trail conditions if there has been heavy rain in the days before your hike.

Finding the trailhead: From the junction of I-70 and I-270 near Frederick, Maryland, drive west 29 miles to I-68 in Hancock, Maryland. Take I-68 26 miles west to exit 64, M. V. Smith Road. Go south (right) at the end of the exit ramp. Cross over I-68, and in 0.3 mile turn right into the state forest headquarters. The trailhead is to the left of the restrooms. GPS: N39 39.920' / W78 26.576'

The Hike

Fifteen Mile Creek slices a 200-foot gorge between Green Ridge and Town Hill on its way to the Potomac River. The 49,000-acre Green Ridge State Forest provides a sense of the wild backcountry only 2.5 hours from Washington, D.C. Considering the hike begins only a few hundred yards from the interstate and then spends the first 0.5 mile in proximity to it, it offers surprising solitude. It also presents a nice opportunity

Shale slabs on Fifteen Mile Creek.

to combine hiking with fly-fishing in one of several shaded holes down in the gorge. The hike travels south on Pine Lick Trail, spending about 2 miles within sight and sound of tumbling water. This is perhaps one of the only hikes in the book that offers primitive overnight camping.

Starting at the state forest visitor center, on the blue-blazed Pine Lick Trail, the first 0.5 mile is an unremarkable scamper through conifer and maple as the trail makes its escape from the intrusion of I-68, sitting practically astride the trail. At the top of a short ascent, reach a junction and go right, still a stone's throw from the highway. Completed in the 1980s to provide a high-speed route west over the rugged Allegheny Front, the highway has succeeded in bisecting key forests and hiking lands. After the trail breaks south away from the road at 0.5 mile, it ascends into eastern cedar and pine along an old forest road. Soon the highway is easily forgotten.

Following the ridgeline at about 1,000 feet, the trail enters a stand of towering chestnut oaks, hickory, and scattered eastern hemlock, signaling a more mature forest of more hardwoods and fewer pines than the trail will follow along the creek. Just beyond a remnant pine grove, the trail passes the ruins of an old cabin, unremarkable except for the tin shard implanted deep into the trunk of an ash tree and, high above the ruins, another sign of the hardwoods reclaiming a forest stripped clean a century ago for charcoal and tanning bark. A nice view to the west across the valley awaits you at just under a mile.

Wood turtle at the campsite.

The pathway ends at a four-way intersection at 1 mile, the high point on the hike at 970 feet. The Twin Oaks Trail moves north (right) through Green Ridge State Forest to Pennsylvania, 6 miles away, and the southern terminus of the Mid State Trail, a 187-mile path through the heart of the Keystone State. To the south, it is 13.7 miles to the Potomac. Looking in that direction, in the leafless months you can catch a revealing view of the regional topography to the left of Town Hill. Following the blue blazes downhill to Fifteen Mile Creek, at 690 feet, is steep but not overly challenging. Notice the rock formations lining the trail, reminders of the volcanic activity that built these mountains.

At 1.3 miles you reach Fifteen Mile Creek and bridge abutments on either side. But the bridge no longer exists and you must wade across. In a dry season it's easy and shallow, but after a big rain, the creek can be roaring, so again use a walking stick and take care. Be sure to check the weather and ask the park managers about conditions.

Following the crossing, the trail cuts sharply left and then travels up and down for 0.5 mile along the face of a ridge. Although none of the climbs is longer than 50 yards, the trail is narrow and difficult to navigate in sections. But the forest is deep here with few invasives, and the sound of falling water and songbirds, coupled with sightings of deer and wild turkey, will be remembered long after the climbs.

Fifteen Mile Creek, Green Ridge State Forest

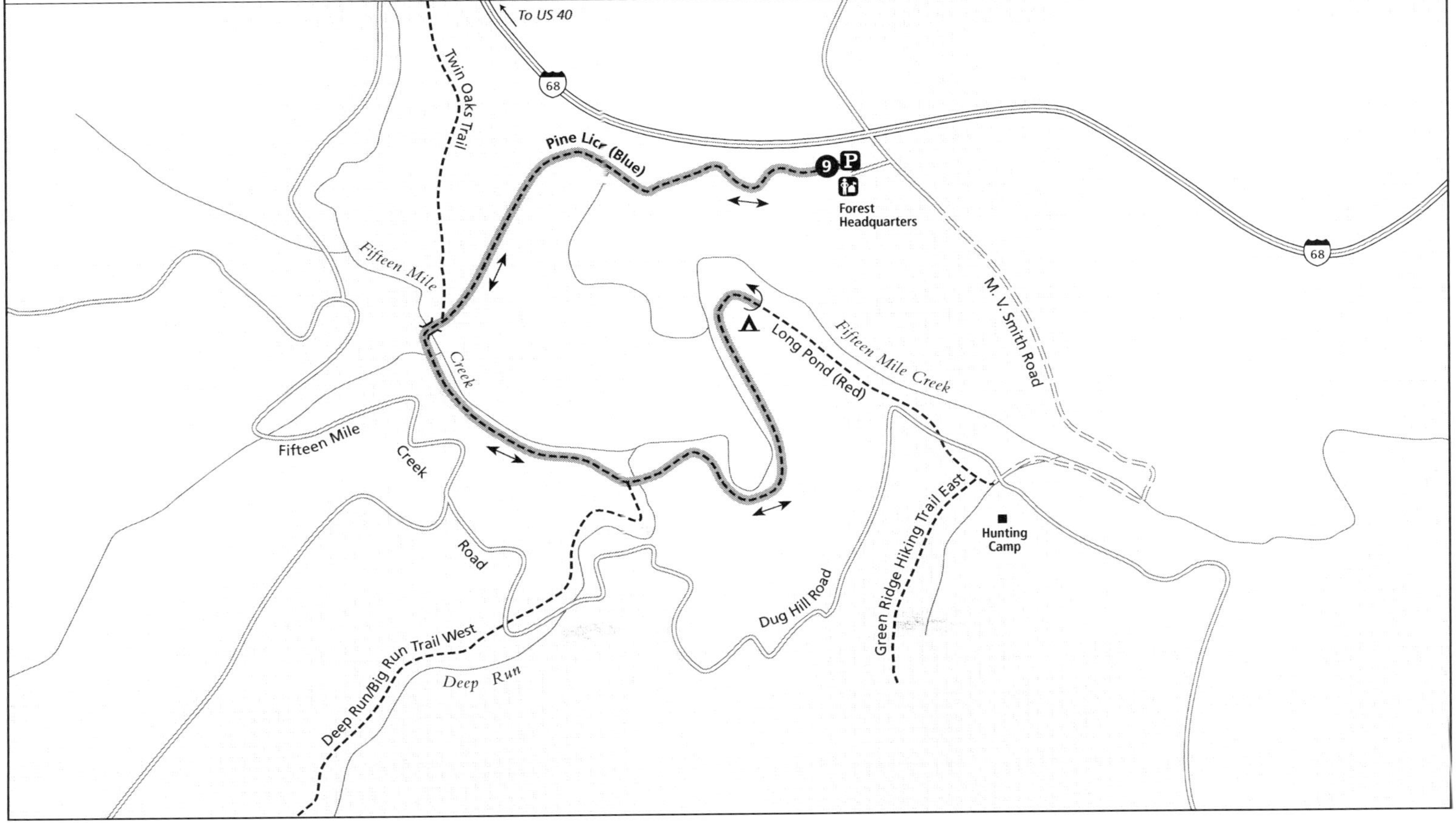

N

Pine Lick (Blue)

To US 40

68

68

Twin Oaks Trail

Fifteen Mile Creek

Creek

Fifteen Mile Creek

Road

Deep Run/Big Run Trail West

Deep Run

Dug Hill Road

Long Pond (Red)

Fifteen Mile Creek

Forest Headquarters

P

9

M. V. Smith Road

Green Ridge Hiking Trail East

Hunting Camp

0   Kilometer   0.5

0   Mile   0.5

In its 2.5 miles along the river—at times down in the gorge astride the river and at times a hundred feet above—the trail passes through one of the more wild, remote landscapes in Maryland. Centuries-old eastern hemlocks, undamaged by the hemlock woolly adelgid, tower above the forest floor. The footpath ascends 80 feet and follows the ridge along the creek. This area is steep and the path is slight—be careful here.

If you have brought rod and reel along, Deep Run, at 1.9 miles, is the place to find a spot where the water runs fast and cool. This is the end of the Pine Lick Trail and the intersection with the Deep Run/Big Run and Long Pong Trails; follow the red-blazed Long Pond Trail left across Deep Run. A sign at the junction says Pennsylvania is a short 6-mile hike to the north. To the south (right), the Deep Run/Big Run Trail climbs a saddle of Town Hill up the headwaters of Deep Run and then descends along Big Run to the Chesapeake & Ohio Canal. Proceed straight ahead on the red-blazed trail heading east.

Crossing Deep Run, Long Pond Trail stays left of the hill for about a hundred yards and then veers subtly right, up the ridge. You will again be following a narrow path along the flank of the ridge and encounter a long ascent. The forest here includes hickory trees, which can be identified by their nuts on the trail. Follow the red markings carefully through the next mile—a couple of false trails and old roads veer from the trail. With the views across the ravine, the sandstone cliffs, and the hemlock stands capturing your attention, it would be easy to stray down a dead end.

As you finally descend the ridge, you are rewarded not only with views of the creek from above but at least two very special wilderness campsites and a swimming hole along Four Mile Creek at 3.1 miles. Even during the busy summer months, it is possible to move downstream and find an out-of-the-way spot for a quiet lunch and a dip. The creek flows beneath dramatic 400-million-year-old shale slabs jutting into the creek from a hundred feet above the gorge. Take a long break here before retracing your steps back to the parking area, or set up camp and spend the night returning the way you came the next day.

Miles and Directions

0.0 Start at the trailhead at the visitor center.

1.0 Reach the junction with Twin Oaks Trail to the north. Begin the descent to Fifteen Mile Creek following the blue blazes.

1.3 Wade across Fifteen Mile Creek.

1.9 Reach Deep Run and the junction with the Long Pond Trail. Continue downstream.

3.1 Reach campsites and swimming holes. Retrace your steps back to the parking area.

6.2 Arrive back at the parking area.

10 Snavely Ford Trail, Antietam National Battlefield

A pleasant circuit walk leads along the surprisingly wild Antietam Creek, one of three fronts in the Battle of Antietam, the bloodiest single-day battle in American history. Wild turkeys, beavers, barred owls, and other wildlife inhabit the stream valley. Cows can often be seen grazing on the other side of the creek.

Start: The trailhead is located at Antietam National Battlefield Tour Road Stop 8 Burnside Bridge overlook. The hike begins at the bottom of the steps leading to the bridge.
Distance: 2.3-mile loop
Hiking time: About 1.5 hours
Difficulty: Easy
Elevation gain: Minimal
Trail surface: Natural dirt path; rolling hills
Best season: Year-round
Schedule: Dawn to dusk. Visitor center hours are 9 a.m. to 5 p.m.
Other trail users: Equestrians
Canine compatibility: Leashed dogs permitted
Land status: Antietam National Battlefield; Washington County, Maryland, about 75 miles northwest of Washington, D.C.
Nearest town: Keedysville
Fees and permits: Entrance fees are collected at the front desk at the visitor center.

Camping: Camping is available to organized groups at Antietam's Rohrbach Campground, by permit only. More information can be found at www.nps.gov/anti/planyourvisit/campgrounds.htm.
Trailhead facilities: None; water and restrooms available at the visitor center
Maps: USGS Keedysville MD
Trail contact: Antietam National Battlefield, PO Box 158, Sharpsburg, MD 21782. Physical address: 5831 Dunker Church Rd., Sharpsburg, MD; (301) 432-5124; www.nps.gov/anti/index.htm.
Special considerations: The creek is stocked with trout in spring; licenses are available at a store near the park. Exploration of the rest of the battlefield and the charming town of Sharpsburg make a fine conclusion to the hike. A hiking ritual: Stop at Nutters in Sharpsburg for ice cream.

Finding the trailhead: From the Capital Beltway, drive north on I-270 to I-70 west. In 25 miles, exit onto MD 65 south. The Antietam National Battlefield visitor center is 10 miles farther, on the left. To reach the trailhead, continue 1 mile to the town of Sharpsburg and turn left onto MD 34. In about 0.5 mile, descend a hill and turn right into the park. At the bottom of the next hill, just after crossing a bridge, turn left. (Turning right leads to Harpers Ferry Road, the route you will take to exit the park.) Parking for Burnside Bridge is at the end of the road. The hike begins at the bottom of the steps leading to the bridge. GPS: N39 27.010' / W77 43.960'

The Hike

The lovely bucolic countryside belies the carnage that took place along Antietam Creek on September 17, 1862. The Battle of Antietam (also known as the Battle of Sharpsburg) took place in three phases over 12 square miles. Down by the creek, Union General Ambrose Burnside tried to move his corps across the bridge to flank the Confederate army. The streamside trail preserves the landscape that saw the

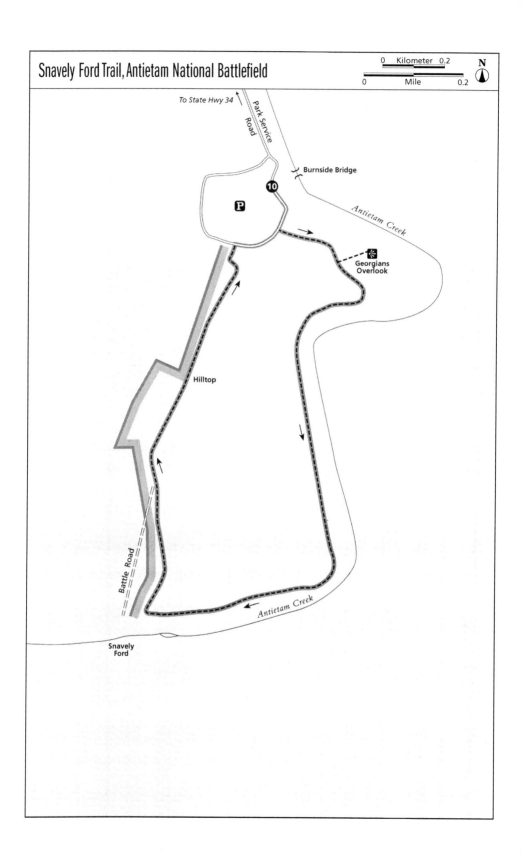

Snavely Ford Trail, Antietam National Battlefield

To State Hwy 34

Park Service Road

Burnside Bridge

10

P

Antietam Creek

Georgians Overlook

Hilltop

Battle Road

Antietam Creek

Snavely Ford

0   Kilometer   0.2

0   Mile   0.2

N

casualties of 600 men. Now it is alive with towering oaks and maples, blackberries on the edges, and the scent of pawpaws by the bank.

From the parking area, descend the steps and follow the Snavely Ford Trail. Take some time to enjoy the overlook, from which Southern troops trained their rifles on Federal troops approaching the bridge. From the overlook, descend to the creek and turn right.

Ancient beech trees line the creek and uplands, while the bottomland is still thick with the lower story of second-generation forest. The hillside to the right is home to wild turkeys, barred owls, and deer. In spring there are Dutchman's-breeches flapping in the breeze; in fall the pawpaws give the forest a banana smell.

At 1.2 miles reach Snavely Ford, the crossing point for a division of Union soldiers, about 3,000 men, on a flanking maneuver. They made their way up the hill toward Sharpsburg here; the road they traveled is still visible to the left, beginning at about 1.3 miles. Uphill, the forest cover changes to thick red cedar. On early evening hikes, you may see several deer leaving the cedar cover to follow the trail down to the creek.

At the top of the hill, stay to the left, passing by the monument to William McKinley, who was at the battle and later became the twenty-fifth president of the United States. The parking area is 0.5 mile down a dirt cart path.

Miles and Directions

0.0 Start at the trailhead at the bottom of the steps.

0.1 Reach the Georgians Overlook cutoff.

1.2 Reach Snavely Ford.

1.4 Views of the battle road begin.

1.8 At the top of the hill, turn left on the cart path to return to the trailhead.

2.3 Arrive back at the trailhead.

11 Hog Rock-Blue Ridge Summit, Catoctin Mountain Park

Take a ramble through hardwood forests and over ridges of Catoctin Mountain, with views of the Blue Ridge and the Monocacy Valley, coupled with a short excursion to Cunningham Falls. In spring, dogwoods and other flowering trees are abundant.

Start: The trailhead is at the far end of the lot to the east.

Distance: 5.2-mile loop

Hiking time: About 3 hours

Difficulty: Moderate but rocky

Elevation gain: 700 feet

Trail surface: Natural packed dirt; rocky in places; Appalachian piedmont

Best season: Year-round

Schedule: Dawn to dusk

Other trail users: None

Canine compatibility: Pets are allowed in Catoctin Mountain Park as long as they are physically restrained on a leash no longer than 6 feet at all times or are otherwise physically confined.

Land status: Catoctin Mountain Park, a unit of the National Park Service; Frederick County, Maryland, about 50 miles northwest of Washington, D.C.

Nearest town: Thurmont

Fees and permits: None

Camping: Camping is offered on a first-come, first-served basis. At adjacent Cunningham Falls State Park, reservations are accepted. Camping is available in campgrounds only; several locations have multiple sites. Cabins are also available. Registration and a fee are required.

Trailhead facilities: Water fountain outside visitor center; bookstore, museum, restrooms, and water fountain inside visitor center

Maps: USGS Blue Ridge Summit PA; Catoctin Mountains, National Park Service (NPS); topo map sold in visitor center

Trail contact: Catoctin Mountain Park, 6602 Foxville Rd., Thurmont, MD; (301) 663-9330, emergency (301) 714-2235; www.nps.gov/ cato. Physical address: 14707 Park Central Rd., Thurmont, MD.

Special considerations: The NPS does not blaze the trails in Catoctin, but this trail is easy to follow in spring and summer. However, in late fall leaves can cover the route, so be sure you're following the path. Wear good footwear. This hike is described as moderate because most of the climbing is done in two short stretches: the first 0.25 mile and the 0.3-mile approach to Blue Ridge Summit Overlook. Most of the rest of the hike is a mixture of level ground and gradual ascents and descents. This is a beautiful hike in winter, especially when using snowshoes after a winter storm.

Finding the trailhead: From the Capital Beltway, drive north on I-270 about 32 miles and exit onto US 15 north. In 17 miles head west on MD 77 (at Thurmont). Watch for the sign to Catoctin Mountain Park; it is a quick right off US 15 after you see the sign. Catoctin Mountain Park Visitor Center is 3 miles farther on the right. GPS: N39 38.020' / W77 26.966'

The Hike

Within a few hours, you can visit a splendid waterfall, enjoy a spectacular view of the Monocacy watershed, and find an intimate cross ridge at Catoctin's summit and South Mountain, all while wandering through a second-growth (almost-old-growth-again)

Young families enjoying the view from Hog Rock.

hardwood forest. But what is the rush? The hike is short enough that extended stays are in order at each highlight.

Starting at the trailhead visitor center, begin ascending toward Hog Rock and Thurmont Vista. The first 0.25 mile is a rude start for automobile-weary legs, but leveler ground is found soon enough. The dogwoods and spicebush, scattered here and there with mountain laurel, are reason enough to take it slow and get your lungs working. This is a scenic hike any time of year, but spring on Catoctin Mountain is a world of flowering trees.

At 0.6-mile Wolf Rock Trail leads east to Wolf Rock, a formation of Weverton quartzite named for its resemblance to the snout and mane of a wolf. You can detour to Wolf Rock without backtracking to this junction: From Wolf Rock, hike north past Thurmont Vista to rejoin this hike at the 1-mile point (Thurmont Vista Trail junction). It will add about 1.6 miles to the hike and a fair amount of up-and-down.

To follow the route without a visit to Wolf Rock, stay straight, following the ridgeline north from the junction with Wolf Rock Trail. The trail flattens out as you walk through beech, poplar, oak, and maple. At 1.2 miles is a four-way intersection where the Thurmont Vista Trail joins the Hog Rock Trail from the right. To the left is Charcoal Trail, which tells the story of the charcoal industry that, along with leather tanning, supported the mountain settlers in the nineteenth century. Bark was gathered and sold to leather tanners, and the trees were felled to make charcoal as a fuel for nearby iron furnaces. The mountain people effectively worked themselves out of an existence, however, because their livelihoods were hardly sustainable once they had denuded Catoctin Mountain of every tree. The story is true for many of the nearby mountains of the Blue Ridge. Still, the process of charcoal production is fascinating and worthy of a detour to Charcoal Trail.

Go straight toward Hog Rock and descend into a small hollow. You will pass through a large section of blown-down trees from the storms of 2012. Pass through a boulder field of Catoctin greenstone, a basalt rock formed from compressed lava flows. Watch for the ragged outcropping to your right. The trail bends around this formation downhill to the right. Then begin a long, slow ascent toward Blue Ridge Summit Overlook, passing another boulder field where rock has tumbled down the mountainside. A section of level ground prepares you for a short, intense rise of about 100 feet over only 200 yards.

A brief respite from ascending follows, then make a quick final ascent to Blue Ridge Summit Overlook at 1.9 miles. A short trail leads to the view over the ledge. From here you can almost reach out and touch Catoctin's summit, at 1,880 feet, about 0.5 mile away on the other side of a narrow hollow. On a clear day you can also spy South Mountain between the ridges, part of the jumbled collection of peaks and hollows that make up the Blue Ridge. In some places the Blue Ridge runs southwest to northwest in one clearly defined ridge. In many others, the naming of one mountain as a separate summit seems almost arbitrary.

From here follow the ridge and gently descend amid mature chestnut oak and beech. On a damp day particularly, the scent of sassafras fills the air. At the Hog Rock Nature Trail junction, at 2.1 miles, there are picnic tables and privies. Crossing Park Central Road, follow Hog Rock Nature Trail on a casual ascent. Mature sugar maples and basswood line the trail. The crosscut wounds on the maples that resemble closed lips are the handiwork of woodpeckers and other insect-loving birds. They cut a horizontal gash in the trunk, which gets the sap running. When insects come to feed on the sap, the birds arrive for their own feeding.

Several interesting rock formations of Catoctin greenstone abut the trail; pignut hickory rise above them. The nuts, once favored by swine turned loose to roam the woods, now attract legions of squirrels and chipmunks. To this day, hickory is a choice wood for tool handles. Before the mountain was cut for bark and charcoal, the hickory here was prized for hammer mauls.

Hog Rock, at 2.6 miles, is a fine rest stop. A huge, flat outcrop of greenstone, it is also the place for a nap—especially on weekdays, when you stand a good chance of having the place to yourself. As was the custom throughout much of the Blue Ridge, in years past mountain farmers let their swine run wild through the woods, allowing them to graze on nuts and seeds and whatever else they could find. In autumn the hogs typically ended up at the base of this rock, feasting on hickory and chestnuts. The farmers would retrieve the fattened animals here at Hog Rock.

From Hog Rock begin a slow 1-mile descent toward Cunningham Falls. There are a few stream crossings and boulder fields amid the towering, misnamed tulip

Hog Rock–Blue Ridge Summit; Wolf Rock–Chimney Rock Loop

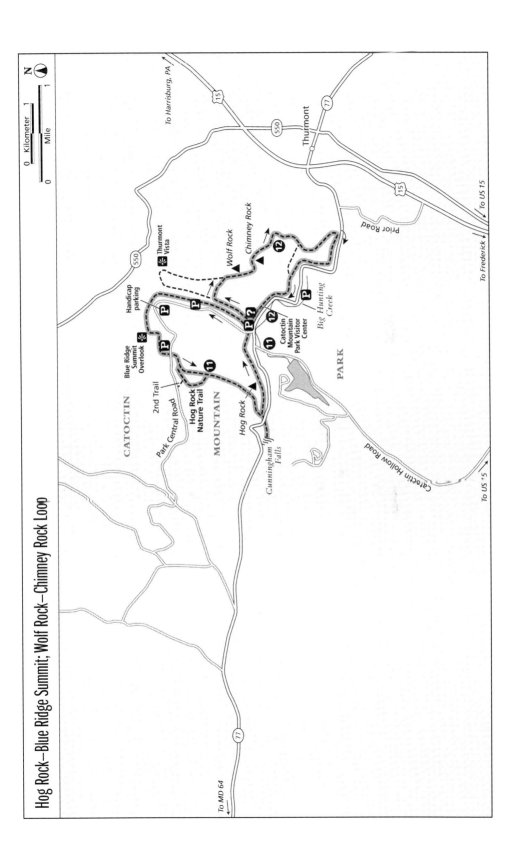

poplars and the occasional, aptly named musclewood trees. The tulip poplar, known by its excellent upright posture and light-gray corrugated bark, actually is not a poplar at all. It is a member of the magnolia family. The musclewood's small stature belies its strength—its wood is so tough, it was once used to make ox yokes. Tiny spring beauties grace the trail in the early spring, to be followed a few weeks later by dogwood, redbud, and mayapples.

Descend more steeply for the final 200 yards to reach the junction with the short trail to Cunningham Falls at 4 miles. Viewing the falls requires a short 0.25-mile detour. Cross MD 77 into Cunningham Falls State Park and follow the boardwalk another hundred yards to the falls. Early morning and late afternoon are the best times to find some solitude at the falls—winter is a great time to visit.

Back on the main trail, the final 1.2 miles are an easy ramble under tulip poplars and beech, with two short ascents over low knobs. MD 77 parallels the trail, so it can be noisy. In the spring local residents forage for edible morel mushrooms on this side of the mountain. (Though morels are a delicacy, know what you're looking for before eating mushrooms.) Cross Hunting Creek and enter the parking lot. The bookstore and museum inside the visitor center make a good finish for this hike.

Miles and Directions

0.0 Start at the trailhead visitor center.

0.6 Reach the junction with Wolf Rock Trail and stay straight.

1.2 Reach the junction with Thurmont Vista Trail and go straight.

1.9 Arrive at Blue Ridge Summit Overlook.

2.2 Cross Park Central Road.

2.6 Arrive at Hog Rock, a good rest stop.

4.0 Reach the junction with the short trail to Cunningham Falls.

5.2 Arrive back at the visitor center.

Option: For a short hike to Cunningham Falls, start at the visitor center and hike west, reversing the final 1.2 miles of this hike.

12 Wolf Rock-Chimney Rock Loop, Catoctin Mountain Park

This somewhat rugged hike climbs to outstanding vistas and a fascinating rock formation known as Wolf Rock. Sturdy footwear is recommended. The hike takes you through hardwoods and abundant mountain laurel.

See map on page 61.
Start: The trailhead is at the far end of the paved lot, past the visitor center.
Distance: 3.9-mile loop
Hiking time: About 2 hours
Difficulty: Strenuous
Elevation gain: 500 feet overall, a lot of up and down
Trail surface: Natural packed dirt, rocky; Appalachian piedmont
Best season: Year-round
Schedule: Dawn to dusk
Other trail users: None
Canine compatibility: Pets are allowed in Catoctin Mountain Park as long as they are physically restrained on a leash no longer than 6 feet in length at all times or are otherwise physically confined. Dogs are not allowed on the Chimney Rock and Wolf Rock formations.
Land status: Catoctin Mountain Park, a unit of the National Park Service (NPS); Frederick County, Maryland, about 50 miles northwest of Washington, D.C.
Nearest town: Thurmont

Fees and permits: None
Camping: In Catoctin Mountain Park and adjacent Cunningham Falls State Park, great quiet camping is available in secluded campgrounds. Several locations have multiple sites. Camping is available by reservation at Catoctin Mountain Park, as are (29) cabins. Registration and a fee are required.
Trailhead facilities: Bookstore, museum, restrooms, and water fountain and bottle filler inside visitor center
Maps: USGS Blue Ridge Summit PA; Cunningham Falls State Park map, NPS maps at the visitor center
Trail contact: Catoctin Mountain Park, 6602 Foxville Rd., Thurmont, MD; (301) 663-9330; https://www.nps.gov/cato/planyourvisit/hiking.htm
Special considerations: This trail is easy to follow in spring and summer. However, in late fall leaves can cover the route, so be sure you're following the path, especially the last few miles. Wear good, sturdy footwear. In addition, you will be in snake habitat so beware and be careful.

Finding the trailhead: From the Capital Beltway, drive north on I-270 about 32 miles and exit onto US 15 north. In 17 miles head west on MD 77 (at Thurmont). Watch for the sign to Catoctin Mountain Park; it is a quick right off US 15 after you see the sign. Catoctin Mountain Park Visitor Center is 3 miles farther up MD 77 on the right. The trailhead is at the far east end of the paved lot. GPS: N39 38.020' / W77 26.966'

The Hike

At the trailhead on the east end of the paved parking lot, begin ascending the Orange Trail on stone steps toward Hog Rock and Thurmont Vista. You'll pass through mature woods of maple, and oak, dogwoods, and spicebush. In spring these blooming trees teem with mountain laurel and rhododendron to create quite a flower show.

Sunning turkey vultures on Wolf Rock.

At 0.6 mile turn right (east), following the sign to Wolf Rock. Ascend a steep switchback to a junction with the pink/purple-blazed Thurmont Vista Trail. A looped side trip to Thurmont Vista, about 1 mile north, offers surprising solitude in this popular hiking area. A hike to the vista presents a view to the east at the beginning of the twenty-first century that is vastly different than it was at the start of the previous century. The fertile farmland of the Monocacy Valley is giving way to houses—intense efforts are under way to preserve the valley's historic farmland as a result. It reconnects with the orange trail in about 1.5 miles.

Follow the orange Wolf Rock Trail south to a formation of Weverton quartzite, named for the resemblance of one of many rock stacks to the snout and mane of a wolf. While the vistas get top billing on this hike, the huge old-growth trees through this section is memorable. Passing along the huge slab of rock, you will reach the turnoff to Wolf Rock overlook at 1.2 miles. Take care climbing on the rocks. This is a good spot for lunch, but please "leave no trace."

From Wolf Rock proceed across level ground and a short uphill to Chimney Rock at 1,400 feet, with another outstanding view to the east of the nearby Monocacy Valley. The peak to the southeast is 1,500-foot Cat Rock, accessible from the trailhead across from the National Park Service headquarters. Reaching it requires an ascent of 700 feet in less than a mile.

Following the white markers, descending from Chimney Rock through the forest, pass a trail cutting right and head downhill to Big Hunting Creek. Reach the creek at 3 miles.

From here, the trail parallels MD 77 for much of the way back to the trailhead. It is a lovely walk along the creek, but you will encounter road noise. Although newly blazed, this section of the trail may not be very discernible in the fall and winter. Be sure of where you're heading. Follow the path, diverging from the creek periodically, back to the parking area.

Miles and Directions

0.0 Start at the trailhead at the visitor center.

0.6 Reach the fork to Wolf Rock and go right.

1.2 Arrive at Wolf Rock.

2.0 Reach Chimney Rock.

3.0 Reach Big Hunting Creek.

3.9 Arrive back at the trailhead.

Honorable Mention

A Fort Frederick State Park Nature Trail

This easy, 1.2-mile loop through a young forest in an area that was previously logged is a great hike for kids or for a field study of forest succession. If your family likes car camping, Fort Frederick is a small gem on the banks of the Potomac River.

Because it is very short and not entirely pristine, Fort Frederick State Park Nature Trail is not a "destination hike." Nevertheless, a walk on the trail could be a nice part of a family outing to the park. In addition to the nature trail, the park boasts Fort Frederick, the national historic monument that played a role in the French and Indian, Revolutionary, and Civil Wars. The historic Chesapeake & Ohio Canal Towpath passes through the park, as does, of course, the Potomac River. With a picnic area by the trailhead, the park is a great place to spend a day exploring the human and natural history of the area.

As you follow the trail through dense thickets and saplings common to recovering forests, and then bend into an older forest of pines and the mixed hardwoods that will one day succeed the conifers, you will have a sense of why this part of the park is called the pine plantation area. The marks of logging are everywhere, but so are the signs of recovery: Note the different stages a forest passes through on its way from clearing to thicket to pine forest to an ever-increasing mix of hardwoods.

Soon the trail travels through more mature woodland. Still young by forest standards, there are nevertheless some big pines, along with sturdy oaks, maples, and sweet gums. You will also pass through grassy meadows where deer browse and stands of bigger hardwoods—mostly tall, straight tulip trees on their way to being stately giants—before returning to the trailhead.

Finding the trailhead: Fort Frederick State Park is located in Washington County, Maryland, about 80 miles northwest of Washington, D.C., and 12 miles southeast of Hancock, Maryland. From I-70 in western Maryland, take exit 12 (Big Pool–Indian Springs) and travel 1.1 miles east on MD 56 to the entrance of Fort Frederick State Park. Turn right into the park; bear left in 0.1 mile and follow the road 0.4 mile to Fort Frederick National Historic Monument. Turn left just past the fort, and travel 0.5 mile to the parking at the picnic area. GPS: N39 36.809' / W77 59.998'

Contact information: Fort Frederick State Park, 11100 Fort Frederick Rd., Big Pool, MD; (301) 842-2155; https://dnr.maryland.gov/publiclands/pages/western/fortfrederick.aspx

West of the Chesapeake Bay and Susquehanna River

Fishing at dusk on the Susquehanna.

13 Hashawha Loop, Hashawha Environmental Appreciation Area

A fine walk rambles through surprisingly deep woods in a county park. There are views of Pars Ridge, the principal geologic feature of Carroll County, and passages through open meadows and cultivated fields. The Bear Branch Nature Center hosts a raptor exhibit where visitors can see the wild birds close-up.

Start: Find the trailhead beyond the lake and up the hill near the Bear Branch Nature Center, at the far end of the parking area.
Distance: 4.7-mile loop
Hiking time: About 3 hours
Difficulty: Easy
Elevation gain: 320 feet
Trail surface: Natural packed dirt; rolling hills
Best season: Year-round
Schedule: Dawn to dusk
Other trail users: Bikers, horseback riders, and cross-country skiers
Canine compatibility: Leashed pets permitted
Land status: Hashawha Environmental Appreciation Area (a county park); Carroll County, Maryland, about 30 miles northwest of Baltimore and 5 miles north of Westminster
Nearest town: Westminster
Fees and permits: None
Camping: On weekends and through the summer months, Hashawha's residential facility is available to rent by groups such as churches,

Scouts, and the like. A group may rent anywhere between 1 and 5 cabins. The minimum group size is 15 people while the maximum group size is 145.
Trailhead facilities: Water and restrooms are available at Bear Branch Nature Center. The facility, which houses wildlife exhibits and offers a wide array of programming, is open Wed–Sat from 11 a.m. to 5 p.m. and Sun from noon to 5 p.m. Hours are subject to change. Call for more information.
Maps: USGS Finksburg MD; county trail map
Trail contact: Bear Branch Nature Center, 300 John Ownings Rd., Westminster, MD; (410) 386-3580; www.carrollcountymd.gov/government/directory/recreation-parks/places-to-go/hashawha-environmental-center-bear-branch-nature-center/; bearbranch@carrollcountymd.gov
Special considerations: When the nature center is closed, no water is available.

Finding the trailhead: Follow MD 97 north from Westminster for 5 miles to John Owings Road. Turn right and go 1 mile to Hashawha Environmental Appreciation Area on the left. Proceed past the lake and up the hill to Bear Branch Nature Center. GPS: N39 38.826' / W76 59.207'

The Hike

Note: As of this writing, the park managers are revising the map, blazes, and trail markers, which are sorely outdated. Ignore the yellow metal signs with numbers and arrows, some lodged into trees long ago. But the following description is accurate. Additionally, the county airport is close by, and a major roadway is to the west so, at times, you will hear planes and road noise.

The author at a log cabin along the trail. PHOTO COURTESY OF RUTH CONNELL

Carroll County is not known as a hiking destination. But the quiet woods, the opportunity to see a fox or hawk hunting in a cornfield or beavers plying the stream, and the extensive variety of wildflowers in the stream bottomland all combine to make this an outing worth traveling for—especially when combined with a visit to Westminster's Main Street or other Carroll County attractions.

Following the white blazes from the rear of the nature center parking area to the Vista Trail, descend the path to a picnic pavilion. Turn right with the blazes, and follow a wide path 250 yards down to the end of the opening. Go left into woods on the Vista Trail, ascending a small knob through oak and dogwood. Go left at the next intersection; stay on the main trail, past the trail leading left back to the picnic area you skirted by a few minutes earlier. Ascend easily through a white pine grove, with a nice view of farmland on the right and a meadow on the left. In the distance is the scenic wooded hillside of Pars Ridge, a narrow crest running from Washington, D.C., into southern Pennsylvania, and the feature that gives the region its famous rolling countryside.

At 0.8 mile the woods open at the raptor center, which houses birds of prey that are brought here following life-threatening injuries. Take the green-blazed Stream Trail right, along the park road. The white-blazed Vista Trail turns left at the raptor center.

In a short distance, go right onto an old farm road and the start of the Stream Trail. Quiet hikers will be rewarded here with views of deer, fox, and rabbits, which favor the edge where the farm fields to the right meet the woods just beyond. Throughout the hike you will witness a number of large uprooted and blown-down trees and especially in this section. At 1.1 miles the yellow-blazed Boundary Trail skirts right into the woods. Before you turn right here, take a moment to examine the 1800s log cabin. In the 1990s the cabin was entirely reconstructed. It is now open during festivals and for group programs. You will have to content yourself with an outside examination because vandals have forced the closure of the building.

From the cabin, follow the yellow blazes leading right on a narrow path between low shrubs and wildflowers, a veritable butterfly alley in summer. On an early August day, you may see a hundred butterflies in these 40 feet of green tunnel.

Enter a pine grove, and ascend through a cool, sweet-scented canopy. When the park was acquired in the 1970s, there were virtually no trees on the property. These white pines were planted through the efforts of Hashawha staff and Carroll County school students and give the grove a plantation-like appearance.

Pass an unblazed trail on the right—do not take it. Continue following the yellow blazes, and descend into a deep hollow; then ascend and emerge into an open field. The corn or other crop that may be planted here is a common feature in many Maryland parks, where park and agriculture coexist. It makes for a pleasurable hike, especially for those remembering childhood hikes through nearby farms. Veer right, and follow the line of trees for 50 yards. Enter the woods again, this time under mixed hardwoods—red oak, poplar, and beech—passing the Warbler (Red) Trail at 1.3 miles. The trail forms a shorter, woodland loop that rejoins the main trail at about 3 miles.

Enter a field with a splendid view straight ahead of the Pars Ridge—the quintessential Carroll County scene. If you reach this spot late in the afternoon, pause at the woods' edge and scan the field for wildlife activity. If you are lucky, you may see a coyote ambling through the field. If you are especially lucky, it will be in pursuit of a rabbit.

Continue straight across the farm field to the midway point, turn left toward the trees, then right, again following the Boundary Trail toward the woods to the east. Descend into the trees, passing the Yellow Loop 2 marker at 1.5 miles. In another 100 feet, pass the Half Car Trail on the left.

Begin a long descent on a wide path until you enter the Big Pipe Creek floodplain. Emerging from the woods, 30 yards to the right is a gated trailhead at Sawmill Road. Make a hairpin turn left and begin walking uphill adjacent to Big Pipe Creek. The creek, one of the largest streams entirely within Carroll County, is 75 yards to the right, beneath the birches and a few cottonwoods. Watch for deer and smaller denizens, such as gophers, scattering at the sound of you.

At 2 miles enter the woods and begin ascending on a wide path. The hillside suddenly drops dramatically to the right, and the creek is 50 feet below you. The next 0.5 mile is as lovely a walk as you will find anywhere in Maryland. With the ridge rising steeply to your left and the stream splashing far below, this is a place to walk slowly and savor your time.

After a gentle descent back to floodplain, turn sharply left, away from the creek, and ascend at 2.5 miles. The trail that continues straight ahead is open to hikers but is managed for hunting in season. Check with the park office for information when hiking from September through March. Fifty yards after turning left, be sure to stay right at the fork, following the yellow blazes. Horse riders go left.

Hashawha Loop, Hashawha Environmental Appreciation Area

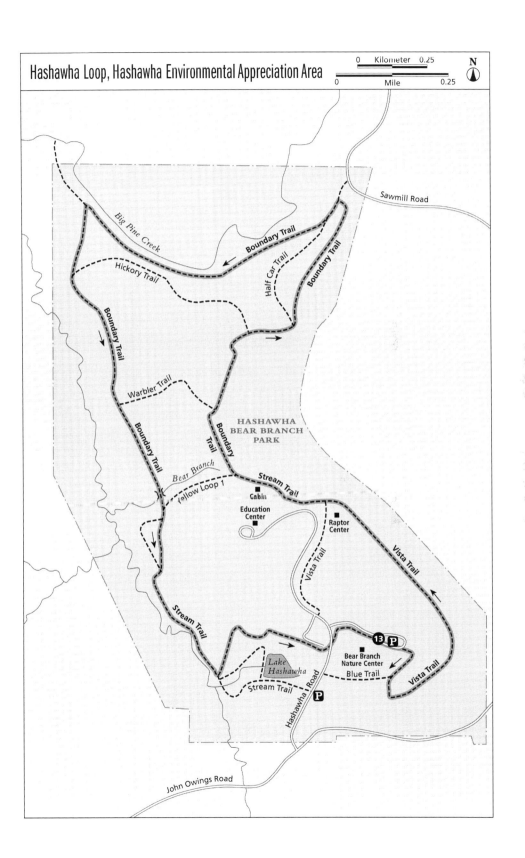

Climb steeply for about a hundred yards, and then find level ground. Over the next 0.5 mile, follow the yellow blazes past the Hickory Trail at about 2.6 miles (look for the shagbark hickory just in front of you) and then the Warbler Trail, rambling over knobs and descending into hollows. From time to time, the trail emerges into small meadows that are lush with blackberries and wildlife-viewing opportunities.

At 3.1 miles descend to a small stream and cross on a footbridge. Continue straight for 20 yards to a junction. The log cabin you passed at 1.1 miles is now 200 yards to the left. Turn right at this junction, following what is now the green Stream Trail in and out of the woods. Presently, you have the option of taking the high trail or low trail at 3.4 miles. The high trail takes a direct route to an open field and Bear Branch Creek, while the low trail ducks into the woods—the distance is about the same, and the two rejoin as the trail enters the field in 200 yards. Watch for the green blazes on a post. Walk into the field, then turn right into its center, then left about 60 yards from the woods. Picnic tables (easily accessible from the parking area just around the corner) are scattered along the creek and in the woods for a very delightful family gathering.

At 3.9 miles reach a clearing at Bear Branch Creek. (A metal bridge over the stream leads to an equestrian trail system.) Follow the green blazes left, up and around a large sycamore tree with its distinctive ghostly white bark. Walk steeply uphill to the white pine grove and large fenced area, then sharply right downhill around the grove and above Lake Hashawha. The path skirts a cluster of beehives and cuts through maintenance buildings to the main road you came in on. Go left at the road and return to the Bear Branch Nature Center via the driveway.

Miles and Directions

0.0 Start at the white Vista Trailhead at the rear of the nature center parking area.

0.8 Arrive at the raptor center. Go right, following green Stream Trail.

1.1 Reach the junction with the Boundary Trail. Examine the cabin before turning right onto the yellow Boundary Trail.

1.3 Pass the Warbler (Red) Trail junction.

1.6 Pass the Half Car Trail to the left.

1.8 Turn sharply left at Big Pipe Creek and ascend.

3.1 Descend to a small stream and cross on a footbridge.

3.9 Reach the clearing at Bear Branch Creek. Follow the green blazes.

4.2 Cross the park road and turn left. Then turn right onto white trail.

4.7 Arrive back at the trailhead.

Options: For a shorter hike of about 2 miles, on the outward leg continue past the cabin on the green trail rather than following the yellow-blazed Boundary Trail. Follow green blazes through new woodlands and seasonal wetlands down in the bottomland of a small stream and connect with the return leg of the hike. Turn left to return to the trailhead. You also can use Warbler and Half Car Trails for a shorter hike. The white-blazed Vista Trail makes a 1.2-mile loop back to Bear Branch, leaving from the raptor area at 0.8 mile.

14 BeeTree Preserve

This hike combines views of the open rural Baltimore County countryside with a circuit through the woods along the Torey C. Brown Rail Trail (TCBRT).

Start: Walk north from the trailhead parking area on the TCBRT with the parking on your right.
Distance: 3.7-mile lollipop
Hiking time: About 2.5 hours
Difficulty: Moderate
Elevation gain: 100 feet
Trail surface: Crush and run (crushed stone) on rail trail; natural soil and leaf litter
Best season: Year-round
Schedule: Daylight hours
Other trail users: Bikers, equestrians, campers; hunting club Oct 1 through Jan 31
Canine compatibility: Leashed dogs permitted
Land status: BeeTree Preserve is along the TCBRT, 18 miles north of Cockeysville, Maryland. The property is in church ownership with public access.
Nearest town: Parkton

Fees and permits: None, but donations are encouraged.
Camping: Camping is available for organized groups with a church-issued permit.
Trailhead facilities: Pay phone, privy
Maps: USGS New Freedom PA; map at www.towsonpres.org/index.php/about-tpc/beetree-preserve
Trail contact: Towson Presbyterian Church, 400 W. Chesapeake Ave., Towson, MD; (410) 823-6500; tpc@towsonpres.org; www.towsonpres.org/about/beetree/
Special considerations: BeeTree Preserve is privately owned by the Towson Presbyterian Church; respect any trail closures related to church-sponsored events. Calling in advance of your hike is requested only for groups of more than 6 people. Hunting is only allowed by membership in a hunting club under lease to Towson Presbyterian Church.

Finding the trailhead: From the Baltimore Beltway (I-695), travel north 17 miles on I-83 to exit 33, York Road. Go north on York Road (MD 45) for 1 mile, and turn left onto Kaufman Road. In about 0.7 mile turn left onto Bentley Road, and proceed 0.7 mile to the parking area on the right. GPS: N39 40.546' / W76 40.126'

The Hike

This hike offers one of the few circuit hikes along the Torrey C. Brown Rail Trail (formerly the Northern Central Railroad Trail), allowing you to hike a little on the wide flat path of the famous Northern Central Railroad (NCRR) through the rolling countryside, then duck into the woods for a ramble around a hilltop nature preserve. The hike's main attraction is the varied experiences that it packs into a short hike—the NCRR, mature and recovering forestland, the babbling of BeeTree Run, associated wetlands, and passage above a scenic stream hollow. This is a particularly enjoyable short ramble in spring, when you will see the varied blooms of wildflowers and trees in the woods and under the NCRR's open skies. In addition, the area

Dogwood, azaleas, and numerous wildflowers abound in the pockets of woodland along the TCBRT. Photo courtesy of Maryland DNR

is home to at least thirty-eight species of forest-dwelling birds and, just north of the junction with the TCBRT, a colony of beavers.

Walk north on the TCBRT with the parking area on your right. If you've never hiked or biked the TCBRT before, this will be enough to entice you to walk or bike its length. In places, the landscape surrounding this former rail line still resembles the countryside of long ago, when the morning milk was sent south to Baltimore by train. Beginning in the 1950s, the line began sending commuters down and back, then it closed altogether.

Turn right onto BeeTree Road at 0.8 mile, and walk straight to the sharp bend in the road a few hundred yards ahead. At the bend go straight to leave the road and follow the fire road behind a gate. Climb a steep hill on the fire road into the woods for 200 yards. The road levels off in a small clearing. Continue north on the fire road for a pleasant walk through recovering woods for 0.5 mile. At a clearing at 1.3 miles, take the hard-left trail (not the middle trail) into the woods. After a short, steep descent, reach a T at the bottom of the hill at 1.4 miles. Turn left and walk with BeeTree Run on your right, leaving the stream and ascending on an old roadbed, while slabbing around the hill. To your right a wide hollow opens up. In spring, flowering redbud and dogwood trees are abundant here.

Continue to climb gradually. At 2.3 miles return to the first small clearing. Take the first right into the woods and follow the yellow blazes across a flat, wide ridge. Pass through Soldiers Ridge campsite, with its four Adirondack shelters and an outhouse. Follow the yellow-blazed trail out of camp 175 yards to another T junction. Go left and descend steeply to a clearing to rejoin the TCBRT at 2.7 miles. Turn left. (Or to see a beaver pond, at 2.7 miles turn right and go north along the TCBRT for about 0.25 mile. View the pond on the west side of trail.)

Traveling south, cross BeeTree Run on a bridge, then cross BeeTree Road at 2.9 miles (this is where you left the TCBRT earlier). Continue down the TCBRT back to the trailhead.

BeeTree Preserve

Not to Scale

N

Miles and Directions

0.0 Start at the TCBRT trailhead on Bentley Road.

0.8 Turn right onto BeeTree Road.

1.3 Take a soft left at the second clearing.

2.3 Return to the clearing; take the first right, following yellow blazes.

2.7 Rejoin the TCBRT.

2.9 Cross BeeTree Road.

3.7 Arrive back at the trailhead.

Option: Park at BeeTree Road and hike the woods circuit only, picking up the route at the 0.8-mile mark.

15 Torrey C. Brown Rail Trail

Named for the third secretary of the Maryland Department of Natural Resources, the Torrey C. Brown Rail Trail follows the former Northern Central Railroad in northern Baltimore County. This wonderful walk travels 8 miles (although you can also do it in shorter sections) of the 20-mile Maryland section of the converted rail trail, following a number of small tributaries of the Gunpowder Falls River through scenic woods and rolling countryside. Stow a bicycle at the south end for a 16-mile hike-bike excursion.

Start: The trailhead for this hike is in Bentley Springs, 17 miles north of the Baltimore Beltway.

Distance: 16 miles out and back

Hiking time: About 8 hours

Difficulty: Easy

Elevation gain: Minimal

Trail surface: Crushed stone that is hard-packed and accessible to people with disabilities; lowlands

Best season: Year-round

Schedule: Dawn to dusk

Other trail users: Bikers, equestrians

Canine compatibility: Leashed pets permitted

Land status: Gunpowder Falls State Park; Baltimore County. The route stretches from the Pennsylvania line to Cockeysville, Maryland, about 5 miles north of the Baltimore Beltway.

Nearest town: Hereford

Fees and permits: None

Camping: Only youth group camping is permitted, with permit (fee charged).

Trailhead facilities: At Bentley Springs there is a pay phone and a privy. The station at Monkton has been restored as an administrative office for the state park. The building also houses a museum and meeting rooms. Restrooms and water are available. Across the trail, refreshments and provisions are available at the store in the Old Monkton Hotel. There is also an outdoors store that sells hiking and biking accessories.

Maps: USGS New Freedom PA; Hereford and Cockeysville MD

Trail contact: Torrey C. Brown Rail Trail, Gunpowder Falls State Park, Hereford Area, 1349 Wiseburg Rd., White Hall, MD; (410) 329-6809 or (410) 592-2897; https://dnr.maryland .gov/publiclands/pages/central/tcb.aspx; customerservice@dnr.state.md.us. Physical address: Baltimore County, Gunpowder Falls State Park, PO Box 480, 2813 Jerusalem Rd., Kingsville, MD 21087. Ranger station: 1820 Monkton Rd., Monkton, MD.

Special considerations: The trail is 10 feet wide and composed of crushed limestone. At the northern section there is plenty of solitude. As you approach Monkton, weekend bicycle traffic can be substantial. Equestrians may also be on the trail, but biking and hiking are most common. If you want the Monkton section all to yourself, travel midweek or, best of all, in winter.

Finding the trailhead: From the Baltimore Beltway (I-695), travel north 17 miles on I-83 to exit 33, York Road. Go north on York Road (MD 45) for 1 mile, and turn left onto Kaufman Road. In about 0.7 mile turn left onto Bentley Road and proceed 0.7 mile to the parking area on the right. GPS: N39 40.546' / W76 40.126'

The Hike

The trail follows the railbed of one of the oldest railroads in America—the Baltimore & Susquehanna Railroad/Northern Central Railroad (NCR) completed the Maryland portion of the line in 1838. It operated as a milk train, taking daily early-morning runs into Baltimore. The passenger line carried Civil War wounded from Gettysburg to Baltimore, then carried the body of President Abraham Lincoln north en route to his burial in Illinois. It later became a commuter rail. The line continued with daily service to Baltimore until 1959. Following its decline in use and damage from Tropical Storm Agnes, the NCR ended its run between York and Cockeysville in 1975.

All along the old railway, you will see mileage markers and other signs. The white posts with the large black "Ws" instructed train engineers to repeatedly sound a whistle (on steam locomotives) or air horn (on diesel-electric locomotives) as they approached a road crossing. Mileage markers, also white but with black numbers painted on each side facing the trail, told the engineer or other railroad workers where they were on the railroad. Facing the marker, the mileage on the right side indicates the distance to Sunbury, Pennsylvania, and on the left side, the distance to the former site of the railroad's Calvert Street Station in Baltimore. The hike from Bentley Springs to Monkton is an easy 3 hours; what's hard is pulling yourself away to walk back.

From the Bentley Springs trailhead, walk south along Bee Tree Run. Bentley Springs is a town of old homes and farmland. It is a former resort, hosting legions of Baltimoreans trying to escape the summer heat. Little Falls joins the trail from the west, and for nearly 0.5 mile Bee Tree Run and Little Falls are in view. The confluence of the two streams, at 0.5 mile, offers some of the best trout fishing around, as well as some of the more picturesque views of the surrounding countryside. After the confluence, Little Falls leaves the trail for a time.

The trail enters Parkton at 2.7 miles. There is trailhead parking in Parkton. The section south of Parkton boasts some of the trail's most dramatic views of Little Falls and the actual falls at 3 miles. Then the landscape rises sharply on both sides, leaving only the stream and the trail in a narrow cut in the landscape. Regale in the quirky "Gnome Village" at about 3.6 miles at the confluence of Little Falls and Third Mine Branch.

The route follows swift-moving Little Falls to the west as it meanders along to a broad bend just above White Hall, at 4.6 miles. Here, Second Mine Branch drains into Little Falls, which disappears behind the tiny village. The subtle changes in the character of the stream valley and trail become more evident in this section. The valley is wider and the woods are denser than in the north. There are farms in the area, but the sense of history here is more of mills than milk. White Hall is a former paper mill town, and the look of the old, as well as the new, architecture ties the area more closely to the city of Baltimore than to the other villages in the area. Look for trout

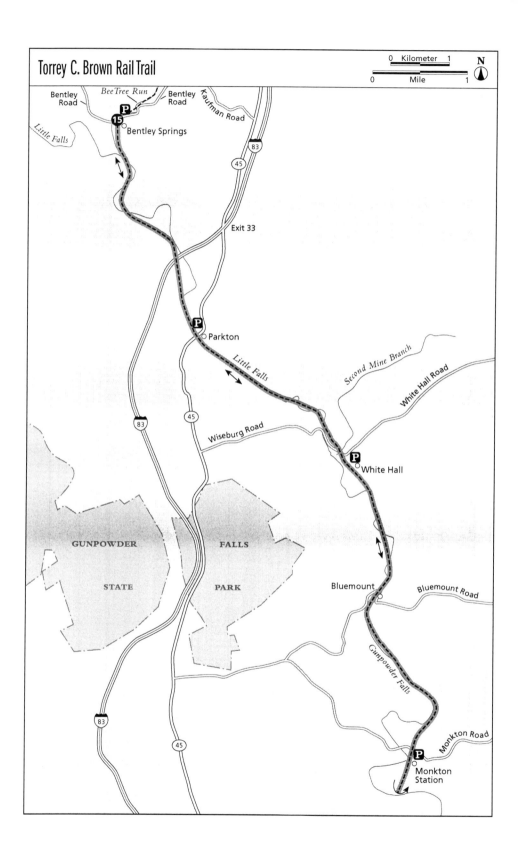

Torrey C. Brown Rail Trail

0   Kilometer   1

0   Mile   1

N

Bentley Road

Bee Tree Run

Bentley Road

Kaufman Road

15

Bentley Springs

Little Falls

83

45

Exit 33

Parkton

Little Falls

Second Mine Branch

White Hall Road

83

45

Wiseburg Road

White Hall

GUNPOWDER

FALLS

STATE

PARK

Bluemount

Bluemount Road

Gunpowder Falls

83

45

Monkton Road

Monkton Station

swimming below as you cross a number of old railroad bridges over Little Falls before reaching Bluemount Road at 6 miles, where the old railway crosses Little Falls for the final time before it empties into the larger Gunpowder Falls. The route now follows Gunpowder Falls.

Moving south, just above Monkton Station, the stone remains of the town of Pleasant Valley can be seen. Only a cross section of a two-story structure marks the old town from the trail.

Gunpowder Falls moves behind a hill to the west, and the trail descends along a rock face into Monkton, one of a dozen historic towns along the old line. If you left your vehicle back at Bentley Springs, this is your turnaround point.

Miles and Directions

0.0 Start at the Bentley Springs trailhead and head south on the rail trail.

0.5 Reach the confluence of BeeTree Run and Little Falls.

2.7 Enter Parkton.

4.6 Reach the village of White Hall.

6.0 Cross Bluemount Road.

8.0 Reach Monkton, the turnaround point.

16.0 Arrive back at Bentley Springs.

Options: There is trailhead parking at each of the historic towns visited on the hike. You can make a shorter trip by walking as far as you like and then returning. Or you can shuttle by leaving a car at a second location. For a truly remarkable day, plant a bicycle at the Monkton Station, the southern trailhead, and make the return by bike. Monkton is a happening spot on weekends. People of all ages congregate, awaiting or finishing their time on the trail. The bike shop is a gathering place, the vegetarian deli dishes up an assortment of sandwiches and sweets, and Lycra-clad cyclists chat it up with safari-shirted birders.

16 Lefty Kreh Fishing Trail and Gunpowder Falls North Loop, Gunpowder Falls State Park

This is a long, worthwhile walk through a diverse and compelling landscape along and above the scenic and renowned Big Gunpowder Falls. If you are an angler, the Big Gunpowder is recognized as one of the best trout streams in central Maryland.

Start: The trailhead is on the south side of Big Gunpowder Falls to the right of the parking area.
Distance: 8.1-mile figure-eight loop
Hiking time: About 5 hours
Difficulty: Moderate
Elevation gain: 300 feet
Trail surface: Natural packed dirt, rocky in places; rolling forested hills
Best season: Year-round
Schedule: Sunrise to sunset
Other trail users: Equestrians. No bicycles are permitted, as the Hereford Area is a protected state-designated wildland.
Canine compatibility: Leashed dogs permitted
Land status: The Hereford Area of Gunpowder Falls State Park; 20 miles north of Baltimore in Baltimore County
Nearest town: Hereford

Fees and permits: None
Camping: None
Trailhead facilities: None. A comfort station, open in summer, is located in the Camp Wood Youth Group Camping Area.
Maps: USGS Hereford MD; state maps available on the website
Trail contact: Gunpowder Falls State Park, PO Box 480, 2813 Jerusalem Road, Kingsville, MD 21087; (410) 592-2897; https://dnr .maryland.gov/publiclands/Pages/central/ GunpowderFalls/Hereford-Area-Trails.aspx; gunpowderfalls.statepark@maryland.gov
Special considerations: Gunpowder Falls is a stocked trout stream; licenses are required. Check at the trailhead in the fall for information on hunting season. If you stay on the trail, you will not enter hunting lands.

Finding the trailhead: From the Baltimore Beltway (I-695), travel north 12 miles on I-83 to the Hereford exit (27). Go west on MD 137 (Mount Carmel Road) 1 mile, and turn right (north) onto Masemore Road. Trailhead parking is 1.6 miles ahead on the right, on the south side of Gunpowder Falls just before the one-lane bridge over Gunpowder Falls. GPS: N39 36.649' / W76 40.951'

The Hike

You can make a day of hiking in the wooded stream valley of the Big Gunpowder Falls and the ridges above it, or you can take one of several shorter loop hikes. Raven Rock Falls, the stone ruins along Panther Branch, and views of hemlocks clinging to the canyon above Mingo Branch are just a few of the sights along the way. You might also encounter red fox, beaver, and wild turkey. If you fish, you could spend all day in the river.

From the parking area, follow the white blazes to the right using stepping stones over a small feeder creek and walk east, downstream, on the Lefty Kreh Fishing Trail.

The trail was dedicated in memory of the famed and beloved Lefty Kreh, Maryland's native son, fly-fishing pioneer, journalist, conservationist, and inspiration to "countless hopeful anglers around the world," as stated on a plaque in the parking lot.

The Big Gunpowder Falls is stocked with trout in the spring, and great numbers can be seen in the pools and shallows another hundred yards downstream. Beavers also inhabit the entire length of the river in this section. If you're lucky, just before sunset you may see them gliding through the cool water. In addition, the hillsides and cliffs along the river are steep enough to provide the cool temperatures and drainage favored by mountain laurel.

Stay with the white blazes as the trail breaks right away from the river at about 0.4 mile and climbs through a stand of mature hemlock. The junction is marked by a small seasonal stream. Do not continue straight. The stream is passable even in wet weather. Go right up the ravine and continue climbing, with the stream now on the right. This is the steepest ascent of the hike, but it lasts only 250 yards and climbs only 150 feet, leveling off in a clearing at the junction with the yellow-blazed Mingo Forks Trail, leading south at 0.6 mile. (Mingo Forks and Bunker Hill Trails create a 3-mile loop back to this spot.)

Staying left at the fork and following the white blazes, descend into ash and maple, with views between the trees to the north slope of Gunpowder Falls. A managed hunting area comes within 50 yards of the trail on the right. A long switchback descends steeply to the crossing, at 1 mile, of Mingo Branch, a 12-foot-wide creek offering plenty of stepping stones, except in high water, when it presents a shin-deep wade.

Ascend amid white pine and black walnut to the yellow-blazed Bunker Hill Trail, which leads right to Mingo Forks Trail and left to a comfort station and a youth group campground. Following the white blazes to the left, cross the paved access road to the comfort station and follow the white blazes downhill to the former Bunker Hill trailhead parking at 1.3 miles. Fifty yards north are the old covered-bridge abutments. Formerly, the bridge enabled a roadway connecting Bunker Hill Road on both the north and south sides of the river, but when the bridge was burned down for the second time, the county chose not to rebuild it, thereby preserving the wild, remote setting. Instead of a throughway, Bunker Hill Road now serves as a quiet trailhead on both sides of the river.

Follow the white blazes to the kiosk and go right, crossing a small bridge just in front of an amphitheater. The amphitheater rests just below a limestone knob where finches and hummingbirds buzz beneath the pines. Just before the amphitheater, the trail goes left to rejoin the river. Stay with the white blazes, following the river and ascending another steep hill. Stay to the left of a stand of white pines at the summit, taking care not to wander right onto the green-blazed Collette Loop. You are still on the white trail, but now you begin to hear the highway in the distance that you cross under in 0.5 mile.

For the next 0.5 mile, the trail hugs the ridgeline until descending via two switchbacks to cross under I-83 at 1.9 miles. It then emerges from the woods to cross York Road at 2 miles. The trail continues through the parking area, crossing York Road (be mindful of traffic), down a hill and right off the grassy area on the banks of the Big Gunpowder. You will see what looks like a weathered stone fireplace, which is just to the right of the trail as it heads back into the woods.

One hundred feet past the fireplace is a junction with the orange-blazed Panther Branch Trail at about 2.2 miles, which heads south, uphill. (This is where, on the return leg, the trail crosses to form the figure eight.) Keep going straight and, in another 100 yards, search for white blazes climbing right, taking care not to follow a false trail that continues along Gunpowder Falls. The trail may be hard to see in the fall with leaves on the ground, but you will know you are on the right track when you see white blazes as you climb uphill. If you lose the blazes and come to an eroded section of path immediately adjacent to the river, turn back to find the white blazes ascending the ridgeline. Although the trail is formally named for Lefty, the trail markers continue to use the old Gunpowder Falls South moniker.

Along the trail over the next 0.5 mile, there are a few spots to step off and enjoy the views of the canyon and, especially in winter, the hillside northwest of the river. Descending on a long switchback, the trail rejoins the river, enters a steep, wooded canyon, and leaves the road noise behind. At twilight the trail through the canyon is a thoroughfare for white-tailed deer and other animals making their way to water. For deer as well as people, there is no easy way up the south slope. Startled animals may make a break across the river, which is deeper and swifter here, forcing an otherwise graceful creature into awkward maneuvers.

The understory opens and great slabs of rock create a fortress on the opposite riverbank. Passing through a tunnel of mountain laurel, reach Raven Rock Falls on the north side at 2.8 miles. This is a popular fishing spot; the falls are accessible via Gunpowder North Trail, with parking areas located off York Road and Big Falls Road. But the best view of the falls is on this side of the river.

For the next mile the trail follows river bottomland, punctuated here and there with jaunts over small knobs. Pass Sandy Lane Trail at 3.2 miles. This trail offers an 0.8-mile shortcut back to York Road.

Passing Sandy Lane, the trail flattens along bottomland with a stand of spruce bisecting the lowlands. Take a minute to watch the many birds flitting in and out of the brush and in the trees here. You may see a redheaded woodpecker, a winter wren, or a white-breasted nuthatch among the buzz of activity. To your right the hillside is covered with Christmas fern, while a junk car and tin roof may surprise you on the left. There is also a very fishy stretch of water 0.25 mile above the junction with the orange-blazed Panther Branch Trail at 3.9 miles.

Here, the white-blazed Lefty Kreh/Gunpowder South Trail continues east 0.5 mile to Big Falls Road. (One option for the return hike is to continue on to

Big Falls Road, cross the road bridge, and then head west on Gunpowder North Trail to York Road. From there the trail follows the same route as this hike does on the return.)

Take a hard hairpin right and follow the orange-blazed Panther Branch Trail west up and over the tip of the ridge you've been walking below. Then move up Panther Branch through a low canyon draped with laurel, black walnut and other "recovery species." The crowded stand of the fast-growing walnut and pine above the dense underbrush is evidence that this side of the stream was at one time cleared for agriculture or settlement. Perhaps because of the steep slope, the mature forest on the other side of the stream was left relatively untouched.

Ruins of earlier settlement are still evident as the orange trail passes the remains of a kiln, a number of stone foundations, and what looks to be the remains of a millrace. At about 4.4 miles there is an unmarked junction. The trail continuing straight ahead, over a stream, is a horse trail that follows Panther Branch from the other side. Stay right, keeping the stream on your left, and continue uphill past numbered interpretative posts until the trail enters an open field.

Crossing the field, just as you reenter a large pine grove, continue straight, following the orange blazes as they duck right onto a narrow footpath off the access road at 5 miles. Follow the orange blazes past the junction with the Sandy Lane Trail at 5.3 miles.

The trail descends to a muddy creek crossing then rises to the top of the ridge and finally descends to York Road at 5.8 miles and the same spot you passed at about 2 miles.

Cross York Road and follow the shoulder north over the bridge for 175 yards until the blue blazes of Gunpowder North Trail are visible on the trees to the left. Cut through the break in the guardrail and follow the blue blazes west along the north bank of Gunpowder Falls on the Gunpowder Falls North Trail. The remaining 2.3 miles trace the north bank through the same territory covered in the first leg of the hike. However, on this side the trail stays close to river level, with no elevation change—you can coast for the last 2.3 miles.

Even though you are covering what is by now familiar ground, the view and experience are quite different. There are three highlights: crossing a cascading stream just before Bunker Hill Road at 6.7 miles; a huge rock outcrop towering 50 feet above the river floor just below the Bunker Hill parking area; and a hillside covered with laurel and studded with more rocky slabs, one that hangs over the river with a tree growing from it just 0.5 mile from the terminus. In early evening you may be treated to the sight of beavers or the sounds of a barred owl setting out for the hunt. At 8 miles cross the one-lane bridge over the Big Gunpowder Falls and return to the trailhead.

Lefty Kreh Fishing Trail and Gunpowder Falls North Loop, Gunpowder Falls State Park

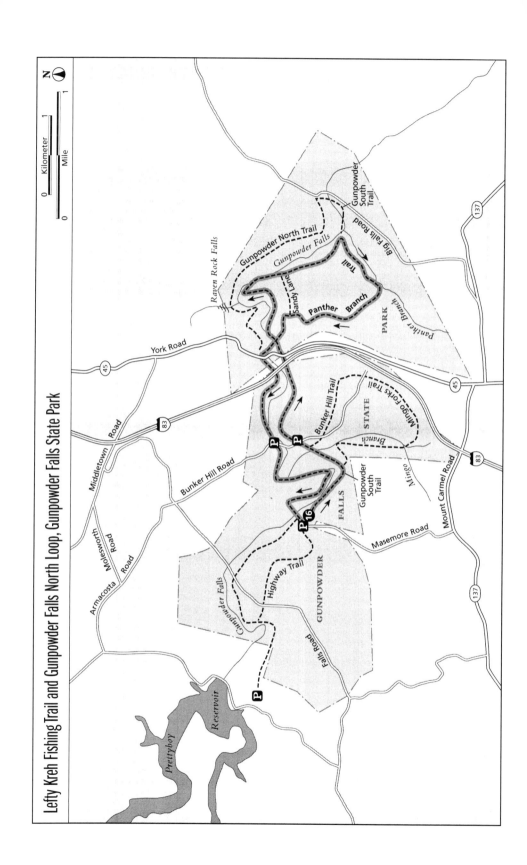

Miles and Directions

0.0 Start at the trailhead off Masemore Road. Follow white blazes east.

0.4 Crossing a small stream, go right uphill away from the river.

0.6 Reach the Mingo Forks Trail junction. Stay left at the fork.

1.0 Cross Mingo Branch.

1.3 Emerge from the woods and cross the access road. Stay with the white blazes.

2.0 Cross York Road and follow white blazes.

2.2 Junction with Panther Branch Trail. Go straight and watch for white trail cutting right uphill.

2.8 Pass Raven Rock Falls.

3.2 Pass the junction with the Sandy Lane Trail (east end).

3.9 Reach the junction with Panther Branch Trail. Make a hairpin right (west) onto the orange-blazed trail.

5.3 Reach Sandy Lane Trail junction (west end). Follow orange blazes left.

5.8 Cross York Road for the second time. Follow the shoulder north to the blue blazes.

6.5 Cross the stream just before Bunker Hill Road.

8.1 Cross the bridge to return to the trailhead.

Options: A 4.4-mile circuit can be made by crossing the river at York Road and heading west on Gunpowder North Trail, skipping the middle 3.7 miles. A 10.4-mile circuit is possible by taking Lefty Kreh/Gunpowder South Trail to Big Falls Road and returning on Gunpowder North Trail. A 2.7-mile loop is possible by heading west from the parking area on Lefty Kreh/Gunpowder South Trail for 1.7 miles, and then returning via Gunpowder Highland Trail.

17 Sweet Air Loop, Gunpowder Falls State Park

This wonderfully quiet hike offers a diversity of experiences: plentiful contact with Little Gunpowder Falls, a small pond in the woods, farm fields, immense tulip poplars, and small pine groves. In late July and early August, blackberries are plentiful. Little Gunpowder Falls contains many species of fish, including smallmouth bass and bluegill.

Start: Find the trailhead at the parking area at the top of the hill, to the left of the trail map.
Distance: 5.5-mile loop
Hiking time: About 3 hours
Difficulty: Easy
Elevation gain: 250 feet
Trail surface: Natural packed dirt, can be muddy; wooded lowlands
Best season: Year-round (July and Aug for blackberries)
Schedule: Sunrise to sunset
Other trail users: Bikers, equestrians
Canine compatibility: Leashed dogs permitted
Land status: Sweet Air Area of Gunpowder Falls State Park; on the Baltimore–Harford County line about 15 miles northeast of Baltimore
Nearest town: Cockeysville
Fees and permits: None
Camping: None

Trailhead facilities: A small picnic shelter with one table is available; a large map of the entire area appears on the information board.
Maps: USGS Phoenix MD; map at kiosk
Trail contact: Gunpowder Falls State Park, PO Box 480/2813 Jerusalem Rd., Kingsville, MD 21087; (410) 592-2897; https://dnr .maryland.gov/publiclands/Pages/central/ GunpowderFalls/Sweet-Air-Area.aspx; gunpowderfalls.statepark@maryland.gov
Special considerations: Bring along a container of frozen cream laced with sugar for blackberries in late July and August. The cream will melt while you hike, making a great dessert. The loop described passes close to private property in one place. Other loops within the park pass close to several houses. The trail also passes through cornfields leased to private farmers. Respect the privacy and property of all. Be aware of equestrian and bike traffic.

Finding the trailhead: From the Baltimore Beltway (I-695), drive 7 miles north on I-83 to the Shawan Road East exit. In 1 mile turn right onto York Road (MD 45); in 0.5 mile turn left onto Ashland Road (MD 145, which becomes Paper Mill Road). Continue straight through the intersection with MD 146, after which Paper Mill Road changes to Sweet Air Road. In 8.5 miles from I-83, turn left onto Green Road. In 1.7 miles turn left onto Moore's Road; about 0.25 mile farther, turn left onto Dalton Bevard Road, the park access road. Proceed to the trailhead parking area at the top of the hill. The physical address is 2840 Dalton Bevard Rd. in Baldwin. GPS: N39 32.161' / W76 30.303'

The Hike

The hike begins from the small picnic shelter at the west end of the parking area. Facing the shelter, locate the yellow-blazed trail at the far right (north end) of the clearing in the woods, following a wide tractor path. Keep an eye out for blackberries in season.

Beyond a row of pine trees, enter a cornfield and continue straight, walking between two sections of the field. When the corn is high, you will walk in a green

One of many thought-provoking postings along the Sweet Air trail.

tunnel scented sweetly with corn; when the corn is low or not yet planted, there is a picturesque view west.

Enter the woods and follow a wide path under large poplars. The understory is white with dogwoods and alive with redbud in spring. Reach Barley Pond at 0.5 mile, a quiet rest stop in a shady place.

To continue, retrace your steps to where you first encountered the pond; then retreat back up the trail 75 feet from the pond and turn left onto an unmarked trail, which leads up the slope of a small hollow to the white-blazed Little Gunpowder Trail at 0.6 mile. Turn left onto Little Gunpowder Trail; in about 160 yards, reach a trail junction and turn right onto a blue-blazed connecter to the red-dot hiker-only trail at 0.8 mile. If you go left, you will shortcut the Red Dot loop and join back up with the main trail down by Little Gunpowder Falls.

Upon reaching a junction of the blue-blazed Boundary Trail, continue straight on the Red Dot Trail, a quiet footpath that hugs the woods and circles a cornfield. Follow the footpath for 1 mile to a junction with Little Gunpowder Trail (white) at 1.8 miles. The Boundary Trail joins from the left at 2 miles. Follow the white-blazed trail straight along the river.

Ferns carpet the ground rising uphill to the right, and in spring, wildflowers surround the small stream. The woods here are quiet and old, with tulip poplars and silver maples towering to 80 to 100 feet. Anglers will find several large pools and a few small falls for plying the waters (check with park authorities for season and license

Exploring the Little Gunpowder.

requirements). At about 2.7 miles stay left with the white trail as it ascends away from the river, leaving the equestrian trail to follow the stream.

Climb steeply, but briefly, to a ledge that moves downstream above a small hollow, and then climb gently. Pass a junction with an orange-blazed connecting trail at 3 miles (you can take a shortcut back to the trailhead by going left here; see "Options").

Continuing on the white trail, follow it above the river and below giant tulip poplars. Then duck deeper into the woods and cross a small stream on a wooden footbridge, before climbing a gentle rise. When you reach level ground, Little Gunpowder Falls will be 100 feet below, about 75 yards west (right). A right side trail at 3.6 miles leads 100 feet to stream access and a few nice pools.

Descend steeply to a junction with the Boundary Trail at 4.2 miles. For a detour to a few very nice pools, you can go right here and follow the blue trail 175 yards. Walk upstream a short distance if you want to play in the water. If relaxing in the inviting pools just downstream of the river crossing, be aware that horses also use the blue trail to cross. You can also continue over the river by rock-hopping to explore the western reaches of the park.

From the junction of the white-blazed Little Gunpowder Trail and the blue-blazed Boundary Trail, turn left (a hard left) and ascend, following the blue blazes. Go right when the trail enters an open field at 4.4 miles; watch for abundant blackberries at the woods' edge as you make your way around the field just outside the woods. Just as a house comes into view, the trail seems to fork; there are no trail markings here.

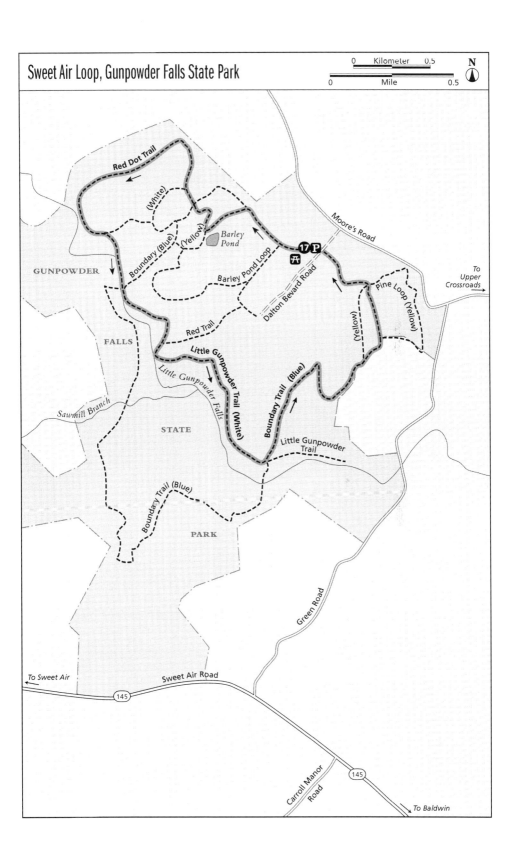

Sweet Air Loop, Gunpowder Falls State Park

Red Dot Trail

(White)

Boundary (Blue)

(Yellow)

Barley Pond

Barley Pond Loop

Moore's Road

17 P

Dalton Bevard Road

Pine Loop (Yellow)

To Upper Crossroads

GUNPOWDER

Red Trail

(Yellow)

FALLS

Little Gunpowder Trail (White)

Boundary Trail (Blue)

Little Gunpowder Falls

Sawmill Branch

Little Gunpowder Trail

STATE

Boundary Trail (Blue)

PARK

Green Road

To Sweet Air

Sweet Air Road

145

Carroll Manor Road

145

To Baldwin

0   Kilometer   0.5

0   Mile   0.5

N

Go to the right, around the field and past the house. Stay left after passing the house (the pathway to the right is private property; please respect it).

Pass through a line of trees, and go right on the edge of another larger field. At the end of this clearing, the trail splits, with the yellow-blazed Pine Loop going left; go downhill, entering the woods and following the blue blazes. Continue straight to a second junction with a yellow-blazed trail. Go left on the blue Boundary Trail, and follow under mixed hardwoods and white and red pine. Blackberries are plentiful from here to the trailhead, and the smell of pine through here is sweet and intense.

Pass another junction with the yellow-blazed Pine Loop at 5.2 miles, and ascend a small knoll (staying to the right at a split in the trail). Emerging from the woods at the park access road, cross the road and proceed to the trailhead.

Miles and Directions

0.0   Start from the picnic shelter.

0.5   Reach Barley Pond.

0.6   At the junction, turn left onto Little Gunpowder Trail.

0.7   Turn right onto the connecting trail (blue blazes).

0.8   Continue straight on the Red Dot trail at the junction with the Boundary Trail.

1.8   Reach the junction with the Little Gunpowder Trail; turn left.

2.0   The Boundary Trail joins the route from the left.

2.3   Arrive at Little Gunpowder Falls.

2.8   Stay left with the white trail, and ascend away from the river.

3.0   Pass the junction with the orange trail (you can use this trail as a shortcut back to the trailhead).

4.2   Reach the junction with the Boundary Trail. Follow blue blazes uphill.

4.4   Go right when the trail enters the field. Look for blackberries here in season.

5.2   Pass the second Pine Loop junction; bear right at the split as the trail climbs a knoll.

5.5   Arrive back at the trailhead.

Options: A shorter, 3.7-mile variation of this hike begins at the junction with the orange-blazed trail at 3 miles. Go left here, then left at the next junction, then right onto the yellow-blazed Barley Pond Loop. A quarter of a mile farther, reach the white trail at the spot at which you first entered the cornfield. The trailhead is 0.2 mile to the right. You can also follow the Boundary Trail, making a western loop that leaves this hike at 1.8 miles and rejoins it at 4.2 miles. This would add only about 0.5 mile but would require crossing the bridgeless Little Gunpowder Falls, which averages about 12 to 18 inches deep at the crossing. A pair of old sneakers in your day pack is all you need.

18 Wildlands Loop, Gunpowder Falls State Park

This rewarding loop follows the upland forests of the fall zone, crossing a few streams and visiting a pleasant cascading water feature, then meanders downstream along Big Gunpowder Falls as it leaves the piedmont. It's a great hike for older children, with a number of places to dip their toes in the water.

Start: The hike begins behind the information board in the parking area.
Distance: 4.5-mile loop
Hiking time: About 2.5 hours
Difficulty: Moderate
Elevation gain: 350 feet
Trail surface: Natural packed dirt, rocky in places; forested lowlands
Best season: Year-round
Schedule: Sunrise to sunset
Other trail users: Equestrians are permitted. Bicycles are not permitted on the Wildlands Trail or Sweathouse Trail, which are in protected state wildlands.
Canine compatibility: Leashed dogs permitted
Land status: Gunpowder Falls State Park; Baltimore County, about 12 miles northeast of Baltimore

Nearest town: Perry Hall
Fees and permits: None
Camping: None
Trailhead facilities: Information board with large map of the area
Maps: USGS White Marsh MD; state park map through the website
Trail contact: Gunpowder Falls State Park, PO Box 480/2813 Jerusalem Rd., Kingsville, MD 21087; (410) 592-2897; https://dnr .maryland.gov/publiclands/Pages/central/ gunpowdercentral.aspx; gunpowderfalls.state park@maryland.gov
Special considerations: The area is very popular on weekends. It is possible to find solitude here early in the day and late in the afternoon. Also, because there are several options for hiking in the park, people tend to disperse.

Finding the trailhead: From the Baltimore Beltway (I-695), take the Belair Road North exit (alternately known as Belair Road, it is US 1). In just less than 5.5 miles, cross the bridge over Big Gunpowder Falls, and then take an immediate right into the trailhead parking area. The hike begins behind the information board. Physical address is 11159 Belair Rd., Kingsville. GPS: N39 25.653' / W76 26.602'

The Hike

Watching Big Gunpowder Falls sliding through several narrow gorges, it is hard to believe that only 5 miles downstream the falls will spread to a broad, delta-like river more than a mile wide. From the information board, walk downhill behind the board to a tunnel under the Belair Road (US 1) bridge. Continue past the junction with the Big Gunpowder Trail (which leads left just beyond the bridge) to a trail junction marking the beginning of the Stocksdale and Wildlands Trails. Straight ahead, the Stocksdale Trail follows the former route of the old Stocksdale Road. (This is the return route of the hike.) Turn right into the woods; follow the pink blazes on the Wildlands Trail over level ground for about 100 yards, and then ascend.

As you climb, steeply at times, you will see that Big Gunpowder Falls sits at the bottom of a narrow ravine. This may seem rather unusual to those accustomed to thinking of Baltimore as more closely linked to the Chesapeake Bay and the coastal plain than to the piedmont north of town. Here, as the falls pass through the transition known as the fall zone, the landscape is still part piedmont, and the steep grade illustrates the point. Perhaps in a few million years, the uplift that created this ravine will erode to a point where it more closely resembles the landscape of Days Cove, an estuarine flatland only a few miles south.

Skirting a housing development to the east and ignoring the road noise along Belair Road, then passing through a beech poplar forest, you reach the end of the Wildlands Trail at the junction of the blue-blazed Stocksdale Trail at 1.3 miles. To the left, Stocksdale Trail takes a shortcut to return to Big Gunpowder Falls, 0.4 mile upstream from the trailhead. Go right, following the blue blazes, and continue through younger woods and fairly open meadow, remnants of the area's agricultural past. In winter, amid the brush, you can still see fence posts and other reminders. The pine trees through this area are plantation planted. Some were planted by former farmers for use as firewood; the younger trees were planted by the State of Maryland at the establishment of the park as a way of protecting the watershed from erosion and runoff.

Stocksdale Trail breaks left at the junction with the yellow-blazed Sweathouse Trail at 2.1 miles—Big Gunpowder Falls is 0.9 mile downhill. The trail to the left is the actual right-of-way of the old Stocksdale Road. To the right it continues out of the park. Take the soft right, following the yellow blazes. Ascend a knoll, and begin a casual descent to Sweathouse Branch. Reach the stream, and follow the trail left for 0.5 mile of very pleasant streamside walking; the stream gurgles and in places tumbles toward the falls. Cross Sweathouse Branch; ascend upstream along a tributary of it for 0.25 mile before crossing the tributary and descending. A side trail leads right 180 yards to a picturesque little cascade on Long Green Creek. In addition to offering a pleasant spot for soaking your feet in one of three nearby pools, the cascade is a fine illustration of the Big and Little Gunpowder Falls topography. The "falls" are casual cascades through the fall zone.

Back on Sweathouse Trail, cross Sweathouse Branch again and continue east, downstream to the Big Gunpowder Falls at 3.2 miles. Rejoin the blue-blazed Stocksdale Trail. There are several places along the way in which the stream valley is more of a steep gorge that drops all the way to the stream, while on the south side of Big Gunpowder Falls, there is gentle bottomland. Continue past a fork where the Stocksdale Trail leads left (uphill) on a loop that eventually leads back to this spot. Cross a small stream, and walk downstream to the tunnel under Belair Road. Pass under the road and return to the trailhead.

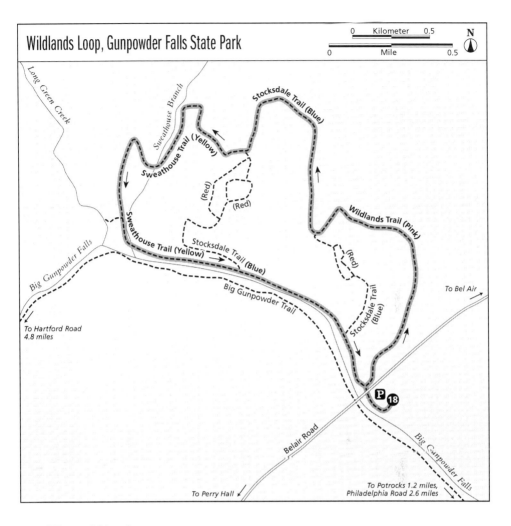

Wildlands Loop, Gunpowder Falls State Park

Miles and Directions

0.0 Start at the trailhead at the information board.

0.1 Reach the Wildlands and Stocksdale Trails junction. Turn right onto Wildlands Trail.

1.3 Go right at the junction with the Stocksdale Trail.

2.1 Reach the junction with the Sweathouse Trail. Take a soft right onto this yellow-blazed trail.

3.2 Reach Big Gunpowder Falls. Watch for a side trail leading 180 yards to Long Green Creek. Head downstream on Sweathouse Trail.

4.5 Arrive back at the trailhead.

Options: For a 3-mile loop, go left onto the blue-blazed Stocksdale Trail at 2.1 miles instead of going right. Follow this blue trail 0.7 mile to the opposite end of the loop made by the Stocksdale Trail. Turn left to return to the trailhead. South of the trailhead are other loops, which are illustrated on a map at the trailhead information board.

19 Susquehanna State Park Loop

This challenging ramble over rocky terrain and through hardwood forest offers great rewards: expansive views of the Susquehanna River, old farm ruins, and the Maryland champion tulip poplar tree. History buffs will be drawn to the restored Rock Run Historic Area, with its gristmill and mansion.

Start: The trailhead is 400 feet up the Susquehanna State Park entrance road on the right. From the historic area, walk back up Rock Run Road away from the Susquehanna River, past the historic mansion, and turn right to enter the woods at the end of the guardrail, following the Mason-Dixon Trail/blue blazes.
Distance: 4.2-mile loop
Hiking time: About 3 hours
Difficulty: Moderate to difficult; the initial mile-plus is uphill. In the heat of the summer, it can be strenuous.
Elevation gain: 300 feet
Trail surface: Natural, rocky, open fields; rolling hills along the river
Best season: Year-round
Schedule: Dawn to dusk
Other trail users: Bikers, equestrians
Canine compatibility: Leashed dogs permitted
Land status: Susquehanna State Park; Harford County, Maryland, about 35 miles northeast of Baltimore on the banks of the Susquehanna River

Nearest town: Havre de Grace
Fees and permits: None
Camping: Camping is available; registration and a fee are required.
Trailhead facilities: Nature center, restrooms, historic buildings
Maps: USGS Havre de Grace MD; park maps are located throughout the park, including at the maintenance shop and historic area.
Trail contact: Susquehanna State Park, 4122 Wilkinson Rd., Havre de Grace, MD; (410) 557-7994; https://dnr.maryland.gov/publiclands/pages/central/susquehanna.aspx; susquehanna.statepark@maryland.gov
Special considerations: There are two stream crossings that can be difficult in high water. Walking sticks are a big help in this instance. Check with the park office if you have a concern. The trail passes adjacent hunting lands. Check with the park office for details when hiking during hunting season. The hike described here starts at the historic area, but you can start at the picnic area just as easily.

Finding the trailhead: From Baltimore drive north on I-95 for 21 miles to the MD 155 exit west, to Churchville. In 2 miles turn right onto MD 161 north. In 0.5 mile turn right onto Rock Run Road. For 4 miles, follow signs to the park, the historic sites, and the trailhead at the river. GPS: N39 36.500' / W76 08.574'

The Hike

This is a fine hike for young hikers—the first 2 miles are challenging, yet there is plenty to see and much to gain. Plan to spend some time along the first ridge overlooking the Susquehanna, enjoying the views of the river, especially when the leaves are off the trees.

To begin, walk back up Rock Run Road away from the river for about 400 feet, and turn right to enter the woods at the end of the guardrail, before the road

Historic Rock Run "House" at the head of the Susquehanna Ridge Trail.

intersection, following the blue discs marking the Mason-Dixon Trail. The trail immediately crosses Rocky Run and heads uphill along the ridge that cradles the Susquehanna River.

You are on the Susquehanna Ridge Trail, marked red, and the long-distance Mason-Dixon Trail, marked blue. The path passes under hardwoods—tulip poplar, chestnut oak—and through the ubiquitous, shrubby, teardrop-leaved pawpaw tree, making a long ascent up the ridgeline. Follow the red markers on the trees. This is where you have views of the river east through the trees. At about 0.6 mile look for a massive poplar on the right with a 4-foot-diameter trunk. It may be 400 years old. It's but one of many large poplars in the park. You will see red blazes on the trees indicating the Susquehanna Ridge Trail.

At 0.8 mile reach the top of the ridge and a junction with the spur trail, heading left across an open field. Stay right, following the river, and begin a slow descent through the woods. Pass a junction with the blue Farm Road Trail and continue right, descending and following the red blazes. Pass another trail that heads right toward the river, stay to the left on the red trail, and continue to the bottom of the descent, scaring deer in the creek that you cross on a stone culvert.

Hike a short up-and-down toward the picnic area. In spring bluebells color the forest floor, while dogwood and serviceberry paint the understory bright white. Pass through two narrow hollows and come to a small hemlock grove followed by a stand of pines. The pines were planted as a lumber crop in the early nineteenth century. The remnant pines are now dying back as the hardwoods mature and block the sun.

Beyond the pines at 1.5 miles is the junction with the blue-blazed Farm Road Trail. The red trail leads across a wood bridge to a Forest Buffer Restoration area and

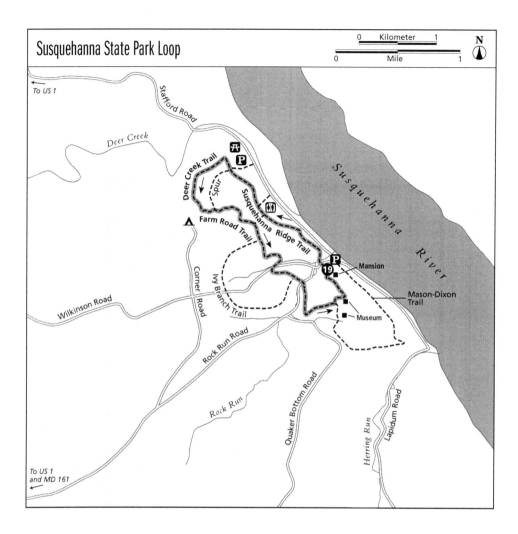

0 Kilometer 1

0 Mile 1

N

To US 1

Stafford Road

Deer Creek

Deer Creek Trail

Spur

Susquehanna Ridge Trail

Farm Road Trail

Corner Road

Ivy Branch Trail

Wilkinson Road

Rock Run Road

Rock Run

Quaker Bottom Road

Herring Run

Lapidum Road

To US 1
and MD 161

Susquehanna River

Mansion

Mason-Dixon Trail

Museum

19

the picnic area. Go left, following the blue Farm Road Trail into the woods, and walk upstream along a small brook on a wide flat trail.

For the next mile, walk quietly upstream through a beautiful narrow hollow with poplar and chestnut oak, sycamore, and beech towering above on both sides. Ferns cover the forest floor. The invasive multiflora rose has yet to invade this segment and the open understory is a welcome sight.

The creek is cold and refreshing, with frogs and minnows. There are a number of paths to the creek to cool your jets.

At the top of the hill, emerge from the woods into a broad field. On a warm summer day, you can smell the hayfield before you reach it. This is a wonderful section, as the trail winds around the field under open sky—but beware of ticks in the high grass. Watch for bounding deer, soaring hawks, birds flittering in the grass, and coyote scat along the trail.

Cut across the field and watch for the spur trail just beyond a tree line dividing the fields at 2.6 miles—it leads left 100 yards to old farm ruins. These ruins are worth taking the time to explore.

Back on Farm Road Trail, continue around the field and ascend a long hill on the field's edge. At the top look behind you for a wonderful view of the fields and the rolling hills beyond, all on the banks of the Susquehanna. In the heat of the summer, this treeless stretch could be a very hot segment. Be sure to have water and a hat.

Just beyond the top of the rise, the unmarked Ivy Branch Trail cuts right across the field to the southwest at about 2.6 miles. Stay straight to the tree line. The Farm Road Trail then cuts through the tree line and quickly forks right into the woods. It's well marked. Slowly descend, following the blue blazes through a very overgrown rocky section.

Cross Wilkinson Road at 3.3 miles, then go uphill past another junction with the Ivy Branch Trail. Continue straight on the blue trail. Coming down the hill, you begin to hear the burbling of Rock Run, accented by the warbling of the wood thrush, and presently arrive at the Maryland Champion Tulip Poplar tree, the "largest tree of its species." Appreciate its mass. It's been around for a long time.

Cross Rock Run Road at 3.7 miles. Cut between the guardrails and down to the creek. This is another beautiful segment along the creek to where you have to cross the creek again. On the other side the Farm Road Trail goes right uphill. But go left at the junction, following Rock Run downstream. Continue straight at the intersection with the Historic Walking Trail past the millpond and below the mansion. The millpond powered the historic mill; it is a great place to stop and cool your feet in the clear cold water at the head of the pond. Past the millpond, walk along the banks of the millrace, circling the historic mansion and the mill, and head back to your car at 4.2 miles.

Miles and Directions

0.0 Start at the historic area parking. Walk up Rock Run Road, turn right at the blue Mason-Dixon marker, enter the woods, and cross Rock Creek.

0.5 Enjoy views of the river.

0.8 Pass the spur trail on the left.

1.5 Junction with the Farm Road Trail; turn left. (The trail straight ahead leads to a picnic area.)

2.5 Reach the spur trail to the farm ruins—worth the time to explore.

3.2 Cross Wilkinson Road.

3.7 Cross Rock Run Road.

4.0 Pass the mansion and other historic sites.

4.2 Arrive back at the trailhead.

Options: You can make this a short, 2.5-mile hike by taking the spur trail shortcut to the farmstead ruins, returning to the red trail, and then heading south back to the trailhead. For an extended hike, you can turn right onto Farm Road Trail after crossing Rock Run, near trail's end.

20 Oregon Ridge Park Loop

An easy but very pleasant walk through a natural museum of Maryland history, along old logging trails under mature second-growth hardwoods with mine pits, a chestnut forest reclamation site, and interludes along a secluded clear-running brook. A great hike for families, ending at the nature center.

Start: Locate a set of log steps at the northeast corner of the parking lot.
Distance: 4.6-mile loop
Hiking time: About 2 hours
Difficulty: Easy
Elevation gain: Minimal
Trail surface: Natural packed dirt; forested rolling hills; can be muddy
Best season: Year-round
Schedule: 10 a.m. to sunset
Other trail users: Bikers, equestrians
Canine compatibility: Leashed dogs permitted
Land status: Oregon Ridge Park; Baltimore County, about 10 miles north of the Baltimore Beltway
Nearest town: Cockeysville
Fees and permits: None
Camping: None

Trailhead facilities: Water and restrooms are available at the nature center, which is open until 5 p.m.
Maps: USGS Cockeysville MD
Trail contact: Oregon Ridge Park, 13401 Beaver Dam Rd., Cockeysville, MD; (410) 887-1818; oregonridgenaturecenter.org; info@oregonridgenaturecenter.org
Special considerations: Trails in the park are effectively marked at major trail junctions. There are several stream crossings without bridges; most are shallow enough to traipse through, and all are narrow enough to rock-hop across. A public beach at Oregon Lake offers a fine finish to a summer hike. As of this writing (2024), within the next two years, the park will embark on a new management plan that may include some new trails and perhaps rerouted trails. Check with the managers at the nature center for more information.

Finding the trailhead: From the Baltimore Beltway (I-695), travel 7 miles north on I-83 to exit 20, Shawan Road West. Follow Shawan Road West, in 1 mile turn left onto Beaver Dam Road, then immediately go right at the fork into the park. Continue past the beach parking area, following signs for nature center parking. GPS: N39 29.640' / W76 41.442'

The Hike

People who grow up in central Maryland usually discover at a young age the bucolic beauty of northern Baltimore County, and many are familiar with the beach at Oregon Lake. Sadly, many never discover the lush woods traversed by the park's excellent trail system. What a shame!

The bedrock beneath the trails is some of the oldest rock in Maryland. The rolling ridges are composed of metamorphic rock known as Loch Raven schist. Created 3 billion years ago from pressurized shale, the sparkly rock is easily identified by

Icicles grace a small pond on the Oregon Ridge loop.

its shiny quartz, feldspar, and garnet crystals. Additionally, you will see Cockeysville marble, a hard gray-white stone without the sparkles.

The ridge supplied iron ore to smelting furnaces formerly located within what are now park boundaries. Little evidence of the open-pit operations remains today, at least to the casual eye, except the large depression you cross at the end of the hike.

From the parking area, locate a set of log steps at the northeast corner of the lot (you passed them as you drove in). Turn right onto the trail; in 100 feet turn left at the fork onto the blue-blazed Laurel Trail. Ascend a gentle grade beneath chestnut oak, accompanied by the mountain laurel often found with this tree. The ridge's well-drained soils offer the perfect conditions for chestnut oak, tulip poplar, and mountain laurel, which dominate the Oregon Ridge forest.

At the top of the ridge, pass into an open meadow, maintained as a gas line right-of-way. It is an unnatural break in the forest cover, but it provides the opportunity for berries to flourish on the woods' edge, drawing deer and other wildlife out for a snack. Back in the woods at 0.5 mile, turn left onto the red-blazed Loggers Trail and follow a wide path through mature, open forest. Horse teams hauling timber from the ridge carved the wide path. Pass the green-blazed Virginia Pine Trail, which breaks left (see "Options"). Just beyond this junction, look to your right for an old stone marker inscribed with a "B." A little farther on is the vestige of an old mining pit on the left at 0.8 mile.

At 1 mile is the junction with the yellow-blazed S. James Campbell Trail, leading southeast to the right. Before turning right onto this trail, continue another 100 feet and follow Loggers Trail left (do not go straight) to an overlook at a ski run and a view across the valley to Cockeysville.

Back on the S. James Campbell Trail, cross a second gas line right-of-way, reenter the woods, and go left at the junction with the green trail, walking below some enormous tulip poplars and red oaks. At 1.5 miles begin a descent via switchbacks; don't follow the remnants of a trail to the right—stay on the yellow-blazed trail. This section can be muddy and slippery in wet conditions. At the bottom of the ridge, briefly walking along the road, the trail becomes a much narrower footpath, following Baisman Run upstream. This is a picturesque little stream through a narrow, wooded canyon—an invitation to slow down and enjoy the scenery, especially at one of the several upcoming stream crossings.

Cross the run at 2 miles, passing a log bench streamside. Over the next 0.25 mile, cross the run, which is glittering with flakes of schist, four more times. The run and trail are in a forest of huge poplars, easily discernable by their towering and very straight trunks. Pass by a number of adjoining trails on the left going up the bank, staying right on the yellow-blazed trail (the trail to the left leads to Ivy Hill Road). Cross a bridge and pass beneath Ivy Hill Pond (a nice stopping point) at 2.5 miles, and begin ascending on yellow Ivy Hill Trail, a wide logging road.

Just past the pond, pass a trail junction leading left over the run and uphill. Stay right, and at the top of the hill, pass briefly into open field over the gas line right-of-way at 2.8 miles. The trail junction at 3.2 miles creates a shortcut right to a return via Loggers Trail. Follow the white blazes left for 0.25 mile to a T intersection, and turn left onto the red-blazed trail. Passing through the right-of-way a final time, turn right and follow the woods' edge 160 yards before ducking left back into the woods, following the red blazes.

Soon you come to a reforestation project where park managers are trying to reestablish the American chestnut. At one time one in four trees in the eastern deciduous forests were chestnuts, before they were wiped out by the chestnut blight. Beginning in 1904, 3 billion to 4 billion trees were lost over a forty-year period. The area is open due to a more recent invasion of the spongy moth (formerly gypsy moth) that destroyed a large area of chestnut oak, but it provides a long view to the west. Continue on the red-blazed trail downhill back into the woods at 3.6 miles.

The tan-blazed Ridge Trail at this junction leads right toward the nature center trailhead—a shortcut to be taken if darkness is falling quickly in the woods. But staying left on the red-blazed Loggers Trail will take you for a final stretch along the sound of water, passing near a small creek. In the springtime look for skunk cabbage and, a little later, mayapples (they're not really apples). The leaves look like tiny umbrellas unfolding from a single stem. The white flowers, hiding under the leaves, can grow to a foot in diameter.

"Forest of Hope" painted by local schoolchildren.

Rising uphill from the stream, the trail bends right to the Forest of Hope. It's an area of trees painted lavishly by students to look like glowing totem poles. It's a joyful sight.

Continue on the Loggers Trail past the tan trail, crossing a wooden bridge over an ancient mining pit to the nature center. From there, follow the paved driveway 150 feet right to the trailhead.

Miles and Directions

0.0 Start at the trailhead near the log steps. Turn right onto the Laurel Trail.

0.5 Turn left onto the red-blazed Loggers Trail.

1.0 Reach the S. James Campbell Trail junction. Walk 100 yards to the overlook before turning right at the junction.

2.0 Cross Baisman Run.

2.5 Pass Ivy Hill Pond, and begin ascending on Ivy Hill Trail.

3.2 Reach the Shortcut Trail junction. Follow white blazes for 0.25 mile, and turn left at the T intersection onto red-blazed trail.

3.6 Chestnut restoration area.

4.3 Forest of Hope.

4.6 Arrive back at the trailhead.

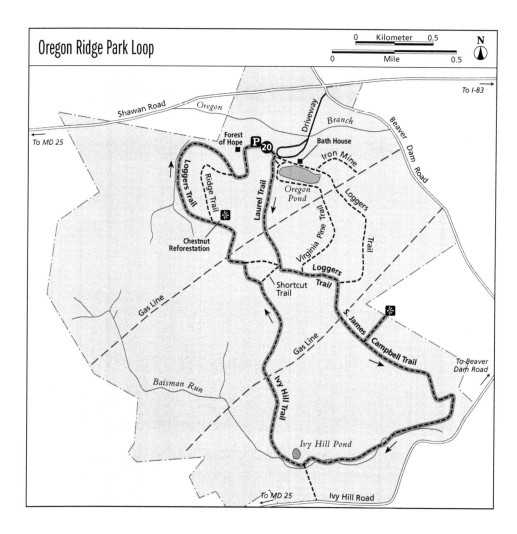

Oregon Ridge Park Loop

Kilometer 0 — 0.5
Mile 0 — 0.5

N

To I-83

Shawan Road   Oregon   Driveway   Branch   Beaver Dam Road

To MD 25

Forest of Hope   P 20   Bath House   Iron Mine

Loggers Trail   Ridge Trail   Laurel Trail   Oregon Pond   Loggers Trail

Chestnut Reforestation   Virginia Pine Trail

Gas Line   Loggers Trail   Shortcut Trail   Trail   S. James Campbell Trail

To Beaver Dam Road

Baisman Run   Gas Line   Ivy Hill Trail

Ivy Hill Pond

To MD 25   Ivy Hill Road

Options: Several color-coded, intersecting trails make a number of shorter loops possible, some of which are pointed out here. You can create a 1- or 1.5-mile circuit past the Oregon Lake beach. Follow the directions above to the Loggers Trail, then turn left at 0.5 mile onto the green-blazed Virginia Pine Trail, or at 0.7 mile continue on the red-blazed Loggers Trail by descending left. Both trails lead to the orange-blazed Lake Trail. Turn left and follow that trail west to the nature center trailhead.

21 Morgan Run Natural Environment Area

This hike is for horseback riders, birders, hikers, and anglers. In the spring you may encounter mating woodcocks; in the summer and fall, you will see a variety of raptors at work as you walk through overgrown farm fields and young forest, followed by an interlude to a steep creek ravine with some of the best trout water in northeast Maryland.

Start: The trail commences at the kiosk in the parking area.
Distance: 3.8-mile lollipop
Hiking time: About 2.5 hours
Difficulty: Easy, with a short downhill/uphill to and from the river
Elevation gain: 250 feet with many short ups and downs
Trail surface: Natural dirt, grass, and gravel in the path descending to the river; rolling hills along the river
Best season: Year-round, but you may want to avoid the area in midsummer due to ticks and heat.
Schedule: Sunrise to sunset
Other trail users: Equestrians, hunters
Canine compatibility: Leashed dogs permitted
Land status: Morgan Run Natural Environment Area; Carroll County, Maryland, 10 miles south of Westminster

Nearest town: Westminster
Fees and permits: None
Camping: None
Trailhead facilities: None
Maps: USGS Finksburg MD; county park map through the website
Trail contact: Maryland Department of Natural Resources, Morgan Run Natural Environment Area, Benrose Lane, Westminster, MD; (410) 461-5005; https://dnr.maryland.gov/public lands/Pages/central/morganrun.aspx; macooper@dnr.state.md.us
Special considerations: The area is open to hunting; check the kiosk for schedules. There is no hunting in Maryland on Sunday. Although the elevation gain is minimal, this hike has many short ups and downs. Be sure to take a map and follow the guide, as there are many confusing, intersecting trails.

Finding the trailhead: From I-70 take exit 76 (MD 97) north. About 2 miles north of I-70, make a right turn onto Bartholow Road, and then turn left onto Jim Bowers Road, followed by an immediate left onto Ben Rose Lane to the Morgan Run entrance. GPS: N39 27.985' / W77 00.036'

The Hike

Much of this walk is through old farm fields and recovering forest, but this hike is for the birds. In the early spring, you may witness the mating dance of the woodcock at dusk in the open fields. Aldo Leopold describes it well in *A Sand County Almanac*. In the woods, you can sit by Morgan Run for an hour listening to the courting wood thrushes.

In the fields red-tailed hawks and kestrels ply their trade with impunity. Barred owls hoot to alert others down-trail of your presence. By the hedgerows, even the shrill killdeer cannot drown the songs of indigo buntings and rufous-sided towhees darting in and out of the thicket.

Except for the wooded sections, the trail system here is a network of mowed paths through and around the overgrown fields (and lots of invasives)—some in succession to forest. When you get to know the area, you can wander without regard to orientation. However, there are no trail signs or blazes, and the hills, tall thickets, and relative sameness of some of the fields make it possible to lose direction. The hike described below offers specific turns to keep you oriented and provides a little of everything Morgan Run Natural Environment Area (NEA) has to offer. If you wander the fields and go astray, walk uphill. From the tree line at the high point, a vista will reveal your location.

From the trailhead kiosk, there are two distinct trails—walk the downhill fork to the right. In less than 200 yards, there is a small clearing. Follow the path at the four-way intersection and go left. At the top of the hill, turn right, following the wide path. At the next junction, at 0.3 mile, go straight. You are making your way to the first tree line at the top of the rise. Hikers often are averse to these types of hikes, and the first section is much more suited to horseback riders, but these fields and thickets teem with wildlife. If you're lucky, you may see a fox cross your path before you even pass through the first line of trees, at 0.5 mile, where you enter the Wildlands area. The tree line demarcates a boundary of two fields. When you pass through the tree line, go right (east) at another four-way and follow the tree line. The trail loops around another old field. Continue straight, descending then climbing with a wooded ravine on your right. The path then emerges at a another multipath intersection. Proceed slightly right until you reach the picnic tables and a towering old oak tree at 1.1 miles. This is the second tree line and a great spot for a snack.

The trail now gets more interesting and challenging. Go past the Big Oak tree, keeping the tree on your left to where the path forks yet again. Take the middle path downhill. Soon enough you dip into the woods and follow a small rivulet on your left. The path flattens as elms and poplars create a canopy above walnuts and serviceberry—a shrub known alternately on the eastern seaboard as shadbush for the reliability of its flowers to bloom when the shad run. A small ridge rises on the left.

At 1.6 miles reach the remains of a concrete privy, two metal barns, and the foundation of a centuries-old farmhouse. Follow the trail past the buildings; go left at the next juncture and left again at the fork past the corn silo on your right. Soon a deep stream gorge opens below and the forest opens a bit from the cloistered path you've been on. In autumn the woods below host great flocks of migratory birds, which stop over and make a racket to rival a hotel full of seniors on a bus tour. Descend steeply to Morgan Run at 1.8 miles. If you brought fishing gear and/or a picnic lunch, this is the spot. Morgan Run has some of the best trout fishing in northeast Maryland, second only to the Gunpowder.

Returning to the trail, go right, downstream, for about 100 feet, and cut right to a T and then left, crossing a narrow creek to the southeast. You are now headed back

Fishing for trout on Morgan Run.

into the woods, passing a pond on the left and into the best section of the hike. If you quietly wander to the pond, you may be treated to glimpses of wood ducks. Look for the distinctive colorful helmet of the male. Back on the path, proceed uphill.

This section is much less traveled and the trail is not as distinct, but the horses do a good job of creating a path to follow. The trail winds up the feeder creek you just crossed into deep woods, where the invasives have yet to take over. The ridge with the farm buildings rises to your right as you walk upstream. There is great solitude among the oaks and poplars for the next 0.4 mile until you reach the Private Property signs. Walking along the property line and crossing the stream once again at 2.3 miles, the trail makes a sharp right, ascending the hollow to the farm buildings you passed earlier. At the top, at 2.6 miles, turn left, passing the buildings along the path you traced earlier to the Big Oak.

From the Big Oak, follow the middle fork of the three paths directly in front of you to the west. In about 1,000 feet at the Y, take the short path to the right through the bushes uphill. Then go right at the tree line to the four-way where you entered the Wildlands at 3.2 miles. From there exit the Wildlands left. Follow this uphill stretch straight back to the parking area cutting off the first loop. Feel like a rabbit yet? It is a warren but one that's fun to explore.

As you follow the path back to your car, listen for the woodcock's *peent* and look for the whirling bird streaking skyward in the closing darkness of a new season.

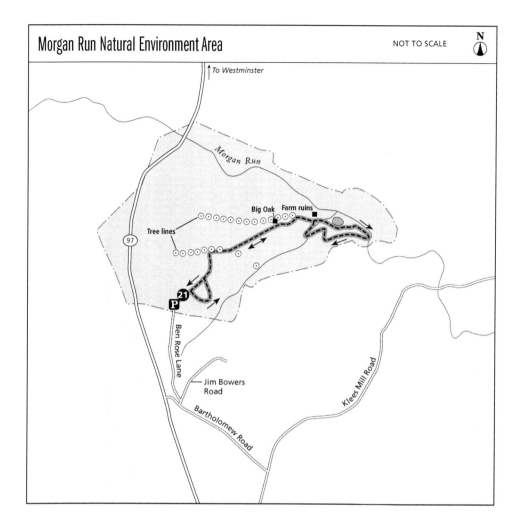

Morgan Run Natural Environment Area

NOT TO SCALE

N

To Westminster

Morgan Run

Big Oak   Farm ruins

Tree lines

97

21
P

Ben Rose Lane

Jim Bowers
Road

Bartholomew Road

Klees Mill Road

Miles and Directions

0.0 Start from the trailhead kiosk.

0.5 Pass through first line of trees and enter the Wildlands.

1.1 Reach the Big Oak and the corner of three fields. Pass to the right of the tree and take the middle path when the trail forks.

1.6 Arrive at the farm buildings.

1.8 Reach Morgan Run at the bottom of the hill.

2.3 Cross a small stream below the farm, which is on the ridge above.

2.6 Pass farm buildings for a second time; go left.

3.2 Reach the Wildlands junction.

3.8 Arrive back at the trailhead.

22 Soldiers Delight East Loop, Soldiers Delight Natural Environment Area

This modest hike through pine forest grasslands and along a meandering creek is more remote than you would think. The natural resources, coupled with the history of the area, make for an unusually interesting hike. See if you can find the pond crowded with wood frogs in the spring. It is also a great birding spot.

Start: Trailhead parking is on Deer Park Road.
Distance: 3.6-mile loop
Hiking time: About 1.5 hours
Difficulty: Easy, with moderate uphill stretches throughout
Elevation gain: Minimal
Trail surface: Hard-packed dirt, crushed rock, rocky; rolling hills
Best season: Year-round, but it can be very hot in the summer.
Schedule: Sunrise to sunset
Other trail users: None
Canine compatibility: Leashed dogs permitted
Land status: Soldiers Delight Natural Environment Area; Baltimore County, 10 miles northwest of the Baltimore Beltway
Nearest town: Owings Mills
Fees and permits: None
Camping: None

Trailhead facilities: None. On weekdays and Sat morning, the visitor center, 0.25 mile past the trailhead on Deer Park Road, is open.
Maps: USGS Reisterstown MD
Trail contact: Soldiers Delight Natural Environment Area, 5100 Deer Park Rd., Owings Mills, MD; (410) 461-5005; https://dnr.maryland.gov/publiclands/Pages/central/soldiers delight.aspx; macooper@dnr.state.md.us
Special considerations: On a hot, cloudless summer day, the area can get excessively warm. Although this hike passes into and out of pine groves and along a stream that offers relief from the heat, it is a lot easier to enjoy the ecology of the area in autumn, winter, or spring. There are two hikes: The first is the white-blazed loop to the east that descends into a stream bottom, and the second is a shorter hike to the west of Deer Park Road in the open savanna-like grasslands.

Finding the trailhead: From the Baltimore Beltway (I-695), drive north on I-795 to exit 7, Franklin Boulevard. Go west on Franklin Boulevard to the light at Church Road and go right. Turn left onto Berrymans Lane. In 0.5 mile turn left onto Deer Park Road. Trailhead parking is on the right in 2 miles. GPS: N39 24.865' / W76 50.146'

The Hike

Cross Deer Park Road and pass through the yellow gate on the red-blazed Choate Mine Trail. Follow the path into a small clearing, and you immediately come to the site of an old chromium mine. The surrounding area was the first chromium mine in the world; the openings on the trail are the last-known shafts. Continue on the path with the mine on the right into a young forest of loblolly pine, blackjack oak, and red

SOLDIERS DELIGHT NATURAL ENVIRONMENT AREA

The 2,000-acre serpentine grassland and oak savanna ecosystem that makes up Soldiers Delight Natural Environment Area is the largest prairie ecosystem in the eastern United States and was once part of the Great Maryland Barrens, covering more than 100,000 acres in the Appalachian piedmont. It was called "barrens" meaning that it was bare of trees. The soil, composed of green magnesium silicate, is so dry it supports only the hardiest grasses and shrubs. A much larger area of northern Maryland once was covered in this unusual grass-and-pine vegetation.

At first glance, the rock-strewn soil and short grasses might seem an unglamorous scrub forest, but a hike through the grasslands reveals a diverse ecosystem of hundreds of plant species. However, it is not the twisting grasses that give the landscape its name. The dull green, mottled mineral that forms the underlying bedrock is serpentine. Because both hikes in the natural environment area start from the same trailhead, information common to both hikes is provided, followed by information specific to each hike.

maple. Enter a small clearing where the multiflora rose has been cleared out to allow for some low-bush blueberries that ripen in the late spring.

At 0.5 mile is a three-way junction where the orange blazes continue right and the red blazes break left. Turn right, following the yellow-blazed Dolfield Trail to another junction, and continue west on the yellow trail. Along this section you are walking atop the serpentine rock the area is known for. The rock was created 500 million years ago, so walk with reverence.

Cross a small stream at 0.9 mile, then ascend through open meadows to the ridgetop, which is checkered with loblolly pine. Watch for fox and coyote scat on the trail. Warblers, wrens, and cardinals raise a ruckus as you pass through the bushes. The trail then makes a long, very gradual descent into and out of the woods along the stream you cross again at 1.2 miles. At the bottom of the hill, walking again on very rocky terrain, the trail takes a hairpin turn left at about 1.3 miles, just before Dolfield Road, which you can hear. The trail heads uphill, through another meadow, where the forest transitions from conifers to deciduous chestnut oaks and maples. The next mile or so is perhaps the most serene segment of the hike. In the springtime listen for wood frogs mating in a small man-made pond off to your left at 1.4 miles. The pond is a very pleasant place to stop and watch hundreds of frogs frolicking in the water. Here the woods are free of invasives and alive with wood thrush, red-bellied woodpeckers, cardinals, and doves. Farther along, ferns carpet the forest floor in pools of bright translucent green.

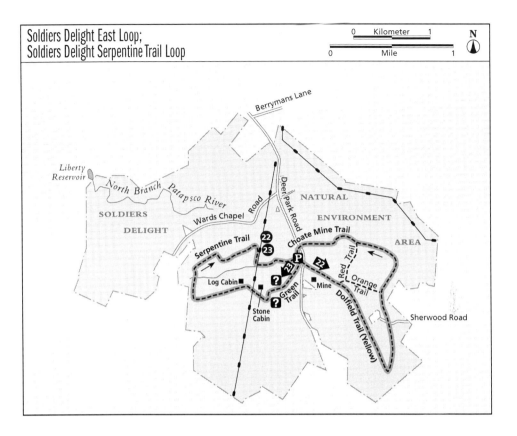

Cross Sherwood Road and reenter the woods at 1.8 miles, following the yellow-blazed trail through the open woods. A trail marker at 2.1 miles shows the way west on the orange Red Run Trail; do not take the red trail; stay on the orange trail.

At 2.3 miles reach the slow-moving Red Run stream, with towering sycamore trees and a farm field beyond, and then cross a small creek. Leave the stream and continue an easy ascent through hickory, poplar, and oak.

Emerge into a beautiful clearing and, as you hike uphill, come to the junction with the red-blazed Choate Mine Trail loop at 2.6 miles. This is a bit confusing, but there is a signpost marked with #6. This is the end of the orange trail.

You can either follow the red Choate Mine Trail left back to the trailhead or veer right, back toward the stream on the red trail. The distance is similar, but an historic mineshaft awaits you to the right. Cross a small stream and emerge into open, sandy grassland. Ascend the "grand staircase" of serpentine rock and reach the mine shaft in 0.25 mile. The ubiquitous birds soaring overhead are turkey buzzards. At the end of the field, the trail follows a narrow "green tunnel," with underbrush and saplings growing close to the trail. At 3.4 miles emerge from the woods onto Deer Park Road. Turn left and follow the road 350 yards back to the trailhead.

Miles and Directions

0.0 Start at the trailhead, crossing Deer Park Road and taking the Choate Mine Trail.

0.3 Reach the first mine site.

0.5 At the junction turn right onto the orange Dolfield Trail.

1.4 Pass a pond with wood frogs and spring peepers in the spring.

1.9 The orange trail joins from the left.

2.1 Turn west at the trail marker; do not continue straight. Stay on the orange trail.

2.6 Reach the junction with red trail again; go right.

3.5 Emerge from the woods onto Deer Park Road; go left.

3.6 Arrive back at the trailhead.

23 Soldiers Delight Serpentine Trail Loop, Soldiers Delight Natural Environment Area

Walk through unique wild grasses and over rugged, rocky serpentine terrain, named for the scaly serpentlike rocks under your feet—rocks that were formed 500 million years ago.

See map on page 109.
Start: Trailhead parking is on Deer Park Road.
Distance: 2.5-mile loop
Hiking time: About 2 hours
Difficulty: Moderate, with a few modest uphill stretches
Elevation gain: 185 feet
Trail surface: Hard-packed dirt, crushed rock, rocky, rolling hills
Best season: Year-round, but spring is best as it can be hot in the summer.
Schedule: Sunrise to sunset
Other trail users: None
Canine compatibility: Leashed dogs permitted
Land status: Soldiers Delight Natural Environment Area; Baltimore County, 10 miles northwest of the Baltimore Beltway
Nearest town: Owings Mills

Fees and permits: None
Camping: None
Trailhead facilities: None. On weekdays and Sat morning, the visitor center, 0.25 mile past the trailhead on Deer Park Road, is open.
Maps: USGS Reisterstown MD
Trail contact: Soldiers Delight Natural Environment Area, 5100 Deer Park Rd., Owings Mills, MD; (410) 461-5005; https://dnr.maryland.gov/publiclands/Pages/central/soldiersdelight.aspx; macooper@dnr.state.md.us
Special considerations: On a hot, cloudless summer day, the area heats 10 to 15 degrees warmer than the hardwood forests several miles away. Although the hike passes into and out of pine groves, offering relief from the sun, it is a lot easier to enjoy the ecology of the area in autumn, winter, or spring.

Finding the trailhead: From the Baltimore Beltway (I-695), drive north on I-795 to exit 7, Franklin Boulevard. Go west on Franklin Boulevard to the light at Church Road, then go right. Turn left onto Berrymans Lane. In 0.5 mile turn left onto Deer Park Road. Trailhead parking is on the right in 2 miles. GPS: N39 24.865' / W76 50.146'

The Hike

This is an odd little hike that leaves you wondering which ecosystem you are in. There are oak-beech hardwoods, open prairie grasses, pine groves, and an almost lunar rocky knoll at the westernmost part of the loop. The trip is somewhat marred by several hundred yards of following a utility right-of-way, but the landscape is so varied that your mind will not focus on the cable lines for long, and the views will help distract you as well.

From the trailhead, walk south along the road until you find the trail leading right into a small grove. Duck into a stand of trees, enjoying the shade while you can, then

The creek drains the higher ground above.

continue through a small field and past the visitor center on the Serpentine Trail, the white trail. The trail is not well marked in places, but it is easily discernable.

Pass right of the visitor center, staying on a dirt road, and come to the Red Dog Lodge, a stone cabin built in 1912, at 0.5 mile. After visiting the cabin, return to the Serpentine Trail and follow it to the right. Soon you come to a clearing at 0.6 mile, where the immense power lines cut a swath through the landscape, offering a bit of irony in the fact that the land here is managed as a natural environment area, but providing an expansive view to the west. (From this perch and as of this writing in May 2023, the remnants of a forest fire that burned a good deal of the area north of the park and into the grasslands is evident. Fires are essential in nurturing new growth and weeding out the invasives.) To its credit, the power company is participating in a management plan to restore the prairie grasses. The native oaks in Soldiers Delight are mostly post oak, with large catcher's-mitt-like leaves, and blackjack oak. This is one of the rarest ecosystems in Maryland, now covering less than 1,000 acres. Enter the savanna at 0.8 mile.

Pass the remnants of an old cabin to the left. Continue descending on the white path through an area of multiflora rose until the path flattens out into an opening of meadows. Take a minute here to consider how unique these seemingly boring spaces of grasses are—in reality, a very rare Maryland ecosystem. Besides the oaks, you may notice sassafras, red maple, and cherry as you pass through a tunnel of multiflora rose.

At the bottom of the hill, go right at 1.3 miles over a rocky section of serpentine rock. Cross a small ephemeral creek at the bottom, then another, larger stream at 1.5 miles, and hike into the savanna. (There is a white trail marker on a post hidden in the bushes on the far side of the creek) Begin a long but modest uphill climb into the grasslands, passing through loblolly pine and hickory.

Were it not for the trees bordering the open area, you would swear you were on another planet. The serrated sedimentary rock forms the terrain, and the open rocky ground takes on ethereal shade in the late-day sun. This is the landscape that lends the name serpentine to the grasslands.

Hay-scented ferns carpet the forest floor.

In an open meadow, continue climbing; the next 0.5 mile is over the open rocks. At the top of the hill, you have a 360-degree panorama of the savanna. A line of oaks offers a brief respite from the sun before you emerge once again into the power line right-of-way at 2 miles. Cross the right-of-way, and reenter the woods for the final leg to the parking area and trailhead at 2.5 miles.

Miles and Directions

0.0 Start at the trailhead, heading south along Deer Park Road to the Serpentine Trail.

0.5 Go right before the Red Dog Lodge cabin.

0.6 Reach the clearing at the power lines.

0.8 Enter the savanna.

1.5 Cross the stream (no bridge).

2.0 Reach the power lines a second time.

2.5 Arrive back at the trailhead.

24 Little Bennett Loop, Little Bennett Regional Park

This wonderful easy loop through several deep forests includes passage through a unique area of huge ant mounds, plus a pleasant stroll along Stoney Brook and Sopers Branch. This hike is a perfect Saturday walk in the woods with kids.

Start: The trail begins at Wilson Mill parking area off MD 121, Clarksburg Road.
Distance: 4.4-mile loop
Hiking time: About 2.5 hours
Difficulty: Easy
Elevation gain: About 50 feet
Trail surface: Natural packed dirt; eastern hardwood forest
Best season: Year-round
Schedule: Sunrise to sunset
Other trail users: Bikers, equestrians
Canine compatibility: Pets must be kept on a leash at all times.
Land status: Little Bennett Regional Park, part of the Montgomery County, Maryland, system; located just east of MD 355, about 25 miles northwest of Washington, D.C.

Nearest town: Clarksburg
Fees and permits: None
Camping: Camping is available; a permit and a fee are required. Call (301) 528-3430.
Trailhead facilities: Water and restrooms at the nature center during business hours
Maps: USGS Urbana MD; downloadable map from county website
Trail contact: Little Bennett Regional Park, Park Manager's Office, 23701 Frederick Rd., Clarksburg, MD; (301) 495-2595; https://montgomeryparks.org/parks-and-trails/little-bennett-regional-park/; info@montgomeryparks.org
Special considerations: The trail can be mucky in spots.

Finding the trailhead: From the Capital Beltway, drive north on I-270. Take exit 18, MD 121, north toward Clarksburg. Proceed through the MD 355 intersection for 6 miles to reach the Wilson Mill parking area on the left. GPS: N39 15.841' / W77 16.915'

The Hike

This splendid little hike offers Washington, D.C., and Montgomery County urbanites an almost instant retreat from the city. Although the woods here have a wild feel about them, the park area actually encompasses the former settlement of Kingsley.

As early as the eighteenth century, the Little Bennett Valley was the scene of farms and small-scale industries capitalizing on the region's abundant resources of timber, water, and vast acreage for farming. Several gristmills and sawmills, a sumac mill, and a whiskey manufacturer were established at various times along the creek. The steep and rocky slopes did not encourage farming, but farmers gave it their best, raising tobacco first, and then grain crops, well into the twentieth century. A small community flourished, which was called Kingsley—named for a prominent

Montgomery County family whose surname, King, now identifies several subdivisions in the region.

Start the hike on the Wilson Mill Trail directly west of the parking area, behind the kiosk, for a short leg to Stoney Brook Trail at about 0.3 mile. You will cross a small bridge on the way built by an Eagle Scout who died shortly afterward at the age of 12. Now you follow the sky-blue blazes. At the junction with Beaver Valley Trail 500 feet farther along are the remnants of Wilson's Sawmill, one of the many sawmills that utilized Little Bennett Creek, which is about a hundred yards east of the trail. Stay right and you come to the Mound Builder Trail a few yards down the path at 0.4 mile.

But before turning left onto the Mound Builder Trail, continue straight for another 50 yards to enjoy a rest stop at Little Bennett Creek. From the bridge over the creek, it is a short hike to Hyattstown Mill Road and the Clarksburg Road trailhead (trailhead for overflow parking).

Back on the Mound Builder Trail, ascend what at times can be a mucky trail, through red cedar and pine. You cannot miss the dirt mounds scattered throughout this area, just off the trail and in the woods. These are huge anthills—by themselves a worthy attraction. This is the largest colony of mound-building ants in the region. However, it is not a good idea to disturb the ant mounds.

As you crest the ridge, the forest turns from poplar and maple to oak and beech. Turn right onto Bennett Ridge Trail, a wide former farm road, at 0.8 mile. Walk through a number of meadows, home to deer, fox, and coyote, and then up along a ridge with wetlands below, perfect bottomland for skunk cabbage in the early spring.

Reach a junction with the Woodcock Hollow Trail at 1.2 miles. Turn left and descend into the woods on Woodcock Hollow, sweeping right and then cutting sharply back left near Sopers Branch, which wanders through open woods dotted with beech, maple, and older red and white oaks. For the next 0.5 mile, walk just above the branch. Follow the Antler Ridge Trail south, descending then rising to the Whitetail Trail at 1.7 miles; stay right and descend on the Whitetail Trail.

At 2.1 miles cross a small stream in an open glade, with princess pine carpeting the forest floor. Reach the nature trail at 2.7 miles, staying left at the fork over the bridge. Ascend the hill, crossing the access road to the campground and walking on to the nature center on a wide, accessible pathway. Find the Big Oak Trail behind the nature center, to the left of the amphitheater, staying on the sky-blue trail.

After passing the Little Oak Trail, in half a mile turn right onto Acorn Hollow Trail, at 3.3 miles, and descend easily into the small valley created by Stoney Brook. Reach the brook and turn left onto Stoney Brook Trail. Walk through the wonderfully quiet hollow, interrupted only by a short rise over a small knob and a crossing of a spring babbling under cover of towering poplars. Look for an ancient iron tractor wheel. Reaching Wilson Mill Trail at 4.1 miles, exit right and back to the parking area.

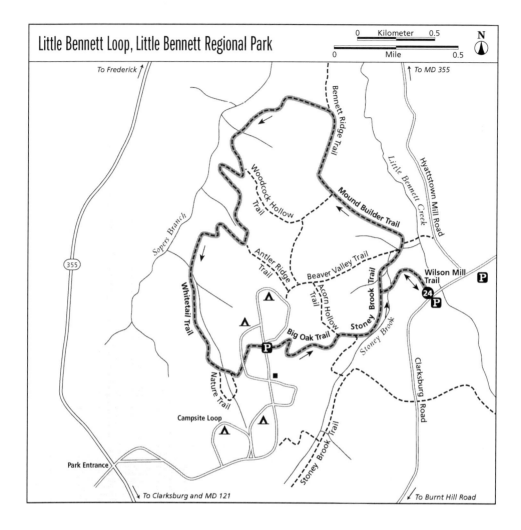

Little Bennett Loop, Little Bennett Regional Park

Miles and Directions

0.0 Start at the Wilson Mill Trail parking off MD 121.

0.3 Turn right on Stoney Brook Trail.

0.4 Junction with the Mound Builder Trail. Go left and up the hill to the mounds.

0.8 Turn right onto Bennett Ridge Trail.

1.2 Reach the junction with the Woodcock Hollow Trail.

1.7 At the Whitetail Trail junction, descend to the right.

2.8 Reach the nature trail. Stay left at the fork and cross the stream.

4.4 Arrive back at the trailhead.

Options: There are several options for short loops in the north section of the park. Site maps are available at the contact station.

25 Schaeffer Farm Trail, Seneca Creek State Park

An easy loop meanders in and out of new and mature woods and farm fields, crossing several creeks, then runs along a high vantage point above Seneca Creek and finishes with a long view west to the Appalachian piedmont. The entire trail system is a haven for mountain bikers.

Start: The trailhead is at the back of the parking area.
Distance: 4.3-mile loop
Hiking time: About 2.5 hours
Difficulty: Easy to moderate, due to a number of ascents
Elevation gain: Minimal
Trail surface: Natural, hard-packed dirt; rolling hills
Best season: Apr–Nov. Intermittent closures are instituted for hunting season and ground freeze from late Nov through early Mar. Call (301) 924-1998 for information regarding trail closures.
Schedule: Sunrise to sunset
Other trail users: Mountain bikers
Canine compatibility: Leashed dogs permitted
Land status: Seneca Creek State Park, Schaeffer Farm Trails System; just off MD 117, 20 miles northwest of Washington, D.C.
Nearest town: Germantown
Fees and permits: None

Camping: None
Trailhead facilities: Portable toilets
Maps: USGS Seneca MD; map boards through the park
Trail contact: Seneca Creek State Park, 11950 Clopper Rd., Gaithersburg, MD; (301) 924-2127; https://dnr.maryland.gov/publiclands/pages/central/seneca.aspx; senecacreek.statepark@maryland.gov
Special considerations: The trails in the system were built largely by members of area mountain-bicycling and equestrian organizations and are maintained cooperatively. Trail use guidelines call for cyclists to yield to hikers, but it is often easier for a hiker to step aside to allow an oncoming cyclist to pass. Be courteous. Summer months are the most popular for trail cyclists here. Trail closures are routine from mid-Dec to mid Mar. Periodically, high water may cause the park to close. Check with the park manager before your hike.

Finding the trailhead: From the Capital Beltway, drive north on I-270 to the MD 118 exit (15B) south. Go 3 miles west and turn right onto MD 117; then almost immediately turn left onto Schaeffer Road and drive through a host of new developments. In 2.5 miles, just as the road takes a hard right, watch for the park sign and turn left into the trail system parking area. The trailhead is at the back of the parking area. GPS: N39 08.590' / W77 18.647'

The Hike

Start at the far end of the parking area, continuing left past a trailhead sign to the white-blazed trail. Turn left into the woods to walk the loop clockwise. Follow white blazes for the entire trail. The terrain is easy, and the trail's path is circuitous, more for aesthetics than necessity. The park is on the edge of Montgomery County's rural preservation area. You may hear voices of soccer players and their fans playing on the soccer fields you drove past on the way in. As you enter a farm field to walk its perimeter, you may be thankful that the county has some of the most protected land per capita in the state and provides this place to escape the growing metropolis.

At 0.4 mile reenter the woods along a seasonal run and begin a stretch of passing into and out of the woods, with a small creek to the right.

Enter mature woods at 0.5 mile and cross two small bridges. At 0.8 mile the trail intersects an unmarked trail; go right downhill. The trail ahead is a citizen trail and not an acknowledged park trail. Cross the same run twice more, and then climb out of the stream valley and enter another field, turning right, with the woods on your right. Circle halfway around the field and cut through a stand of cherry into yet another field. These farm fields are currently not cultivated and very overgrown.

At 1.1 mile the orange trail splits off to the right; stay left (uphill), following the white and orange trail markers for a short way. Cross a bridge and walk 0.25 mile to the next junction to where the orange trail splits off again to the left. You're now in sight of the Black Rock Road entering the woods beside a giant red oak surrounded by a grove of white pine. As with the fields, this area is totally overgrown and mangled, signs that the farmer gave up maintaining this area long ago.

At 1.7 miles cross the Button Farm driveway, with the farmhouse visible to the right. Still in the pine, pass below the farmhouse, and then ascend toward the open field. This is a perfect location for spotting deer and fox. Watch for animal scat on the trail.

At about 2.1 miles, the trail bends right. Finally away from the road, the hillside drops dramatically to the left. You can see and hear Seneca Creek 300 yards south and 90 feet below. Perhaps the most serene segment, the path hugs the slope high above the creek through open woods for more than a quarter mile. The forest is primarily tulip poplar here, peppered with swamp oak, red maple, beech, sycamore, and an occasional cedar.

The trail then moves up the ledge of a narrow hollow containing a stand of huge, mature red oaks. At the top of the hollow, the trail cuts right on the backside of a field, then ducks back into the woods at 2.4 miles. To the left is a dirt bike course, crossing steeply back and forth across the stream trace. Stay to the field side, following white blazes as the trail bends around the course at the top of the run, and intersects with the orange trail again at 2.6 miles. Go left through remnant fence posts. Stay right past the Seneca Ridge Trail—save that for your next visit. You can see the remnants of the derecho that tore through here in 2012: huge oaks and poplars blown over or just snapped off, now decaying back into soil.

In another quarter mile, cross a utility right-of-way as the trail descends, following a line of mountain laurel. The orange posts infringe somewhat on the scenery, but the clearing brings berries and other edge-loving plants that attract wildlife. Then the woods open into a beautiful stream valley. The woods are open here, and it's as peaceful a place as you will find on this trail; a great spot to rest and watch for wild turkey and deer. At the bottom, cross two small streams just above their confluence. Pass the green trail to begin climbing steeply, with the streams on the right.

At 4 miles reach the intersection with the yellow trail as the white trail follows mostly level ground punctuated by gentle descents and rises over small knobs. There

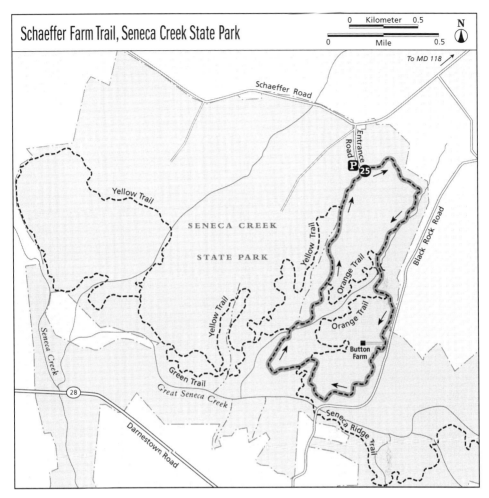

Schaeffer Farm Trail, Seneca Creek State Park

are dogwood, redbud, and green spring farm fields to either side. Here you can look through the trees, west across a farm field, to the piedmont in the distance. Follow the route with the white blazes back to the trailhead at 4.3 miles.

Miles and Directions

0.0 Start at the trailhead at the far end of the parking area.

0.5 Enter the woods and cross two small footbridges.

1.7 Cross farm driveway.

2.6 Intersect the orange trail (again); stay on the white-blazed trail.

3.0 Cross the utility right-of-way.

4.0 The yellow trail enters from the left; stay right on the white trail.

4.3 Arrive back at the trailhead.

Options: There are several color-blazed trails in the park system. Contact Seneca Creek State Park for information about these other trails.

26 Northern Peaks Trail, Sugarloaf Mountain

Sugarloaf Mountain is arguably the best hike within an hour's drive of Washington, D.C. The mountain is privately run and meticulously maintained. The trail takes you through thick woods and to outstanding views. It's long but well worth the effort.

Start: The blue-blazed trailhead is on the west side of the circle at the head of the West View parking lot.
Distance: 5.6-mile loop
Hiking time: About 3.5 hours
Difficulty: Strenuous; a lot of climbing between 4 peaks
Elevation gain: 560 feet from the low point to the highest point
Trail surface: Packed dirt, rocky; rocky monadnock
Best season: Sept–June
Schedule: 8 a.m. until 1 hour before sunset; hikers must be out before dark
Other trail users: None
Canine compatibility: Leashed dogs permitted
Land status: Sugarloaf Mountain is run by a private foundation; located in Dickerson, Maryland, about 45 miles northwest of Washington, D.C., and a few miles east of the Potomac River.
Nearest town: Dickerson
Fees and permits: None
Camping: Camping is prohibited.
Trailhead facilities: Portable toilet
Maps: USGS Buckeystown MD; downloadable map at www.sugarloafmd.com
Trail contact: Sugarloaf is owned and maintained by Stronghold Incorporated, a not-for-profit corporation. Help support the organization by becoming a member; visit the website for more information. Stronghold Incorporated, 7901 Comus Rd., Dickerson, MD; (301) 874-2024; www.sugarloafmd.com; www.poolesvillemd.gov/340/Sugarloaf-Mountain.
Special considerations: The trail is rugged, so good footwear with firm soles is recommended.

Finding the trailhead: From Washington, D.C., take I-270 north to exit 22, Old Hundred Road. Circle around west, going under the highway, toward Comus. In 2.9 miles go right on Comus Road (at the Comus Inn, a great place for late-day food and beverages). Pass the vineyard and enter the park in 2.3 miles. Go right, through the entrance, and follow the one-way road winding up the mountain. Go left to the West View parking lot, where you will find the trailhead. GPS: N39 15.671' / W77 23.800'

The Hike

The history of Sugarloaf Mountain is a remarkable story of halting exploitation followed by enlightened land conservation. Geologically, the mountain is a monadnock, a "mountain that remains after the erosion of the surrounding land"—a 14-million-year process. Native people used the mountain as a lookout. Early settlers timbered the mountainside for fuel to feed the iron furnace at Point-of-Rocks on the Potomac River. Later, local farmers also took advantage of the woodlands and continued the denuding of the mountain, leaving the quartzite rock barren and shining in the sun.

At the turn of the twentieth century, a D.C. lawyer named Gordon Strong bought the mountain. Strong loved the mountain and built a log cabin on its flank, but his

The view across the valley from White Rock overlook, Sugarloaf Mountain.

wife didn't want to live in a log cabin, so he built her a mansion, which you pass on the way out. To accommodate his D.C. visitors, Strong built stone steps (the Green Trail) to the top of the mountain. By the time he died, Strong had created a trust to ensure the preservation of the mountain for future generations.

Leaving the circle, the trail heads sharply downhill. The blue-blazed Northern Peaks Trail is very well marked and includes mile markers every 0.5 mile. At 0.2 mile go right, following the blue and white trails, and continue downhill through predominately red and white oaks, with poplar and black gum mixed in. Notice the declining state of the oaks due to the spongy moth (formerly gypsy moth) invasion.

The route circumnavigates the mountain clockwise, starting low and reaching the higher elevations as the hike progresses. Presently, the trail bends right and starts a slow ascent through maple and mountain laurel. When the trees are leafless, you will be treated to wonderful views of the rolling farmland to the west between Sugarloaf and the mountains to the west. At 0.6 mile the trail forks; follow the blue trail left, down the slope into a hollow with a seasonal creek. Just before the creek is a stand of very large tulip poplars and a smattering of hickory in an open forest. The creek is loaded with skunk cabbage in the early spring.

At 1.6 miles you reach Mount Ephraim Road, where you go right, following the blue blazes past the parking area and back up into the woods to the right, just beyond Bear Branch. The trail now gets more challenging, ascending to the higher elevations and the first overlook at White Rocks, but there are plenty of rest spots and no prolonged uphill segments. Reach the White Rock overlook at 2.5 miles and enjoy the expansive view west across the Monocacy River valley. (Please be respectful and steer clear of the private residence off the trail just before the overlook.)

Return to the blue trail, heading northeast to the first of four 1,000-foot-plus knobs that make up Sugarloaf Mountain. Sugarloaf gets its name from the huge

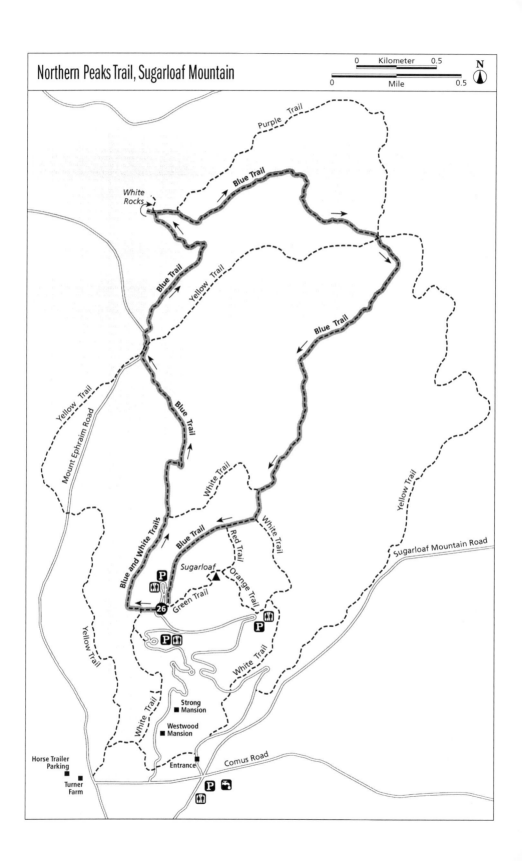

Kilometer

Mile

N

White Rocks

Purple Trail

Blue Trail

Blue Trail

Blue Trail

Yellow Trail

Yellow Trail

Mount Ephraim Road

Blue Trail

White Trail

Blue Trail

Red Trail

White Trail

Yellow Trail

Yellow Trail

Sugarloaf Mountain Road

Blue and White Trails

Blue Trail

Sugarloaf

Orange Trail

Green Trail

26

White Trail

Yellow Trail

White Trail

Strong Mansion

Westwood Mansion

Horse Trailer Parking

Turner Farm

Entrance

Comus Road

quartzite "loaf" on the top of the highest knob, at 1,282 feet. After the Civil War the mountain was timbered such that the quartzite outcrop could be seen for miles, and some thought it resembled the granulated sugar coating people would apply to birthday loaves of homemade bread.

Be sure you make the turn left back on the blue trail, and cross a saddle to begin ascending the first knob. Look over your shoulder to the ridge on your right, which you will be on in about 0.75 mile. Pass through a grove of Virginia pine and pitch pine just before you reach the top of the knob marked by a huge pile of rocks at 3.2 miles.

After taking a break on the knob, head down the switchbacks on the other side and peer through the trees to a view of the Dickerson power plant on the banks of the Potomac River. The trail is notable for its lack of blowdowns and invasive species. In this segment the trail has a very wild and isolated feel, remarkable when you consider the proximity to Washington, D.C. The area is host to over 500 species of plants, including many wildflowers that bloom in the spring.

Come to a five-way junction at 3.6 miles and follow the blue blazes through a tunnel of mountain laurel as you begin the ascent to the second knob. At the top of the knob, enjoy the 360-degree panorama before descending through another saddle and around the east side of the third knob.

Follow the roller-coaster trail up and down until it descends steeply left to the junction with the white trail at 5.3 miles. Follow the blue and white trail to another intersection, and then go right on the blue trail. You are now going west, below the highest point. Come to the red trail, which climbs to the top. If you have the time and energy, you can hike to the top of the "loaf," or you can proceed on the easier route below the peak, following the blue trail as the quartzite outcrop towers above you.

Return to the parking area at 5.6 miles.

Miles and Directions

0.0 Start at the blue-blazed trailhead.

0.2 At the junction with the white trail, go right.

0.6 Follow the blue trail downhill at the fork.

1.6 Reach and cross Mount Ephraim Road.

2.5 Reach the White Rock overlook.

3.2 Climb on top of first knob.

3.6 At the five-way junction, follow the blue blazes.

5.3 At the junction with the white trail; follow the blue/white trail; go right at the next junction on the blue trail.

5.6 Arrive back at the trailhead.

Options: There are a number of other equally enticing trails in the park; consider returning and exploring these trails. As you depart, stop by the winery just outside the park and/or the Comus Inn, with a wonderful view of the mountain, to refresh and consider your day's effort.

27 Billy Goat Trail, Great Falls

The Billy Goat Trail, located just outside Washington, D.C., is one of the most iconic hikes along the Potomac River in the region. Beginning at C&O Canal National Historic Park, the entire trail follows the Potomac River, passing south through Mather Gorge and then back north on the towpath, totaling about 8 miles. This description details Section A, a most dramatic 5-mile loop that encompasses bouldering, flat walks on the canal towpath, and beautiful views of the river.

Start: The trail begins on the C&O Canal towpath just past the Great Falls Tavern Visitor Center.

Distance: 5-mile loop

Hiking time: About 3.5 hours

Difficulty: Strenuous

Elevation gain: Modest

Trail surface: Much of the trail is very rocky; also includes an easy segment on the towpath that is packed gravel; rocky river gorge

Best season: Year-round, except in extreme weather conditions

Schedule: 7 a.m. to sunset

Other trail users: None

Canine compatibility: Dogs not permitted

Land status: C&O Canal National Historical Park; about 18 miles northwest of Washington, D.C.

Nearest town: Potomac

Fees and permits: None

Camping: None

Trailhead facilities: Visitor center with books and maps; restrooms and water located at trailhead

Maps: USGS Falls Church, VA; www.nps.gov/choh/planyourvisit/billy-goat-trail.htm; https://home.nps.gov/choh/planyourvisit/upload/GreatFallsHikingTrailsMap_BGBClosed-Descriptions.pdf; or pick up a map at the Great Falls Tavern Visitor Center.

Trail contact: Chesapeake & Ohio Canal National Historical Park, 11710 MacArthur Blvd., Potomac, MD; (301) 767-3714; emergency (866) 677-6677; www.nps.gov/choh/index.htm

Special considerations: The trail is very rocky, with a good deal of rock-hopping required. In addition, the river itself is very dangerous in this section. Signs that warn hikers to stay out of the water should be heeded. The hike is mostly exposed, with no drinking water available; on hot days carry plenty of water and a hat and use sunscreen. Hiking poles are not recommended, as they can get stuck in the rocks, cause loss of balance, and be an unnecessary distraction. Because of the difficulty of the terrain, hiking with small children is not recommended.

Finding the trailhead: From I-495 in Maryland, take exit 41 (Carderock/Great Falls, MD). Follow the Clara Barton Parkway to its end. At the stop sign, turn left onto MacArthur Boulevard. Follow MacArthur Boulevard approximately 3.5 miles into the park, where it ends.

From Virginia: Cross into Maryland over the American Legion Bridge (Beltway inner loop), and take exit 41 (Clara Barton Parkway) westbound, left at fork. Follow Clara Barton to the end. At the stop sign, turn left onto MacArthur Boulevard. Follow MacArthur Boulevard approximately 3.5 miles into the park.

From Washington, D.C.: Take M Street to the fork. You can follow either MacArthur Boulevard (the right fork) or Canal Road (the fork to the left) to the trailhead.

The C&O Canal National Historical Park is on the Maryland side of the river; Great Falls Park is on the Virginia side. Park in the lot and walk south to Great Falls Tavern. The trail begins adjacent to the Tavern Visitor Center, on the C&O Canal towpath. GPS: N39 00.141' / W77 14.799'

The Hike

Because of its proximity to the nation's capital and because of the dramatic falls along the Potomac River, this hike can be crowded, but let this not deter you from making the trip. On a clear day, this is a most entertaining and rewarding hike just a stone's throw from the capital. In addition, you can teach a course on American history just through the story of the C&O Canal.

The Great Falls of the Potomac have drawn people to the river's shore for centuries. Native Americans gathered here before the colonists. After the Revolutionary War, George Washington had a vision to use the Potomac as a gateway to the West and formed the Patowmack Company in 1785. Making the river navigable was an arduous task, and the Great Falls created perhaps the most difficult roadblock. It took the company seventeen years, using hand tools and horse power, to construct the canal and system of locks around the impediment. This was, and remains, an engineering marvel. Unfortunately, cost overruns and financial hardship drove Washington to sell the company to the Chesapeake and Ohio Canal Company in 1828. The company expanded Washington's vision by circumventing the river entirely and building a canal all the way to Cumberland. The history of the canal reflects the burgeoning history of the country and is a fascinating story. The path you take is a path of history.

To begin, pass the tavern and follow the towpath for 0.4 mile to the sign for the Great Falls Overlook. Go right on the accessible boardwalk, crossing two bridges over the river as it crashes down the fall line. In high water these bridges can be underwater.

Reach the overlook at Olmstead Island in 0.9 mile, and inhale the view up and down the river. It is a powerful scene. Imagine what it looks like when great volumes of rain are dumped on the area by a hurricane and the river has swollen out of its banks. Here the river gorge funnels the Potomac down, over, and through a jagged stretch of metamorphic rock into Mather Gorge, below and less than 0.25 mile wide.

Back on the towpath, pass another lock and turn toward the river at the trail sign for the Billy Goat Trail, just before the covered "Stop Gate." Mules used the towpath to drag barges loaded with flour, whiskey, tobacco, and iron downstream, and cloth, hardware, firearms, and other manufactured products upstream. Downstream took three to four days; upstream took three times that long.

Now on Bear Island, you will recognize how the trail gets its name as you begin rock-hopping along the sky-blue blazed path. For the next 1.5 miles, walk above the river, traversing the cliff top under stunted loblolly pine and swamp oak, with steep cliffs and Virginia to your right. Be careful and take your time. Paddlers and rafters ply the swift waters below, while rock climbers claw up and down the cliffs across the way. It's a recreational hotspot. There are a number of places to view the activity—but again, be careful.

Passing Marker One, the path takes a short break from the rocky section and heads back into the woods on a dirt path, descending to the river. You can cool your toes here or you can wait for the next river encounter, a little farther along, with much

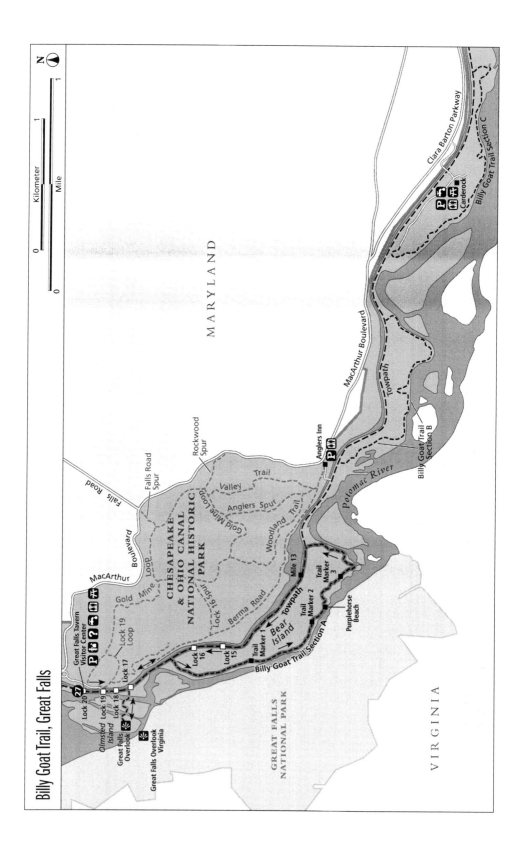

Billy Goat Trail, Great Falls

easier and safer access, at Purplehorse Beach. A steep incline up a rock face takes you back to the top of the gorge. It looks harder than it really is. Have your hands free and take your time.

At 2.4 miles, at Marker Two, a cutoff trail exits left from the Billy Goat back to the canal. If you have had your fill, this is your opportunity to head back to the car, cutting about 1.5 miles from the hike. Beyond the marker, you descend to the gravelly Purplehorse Beach, a quiet spot at the river's edge. This is the best place to rest, eat, people-watch, and relax. The water is inviting, but do not swim; instead take your hiking shoes off and dangle your feet in the water.

Follow the blue blazes up and out of the gorge, back into the woods, and past Marker Three. Go around a stagnant pond created when the river is high to a freshwater pond that is fed by the canal. Go over the outlet on a log bridge, climb a small rise, and head away from the river on your way back to the towpath.

The next section of trail yo-yos up and down, through gullies that are also fed by an overflowing canal in wet weather. Detritus from past storms hangs overhead in the branches, providing another reminder of how high the water can rise.

Reach the towpath at 3.3 miles, where the canal resembles a small pond, and turn left. Here you may see white-tailed deer, raccoon, great blue heron, and giant snapping turtles at the water's edge. You will also encounter people. Follow the towpath past half a dozen locks and Mile Marker 13 (denoting the distance in miles from Washington) to the tavern and your car. Look for slots in the stone blocks at the last lock carved by the ropes tethered to mules hauling the barges.

Miles and Directions

0.0 Begin at the trailhead in the parking lot on the towpath.

0.6 Reach the trail to Great Falls Overlook. Continue on the towpath.

1.4 At the junction with the Billy Goat Trail (Section A), take the Billy Goat Trail.

1.9 Pass Marker One.

2.2 Pass the first descent to the river.

2.4 Pass Marker Two and the cutoff trail back to the towpath. Remain on the Billy Goat Trail.

2.5 Reach Purplehorse Beach.

2.6 Pass Marker Three.

3.3 Reach the towpath and go left.

5.0 Arrive back at Great Falls Tavern and the trailhead parking area.

Options: From the towpath, you can turn right to hike Sections B and C of the Billy Goat Trail. These sections are easier but more remote, traveling through a floodplain forest and past a small waterfall. Each section is connected to the towpath, so you have the option of doing one or both. Hiking both adds about 5.5 miles to the hike. Pick up a map at the tavern for more details.

28 Sawmill Branch Trail, Patapsco Valley State Park, Hilton Area

A surprisingly rugged and remote descent drops into a wooded stream valley, past a stone railroad bridge/tunnel leading to the Patapsco River. The hike finishes with a walk through an eastern hardwood forest—a great way to spend the day with Scouts or friends.

Start: Look for the trailhead behind Shelter 245, 100 yards down the park access road.
Distance: 2.5-mile loop
Hiking time: About 2 hours
Difficulty: Moderate, with a number of short hills
Elevation gain: 300 feet
Trail surface: Rocky and natural packed dirt; rolling hills above stream valley
Best season: Year-round
Schedule: 9 a.m. to sunset
Other trail users: Bikers
Canine compatibility: Leashed dogs permitted; pets prohibited in the Hilton Area campground
Land status: Patapsco Valley State Park, Hilton Area; a few miles outside the Baltimore Beltway near US 40
Nearest town: Catonsville
Fees and permits: Fees are collected Apr–Oct; Nov–Mar the "honor system" is in effect.
Camping: Developed campsites are available; check with the park office. For reservations call

Maryland's statewide reservations line for state parks and forests, (888) 432-2267.
Trailhead facilities: A spigot at the comfort station, 50 yards before the parking area; restrooms; a playground
Maps: USGS Ellicott City MD; https://dnr .maryland.gov/publiclands/documents/ patapsco_avalonmap.pdf
Trail contact: Patapsco Valley State Park, 8020 Baltimore National Pike, Ellicott City, MD; (410) 461-5005; https://dnr.maryland.gov/ publiclands/Pages/central/patapsco.aspx; patapsco.statepark@maryland.gov
Special considerations: The parking area may be crowded on weekends. Throughout the hike, remnant junctions from older versions of these routes sometimes cause misdirection, especially at the bottom of Sawmill Branch. Stay with the fresh blazes. If you are hiking with children, be prepared to go slowly. The area is very popular with mountain bikers, so be prepared to share the trail. Hiking poles will come in handy on this loop.

Finding the trailhead: From the Baltimore Beltway (I-695), take MD 144/Frederick Road west (exit 13). Drive 1 mile and then turn left onto South Rolling Road. At the first intersection, bear right onto Hilton Avenue. The Hilton Area entrance for Patapsco Valley State Park is 1.5 miles ahead on the right. Once inside the park, take the first right and proceed to Shelter 245. The trailhead is 100 yards down the access road to the camping area. GPS: N39 14.781' / W76 44.696'

The Hike

From the trailhead, follow the road behind the picnic pavilion 100 yards to where the white-blazed Santee Branch Trail branches to the right and left; follow it downhill

Young Scouts enjoy a spring hike on the Sawmill Branch Trail.

to the left, through the woods and then back across the road. The rocky trail parallels the road through beech, red and swamp oak, and maple and again crosses the road a second time at a large oak tree and reenters the woods—and then the hike truly begins. Beware of mountain bikers, as they share much of the trail.

Pass the Pig Run Trail to reach the Charcoal Trail, a 0.75-mile loop around the campsites on the top of the ridge, at 0.5 mile. Stay left on the white/red trail. Continue straight, passing the Charcoal Trail again at 0.7 mile. After passing this junction and crossing under power lines in an open meadow, the trail continues under a canopy of huge, mature red oaks, some of which are nearly 3 feet in diameter. Dogwoods cling to the rocky soil, and everywhere on the open knobs, there is moss and lichen. Continue the rewarding, casual descent, following the white blazes toward Sawmill Branch at 1 mile.

The sound of Sawmill Branch takes over, rising above the occasional knock-knock-knock of a pileated woodpecker or the sounds of smaller birds hobnobbing in the undergrowth. The trail meets Sawmill Branch just below its confluence with Pig Run. Cross over the stream and head ever downward, now on the hiker-only and red-blazed Sawmill Branch Trail. Continue along the stream and cross under power lines one last time. Although you are surrounded by civilization, this section feels isolated and remote. The trail runs above the creek on a fairly steep slope with great views through a forest devoid of invasives. Follow the blazes on the rocks, but watch

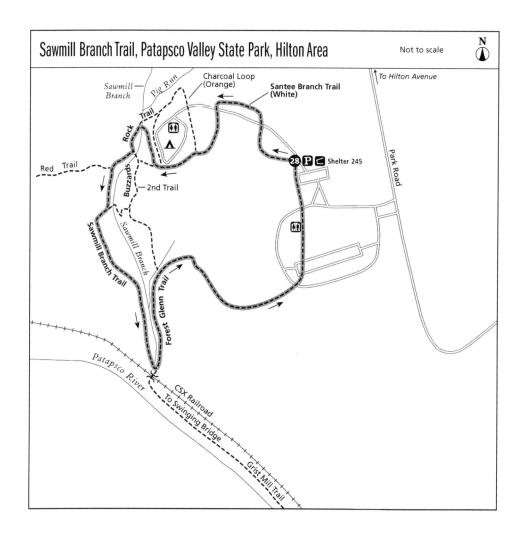

your footing. There are many pools below this stretch ideal for wading and a picnic. Look for three huge poplars to the left as the trail levels off.

The sound of freight trains leads you past another pool, a small waterfall, and finally to the railroad bridge at 1.6 miles. This marvel of stone construction creates a tunnel through which Sawmill Branch passes and Grist Mill Trail begins its southeast route along the Patapsco River. If it's open, take a few minutes to wander through the tunnel and explore the Patapsco, perhaps finding another sunny spot for a picnic or a splash around on the shore.

Here Sawmill Branch Trail crosses the creek over stones, and you now follow the blue-blazed Forest Glenn Trail, which climbs uphill on the opposite side of the creek valley.

The trail makes a long ascent on what feels like a much-less-traveled path on this side of the branch, and for the next half mile, you will hike above and next to Sawmill Branch through an open, older-growth deciduous forest. A monster poplar, maybe 500 years old, awaits you at the top of the rise. Follow the path through a characteristic Maryland hardwood forest and reenter the parking area south of where you came in. Cross the park to your car.

Miles and Directions

0.0 Start at the trailhead behind Shelter 245.

0.1 Follow the Santee Branch Trail left off the road.

0.5 At the junction with the Charcoal Trail loop, go straight.

1.0 Reach Sawmill Branch. Head downstream on the red-blazed Sawmill Branch Trail.

1.6 Reach the railroad bridge and Patapsco River. Cross Sawmill Branch and head uphill on the blue-blazed Forest Glenn Trail.

2.5 Arrive back at the park.

Options: The park map outlines a few shorter options.

29 Wincopin–Quarry Run Loop, Savage Park

Take a short ramble along the Middle Patuxent River to its confluence with the Little Patuxent River, then head upstream and return via an abandoned quarry road. Remnants of the quarrying industry can be seen along this loop. Much of the hike follows along the two rivers.

Start: Find the trailhead off Vollmerhausen Road, just over the bridge crossing the Little Patuxent River.
Distance: 2.9-mile loop
Hiking time: About 1.5 hours
Difficulty: Easy
Elevation gain: Minimal
Trail surface: Natural packed dirt, rocky in places along the river; stream valley
Best season: Year-round
Schedule: Sunrise to sunset
Other trail users: Bikers
Canine compatibility: Leashed dogs permitted
Land status: Savage Park (a county park); Howard County, Maryland, about 20 miles north of Washington, D.C.
Nearest town: Savage
Fees and permits: None
Camping: None

Trailhead facilities: Kiosk with map of area
Maps: USGS Savage MD; www.howardcounty md.gov/sites/default/files/2021-11/ Wincopin%20Trail.pdf
Trail contact: Howard County Recreation and Parks, Savage Park, 9299 Vollmerhausen Rd., Jessup, MD; (410) 313-4700, ranger (410) 313-4672; www.howardcountymd.gov/ recreation-parks/parks-playgrounds-trails
Special considerations: The first mile of the hike is within loud earshot of I-95, which intrudes upon the remote feeling of the river bottomland. Still, considering its proximity to the few million residents of the Baltimore–Washington corridor, the trail provides a quick escape into the woods. Nearby restored Savage Mill is a great spot for an after-hike lunch or beer.

Finding the trailhead: From the Capital Beltway, drive north on I-95 (from the Baltimore Beltway, drive south on I-95). Exit onto MD 32 south. In 2.5 miles turn south onto US 1. In 0.25 mile turn right onto Howard Street, then left onto Baltimore Street. Take the third right onto Savage Road. In 1 mile go left onto Vollmerhausen Road. The trailhead is 0.25 mile farther on the left, just over the bridge. The parking area is small and crowded on weekends. GPS: N39 09.000' / W76 50.073'

The Hike

Within minutes of setting off, you will be transported from one of the most densely populated suburbs in America to a lovely woodland watered by two former mill-streams. Sandwiched between I-95 and US 1, Savage Park is a population epicenter in the Baltimore–Washington corridor; however, you would never know it on this hike (except for the intrusion of highway noise until you reach the river).

From the Vollmerhausen Road trailhead, follow the red blazes along a paved trail that turns to a dirt footpath in 100 yards. Enter the woods, passing through a tangled

Visiting the "stone-finishing plant" in early spring.

thicket of multiflora rose, grapevines, and tumbled-down trees to the first intersection. In a quarter mile, follow the trail past a junction on the left with the green-blazed Quarry Run Trail; pass the blue trail, and at 0.5 mile go left at the second junction with Quarry Run Trail, following the green blazes along the ridge. Take some time at the overlook, which offers a stunning view of the Middle Patuxent bottomland. This is an especially nice view in winter, when the trees are leafless.

About 500 feet from the overlook, reach the "old" green trail, which descends the embankment to the river. It is no longer on the official map and is unmarked. The new green trail heads uphill to a four-way junction with the blue trail. Now you follow the blue-green trail to the right above the river through open woods of beech, poplar, shagbark hickory, and chestnut oak. (If you should take the old green trail, it will reconnect with the new green trail in about a quarter mile.)

Walk uphill to the top of the ridge, pass the next blue-green intersection, and then begin the downhill leg, sweeping around a sharp bend to the right to reach the floodplain and the old green trail. Go left following the river southeast on the now-green trail.

Watch for deer in the bottomland and, in the summer, copperheads along the riverbank. Look for a huge sycamore leaning out over the river just before the bridge abutment at 1.3 miles. A short spur below the old bridge abutment offers an outstanding view of the river and the confluence with the Little Patuxent. You can't help but notice the phone with a message to call someone you've missed or never said good-bye to!

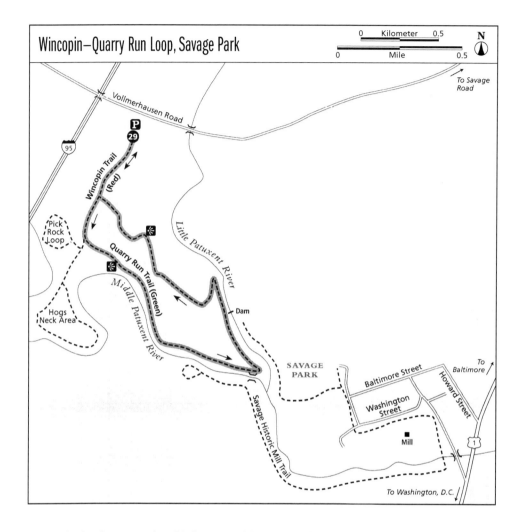

Wincopin–Quarry Run Loop, Savage Park

At the bridge again, head left on an old road, still following green-blazed Quarry Run Trail, along the Little Patuxent, which is about 50 yards to the right and will emerge in about a hundred yards. In this stretch, following the dirt road under a canopy of oak and sycamore, in another quarter mile come to the remains of a "stone finishing plant" that looks like an Aztec ruin.

At 1.9 miles, just past the remnants of a stone crib dam, the dirt road continues straight and the green trail switches back abruptly left and climbs. Do not continue straight. Ascend steeply for 150 yards as the trail finds level ground above the river. Pass the blue trail junction and look for the red trail spur to the right at 2.3 miles that leads to a spectacular overlook. Rewardingly, there are few invasives here to mar the view in all directions.

The green trail ends at an intersection with the red trail at 2.6 miles near where you started. Turn right to return to the trailhead.

Miles and Directions

0.0 Start at the trailhead on the red-blazed Wincopin Trail.

0.5 Reach the second junction with the green Quarry Run Trail; turn left on Quarry Run.

0.6 Arrive at the overlook.

1.3 At the bridge abutment, turn left onto the dirt road.

1.9 Follow the green trail on an ascent to the left.

2.6 Turn right at intersection on the red Wincopin Trail.

2.9 Arrive back at the trailhead.

30 Cash Lake Loop, Patuxent Research Refuge

Walk through pine forests and near marshy lakes in an area that is host to waterfowl, migrating raptors, and songbirds—all within 75 miles of Washington, D.C. The wildlife refuge is an excellent outing for families and Scout troops interested in learning more about local flora and fauna.

Start: The trailhead is adjacent to the refuge exit road, just where the road leaves the parking area.

Distance: 3-mile double loop

Hiking time: About 1.5 hours

Difficulty: Easy

Elevation gain: Minimal

Trail surface: Natural packed dirt; lowland forest

Best season: Sept–May

Schedule: Sunrise to 4:30 p.m. daily

Other trail users: None

Canine compatibility: Dogs are permitted on the trails but must be kept on a leash no longer than 10 feet and must be under control at all times. Take pet waste or trash out of the refuge with you and dispose of it properly.

Land status: Patuxent Research Refuge (a federal wildlife refuge); Prince Georges County, about 10 miles north of Washington, D.C.

Nearest town: Laurel

Fees and permits: None

Camping: None

Trailhead facilities: The visitor center has wonderful exhibits on wildlife habitat and other topics important to world ecology. There are restrooms, water fountains, and a gift shop featuring natural history books.

Maps: USGS Laurel MD; map at the visitor center

Trail contact: Patuxent Research Refuge, National Wildlife Visitor Center, 10901 Scarlet Tanager Loop, Laurel, MD; (301) 497-5772; www.fws.gov/refuge/patuxent-research/visit-us/trails; Amy_Shoop@fws.gov

Special considerations: Because the area is managed for wildlife research, Leave No Trace is especially important. No picnicking is allowed along the trail; bring water but leave the food at home. Rain sometimes makes the south section of the Cash Lake loop impassable. When this is the case, after visiting the fishing pier, retrace your steps to continue your hike via the northern section. Also, the south side of the Cash Lake Trail is closed mid-Oct to mid-Mar to provide undisturbed lakeshore for wintering and nesting waterfowl. Finally, be sure to pick up the *Discovery Hike* guide at office before starting—it will come in handy.

Finding the trailhead: From Washington, D.C., travel north 3.5 miles on MD 295, the Baltimore–Washington Parkway (from Baltimore, travel south on MD 295). Exit onto Powder Mill Road East. In 2 miles turn right into the National Wildlife Visitor Center. The hike begins from the parking area in front of the center. The trailhead is adjacent to the exit road, just where the road leaves the parking area. GPS: N39 01.652' / W76 47.955'

Patuxent Research Refuge has two entrances open to the public. The South Tract entrance is home to the National Wildlife Visitor Center trail system described in this guide. The refuge also has a North Tract entrance, which is located off MD 198 between the Baltimore–Washington Parkway and MD 32 in Laurel. It offers more than 20 miles of trails and roads, six fishing areas, and a wildlife-viewing area. Visitors can enjoy hiking, biking, horseback riding, cross-country skiing, wildlife viewing, photography, fishing, and hunting in the refuge.

Canada geese on Cash Lake Trail in Patuxent Research Refuge.

The Hike

Follow the wide Fire Road Trail through pine and hardwoods dominated by beech and red oak. The odd-looking cuts in the forest are remnants of research on the regeneration of forest species. Cross the exit road and reenter the woods at 0.7 mile. At 0.9 mile cross the old telegraph road and reach the junction with Laurel Trail. The woods seem to get a little wilder here as you walk through a thicket of American holly, which remains green in the winter. You will also notice the prolific work of the various woodpecker species on the dead trunks along the trail.

Just beyond, go left on the Valley Trail, traveling east. Mature oaks and beech tower above, and a woodland valley opens below. It is hard to believe the Baltimore–Washington Parkway is less than 2 miles away, but you can hear the road as you approach the lake.

At 1.5 miles turn left onto the Cash Lake Trail, crossing two wooden bridges and then passing a fishing pier right off the trail. This is a great spot to watch the amazing variety of waterfowl, and possibly beavers building their lodges. To make the most of your viewing, consider stopping at the visitor center to purchase a booklet to help identify the birds.

From mid-March to mid-October you can round the lake to the south side, crossing a bridge over an arm of the lake to a peninsula. Cross another bridge, now just

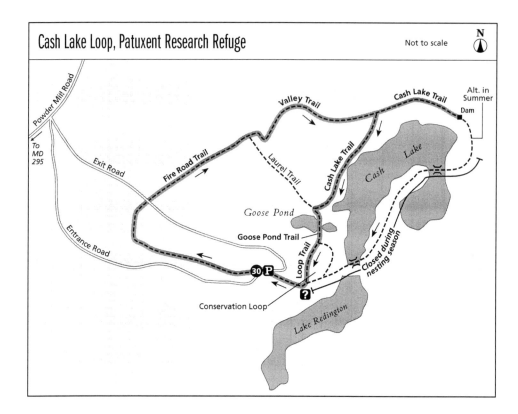

Cash Lake Loop, Patuxent Research Refuge

Not to scale

N

Powder Mill Road

To MD 295

Valley Trail

Cash Lake Trail

Alt. in Summer

Dam

Exit Road

Fire Road Trail

Laurel Trail

Cash Lake Trail

Cash Lake

Goose Pond

Goose Pond Trail

Entrance Road

Loop Trail

Closed during nesting season

30 P

?

Conservation Loop

Lake Redington

below the visitor center, and turn right onto the paved Conservation Heritage Loop at 2.5 miles.

When that leg of the trail is closed, retreat and pick up the Cash Lake Trail again along the north side of the lake. On this quiet walk, interpretive signposts depict interesting aspects of the forest. Be sure to pick up the *Discovery Hike* guide at the refuge office before starting.

At 2.6 miles the beautiful Laurel Trail joins from the right. In late spring this area is alive with the sounds of songbirds and the bloom of the countless mountain laurels. The Laurel Trail is also known to local birders as Robbins Trail. It is dedicated to Chandler S. Robbins, a researcher whose more than fifty years of work greatly expanded the knowledge of migratory birds and the effects of habitat fragmentation on their populations. Take a short stroll up the trail and see what is to be found.

Go left on the Goose Pond Trail, reaching the pond in 250 feet. Plan to spend some time here. There are waterfowl coming and going and interesting demonstrations of wildlife management practices. Follow the Goose Pond Trail out of the woods to a paved path—the Conservation Heritage Loop. This interpretive trail highlights the greatest conservationists of our time. It is well worth the short stroll to learn about the history and contributions made by visionaries to the conservation movement. Return to the visitor center to enjoy other educational displays.

Miles and Directions

0.0 Start at the Fire Road Trailhead adjacent to the exit road.

0.9 Cross the old telegraph road to the junction with Laurel Trail, and then the Valley Trail. Continue on the Valley Trail.

1.5 Reach Cash Lake Trail junction and turn left.

2.6 Reach the junction with the Laurel Trail. Go left to Goose Pond.

2.7 Reach Goose Pond.

2.9 Follow the Conservation Heritage Loop.

3.0 Arrive back at the visitor center and trailhead.

Option: In the winter months, follow the Cash Lake Trail across the dam and around Cash Lake, returning to the visitor center and adding about a mile to the hike. This section can be the most rewarding and remote area of the refuge.

31 Druid Hill Loop, Jones Falls Trail, Baltimore

This is an unusual walk through Druid Hill Park in central Baltimore marked by surprisingly deep woods, open parkland, historic sites, and a Zen garden.

Start: The trail starts on Parkdale Avenue just south of Clipper Park Road.
Distance: 4-mile loop
Hiking time: About 2.5 hours
Difficulty: Easy
Elevation gain: 200 feet but a lot of up-and-down
Trail surface: Mostly paved with some packed dirt
Best season: Year-round
Schedule: Dawn to dusk
Other trail users: Cars on some sections, bikers

Canine compatibility: Leashed dogs permitted
Land status: City park
Nearest town: Baltimore
Fees and permits: None
Camping: None
Trailhead facilities: None
Maps: https://baltimorecityparks.com/druid-hill-park/
Trail contact: Ron Rudisill, Ronald.Rudisill@baltimorecity.gov
Special considerations: None

Finding the trailhead: From Towson, take I-83 south to exit 9A-B, and turn right on West Cold Spring Lane. In 0.8 mile go left on Greenspring Avenue, and then left on Druid Park Drive in 0.3 mile. Turn right onto Parkdale Avenue, and park anywhere on the street. The trail begins about 200 feet south on the intersection of Parkdale and Clipper Park Road. GPS: N39 19.872' / W76 38.859'

The Hike

The walk/hike begins on Jones Falls Trail but diverges from the trail about halfway around the park. You start by walking up a winding paved switchback through towering tulip poplars, sycamore, and oaks. This is also a short segment of the East Coast Greenway, a long-distance trail from the Canadian border in Maine to Key West, Florida. Look for the fading JFT green ovals and arrows printed on the pavement or curbs. The Olmstead brothers, sons of the famous landscape architect Frederick Law Olmsted, designed the 745-acre park in 1860. It's the largest park in Baltimore. Notice the high fence that protects the park's forest from humans and marks the Maryland Zoo boundary. Soon you will come to said zoo.

As you approach the top of the hill, bear left on the paved road through a Frisbee golf course and the transition to open parkland. Following the road and the JFT signs, your path bends around to the crescent-shaped stone-and-slate Grove of Remembrance Pavilion at about 1.1 miles. The pavilion overlooks the Grove of Remembrance, a landmark where one tree was planted for each state in the union—forty-eight at the time—along with additional trees representing the city of Baltimore, the allies of the United States, and President Woodrow Wilson. This is one of a number of small, architecturally unique pavilions all along the walk.

Grove of Remembrance Pavilion.

Passing the pavilion through the parking lot to the right, the trail runs adjacent to Beechwood Drive to the Maryland Zoo, one of the oldest zoos in the country. Across the park to the west, you will see the dome of a historic Jewish synagogue. A tennis court to your right is another piece of history, where authorities disallowed mixed-race games until 1952 when the park was desegregated. Walking the zoo boundary still on the JFT, you pass a pond with an Asian-style pavilion, the sight for social gatherings at the turn of the century. A similarly painted yellow building on the hill above the pond once housed the zoo's aviary collection but today is used for weddings.

Continuing along, notice the large metal elephant sculpture to the west and the superb architecture of the stately townhomes along Druid Hill Avenue. A series of columns dedicated to the young people of Baltimore stands before you, and in the distance is the Howard Rawlings Conservatory. To your west is Gwynns Falls Parkway, an avenue with a wide tree-lined median. Part of the Olmstead concept was to link the park with green streets. This one takes you to Gwynns Falls Park but also to Mondawmin Mall, where rioting took place during the Freddie Gray uprising in 2015.

Passing the stunning conservatory, the JFT bends to the east and around the George Washington statue. Crossing Swann Drive, you leave the JFT and continue east to the statue of William Wallace at 1.9 miles, with Druid Lake behind it. In 1305

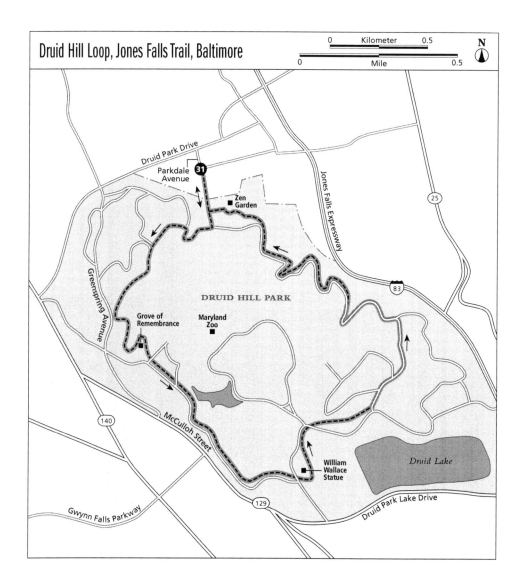

Wallace, a Scottish knight, became one of the main leaders during the First War of Scottish Independence. It may be the largest statue dedicated to Wallace outside of Scotland. Circling back across the lawn, go north a few hundred yards toward the Christopher Columbus statue, which is at the head of Druid Lake. The lake is now being partially covered to ensure higher water quality to the citizens of Baltimore.

Cross Swann Drive again, head east overland past the Lakeside Pavilion, and go left onto Red Road. As you walk along the road, you can see the tops of the buildings in Baltimore Harbor to the east. Years ago, Baltimore built a model streetscape to teach children how to navigate city streets. It's a quirky facility, but see if you recognize Fort McHenry and the blue harbor.

Pass a cemetery and ball fields to the intersection with Mountain Pass Road and go left. You now return to the woods, beginning the steepest stretch of the trail. On the back side of the zoo property, through the trees to the north, you can see and hear I-83, with Jones Falls running below, and some of the old stone warehouses that are being reinvented as office space, restaurants, and housing. At the hilltop, follow Prospect Drive to the right until you reach the red trail, where Prospect and Poplar meet. Follow the red blazes downhill to the Zen Garden at 3.6 miles. The garden was created and is maintained by a nearby resident. As you leave the garden on the red trail to the west, look for the inscription "Nothing" on a large pile of granite castoffs, as in "Nothing is written in stone."

Cross a tiny stream and rejoin the JFT in a few hundred feet, and arrive back at your car at 4 miles.

Miles and Directions

0.0 Start on Jones Falls Trail at the end of Parkdale Avenue.

1.1 Grove of Remembrance.

1.9 William Wallace statue.

3.6 Zen Garden.

4.0 Back at JFT and your car.

Option: If you want more walking through the woods, look for the red trail skirting off the path to the right at about 3 miles. It meanders mostly parallel to the paved trail to the Zen Garden.

32 Cedarville State Forest Loop

On this easy walk through a deep, shady forest along the banks of meandering creeks, you may see the industrious activities of a local beaver colony.

Start: The trailhead is in the parking area off Forest Road in the center of Cedarville park.
Distance: 4.5-mile loop
Hiking time: About 2 hours
Difficulty: Easy
Elevation gain: Minimal
Trail surface: Mostly packed dirt through lowlands, marsh, low hills, forest
Best season: Year-round
Schedule: Dawn to dusk
Other trail users: Equestrians, bikers
Canine compatibility: Leashed dogs permitted
Land status: Cedarville State Forest; few miles east of Waldorf, Maryland, and about 20 miles southeast of Washington, D.C.
Nearest town: Waldorf

Fees and permits: Fees are charged and permits required.
Camping: Youth group camping is permitted with advance registration. There are also a number of improved campsites with electrical hookups and a bathhouse. Reservations are encouraged; call (888) 432-2267.
Trailhead facilities: Portable toilets
Maps: USGS Bristol MD
Trail contact: Cedarville State Forest, 10201 Bee Oak Rd., Brandywine, MD; (301) 888-1410; https://dnr.maryland.gov/publiclands/Pages/southern/Cedarville/Trails.aspx; Park-Cedarville@dnr.state.md.us
Special considerations: During hunting season, check with forest managers to see which trails are open and safe.

Finding the trailhead: From Washington, D.C., take I-495 to exit 7A. Travel 11.5 miles south on MD 5 to Cedarville Road. Turn left, go 2.1 miles, and turn right on Bee Oak Road into Cedarville State Forest. Follow Bee Oak Road 1.7 miles to Forest Road. Turn right onto Forest Road and go 0.1 mile to the trailhead parking area on the right. From the Baltimore area, take MD 301 south and turn left on Cedarville Road, then follow the directions above. GPS: N38 38.591' / W76 49.077'

The Hike

On a hot summer day, there is a drowsy, languid feel to the creeks that run through Cedarville State Forest. They are known to rise up and wash out bridges, and if their steeply cut banks are any measure, they have done so often. But there is little babble to these sandy-bottomed brooks. Walking by them through stands of hardwood and meadows of lush ferns, you are more likely to hear a breeze in the trees than a wild torrent. Watch for the activities of beavers in the lowlands. It is a good setting for a tranquil afternoon stroll and a surprising find so near to busy, congested US 301 and the strip malls of Waldorf.

When you enter the woods from the trailhead parking area, you immediately come to the blue-blazed trail with signs pointing in both directions; it's a loop, and this is the beginning and the end of the trail. Turn left onto the blue trail, and follow the entire loop counterclockwise.

Beaver dam, Cedarville State Forest.

Descend with placid Wolf Den Branch on your right, staying left where the orange-blazed trail goes right, and follow the blue trail through the lowlands along the creek. This is the perfect habitat for beavers. One of nature's great engineers, they build dams along Wolf Den Branch and flood the area, creating pools and habitat.

The trail soon meets Sunset Road, goes right over Wolf Den Branch, and cuts back left into the woods at 0.4 mile. Follow the blue markers along a small ephemeral creek through oak and hickory, with an understory of holly. In the spring, skunk cabbage pokes up along and in the creeks and princess pine blankets the open forest floor, while the summer brings fern-covered meadows, giving the woods the lush feel of a Pacific Northwest rainforest. The remote area may also have provided cover for moonshiners who once used the area's creeks and streams for their subtle art.

Climbing slightly along a ridge, look to the right to see the wetlands from above, through the trees. At 0.8 mile, bridge another feeder creek. Look 25 feet to your left to a huge old oak tree marred by horizontal drilling, likely the work of the yellow-bellied sapsucker, which bores these holes not for insects but for the sap that then attracts and traps the insects.

At 1.2 miles cross another small bridge. To the right, just 50 feet off the trail, you will see significant beaver activity. It's an easy bushwhack through an open understory to a large beaver dam on Wolf Den Branch, but also watch for snakes sunning by the branch. At 1.4 miles the trail bends to the left, leaving the moist woods by the creek and heading east. As you crest the hill, come to an area devastated by the storms of

Wolf Den Branch bridge, Cedarville State Forest.

2012. You will see the remnants of the tremendous destruction winds in excess of 80 mph can bring. Proceed through stands of young pine on a drier, sandier trail.

At 1.7 miles go across Cross Road and follow the blue blazes through an area used for archery target shooting. The trail bends gradually left, traveling through young oak mixed with large, gray-barked beech, meeting Zekiah Swamp Run, another languid watercourse. In the spring, listen for the unmistakable call of spring peepers as you approach the swampy area adjacent to the run.

Turn left and cross Forest Road at 2.2 miles, then duck left back into the woods, crossing Mistletoe Road at 2.4 miles. Throughout this area, look for small round pools along the creeks. These clear springs harbor small frogs and feed the nascent streams. After passing over Cross Road again at 3.3 miles, enter a young, cut-over area, and then a beautiful stand of mature oak and poplar with a holly understory. Travel through the venerable trees slowly to enjoy their stature; then turn right, following blue blazes, and continue to Wolf Den Branch at 3.8 miles.

Cross the bridge over the branch and go right on the other side, following the blue and orange markers. In 0.2 mile go left. Reach Forest Road at 4.2 miles. Follow the road briefly; then cross the road and reenter the woods, following the blue blazes back to the trailhead.

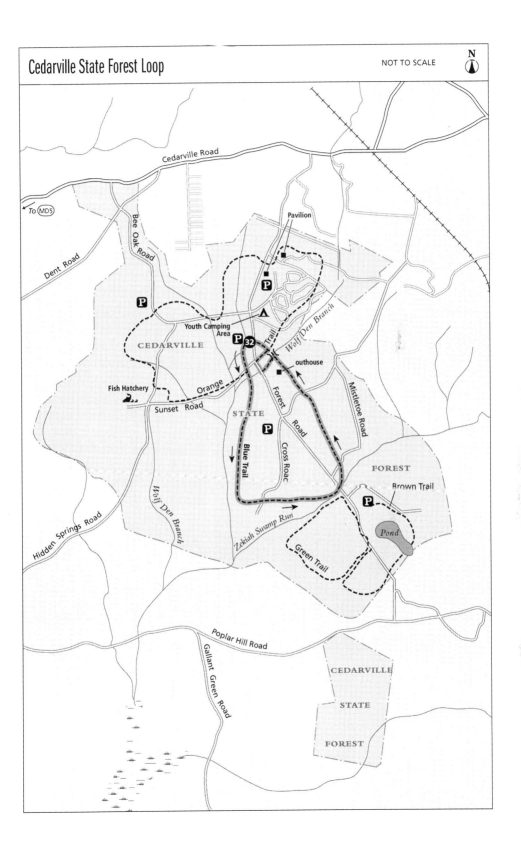

Miles and Directions

0.0 Start at the trailhead parking area, on the blue-blazed trail.

0.4 Cross Wolf Den Branch.

1.7 Go across Cross Road.

2.2 Turn left at Zekiah Swamp Run and cross Forest Road.

2.4 Cross Mistletoe Road.

3.3 Go across Cross Road a second time.

3.8 Cross the bridge over Wolf Den Branch.

4.2 Reach Forest Road. Follow the road briefly, then cross it to reenter woods on the blue trail.

4.5 Arrive back at the trailhead.

Options: There are 14 miles of trails at Cedarville State Forest. For a long hike, you can include most of them in a bigger loop. Families can picnic and fish at Cedarville Pond.

33 Parkers Creek Loop, American Chestnut Land Trust

This hike offers a combination of upland forest, transitional hillsides of holly trees and pines, wetland woods, and the broad marsh along Parkers Creek. Beavers make their home at the top of the creek. The area is called "Chesapeake in miniature" because of its complete estuary, with a broad range of habitats running from brackish water to freshwater at the head of the creek.

Start: From the parking area, walk toward the timber-frame barn. The Turkey Trail is to the right of the barn.

Distance: 3.8-mile loop, not including the Turkey Spur (0.3 mile each way)

Hiking time: About 2.5 hours

Difficulty: Moderate

Elevation gain: 200 feet

Trail surface: Natural packed dirt; rolling forested hills above creek; lowlands/marsh

Best season: Spring and autumn

Schedule: Dawn to dusk

Other trail users: None

Canine compatibility: Leashed dogs permitted

Land status: Parkers Creek Loop is in the northern tracts of lands owned or managed by the American Chestnut Land Trust (ACLT),

a private land trust. ACLT is located in Calvert County, Maryland, about 40 miles southeast of Washington, D.C.

Nearest town: Prince Frederick

Fees and permits: None

Camping: None

Trailhead facilities: Privy, kiosk

Maps: USGS Prince Frederick MD; North Side Trail Guide is available at the trailhead kiosk or online.

Trail contact: American Chestnut Land Trust, PO Box 2363, Prince Frederick, MD 20678; (410) 414-3400; acltweb.org; info@acltweb.org

Special considerations: Hunting is authorized, and hikers are encouraged to check the ACLT website (www.acltweb.org) for details during hunting season.

Finding the trailhead: From Baltimore drive south on I-97 to US 301; then go south 19 miles to MD 4. Turn left, and drive 23 miles to Prince Frederick. Turn left on Dares Beach Road and go 2 miles. Turn right on Double Oak Road and go 1 mile. At the fork in the road, turn left onto the gravel driveway and proceed past the house to trailhead parking. Look for the Turkey Trail/Parkers Creek Loop trailhead to the right of the barn, just past the parking area. GPS: N38 32.831' / W76 31.985'

From Washington, D.C., exit onto MD 4 from the Capital Beltway (I-495). Go 32 miles to Prince Frederick, and then follow the directions above.

The Hike

It is hard to prefer one time of year over another at the Parkers Creek Loop, but it is also hard to imagine a better place to spend a late-autumn morning. The understory has opened for winter, revealing views of Parkers Creek marsh while you are still deep in the woods. The last of the migratory birds darken the sky above the marsh like a pointillist moving picture, the final colors of the canopy perform hang-gliding routines from the ledges. With the pace of growth in Calvert County, it is hard to say what the landscape out on MD 4 will look like in the future.

A scenic rest stop along Parkers Creek Trail.

Fortunately, along this stretch of Parkers Creek watershed, nature will have the say in what types of changes transpire.

From the parking area, walk away from the entrance road toward the barn and ACLT's 1-acre sustainable farm. Look for the Turkey Trail/Parkers Creek Loop trailhead to the right of the barn. Duck right into the woods, following purple blazes on the Turkey Trail. The hardwood trees around you include southern red oak, black cherry, ash, and northern red oak. A great poplar graces the trail, but all around is evidence of the storms that have torn through the area over the past decade. Songbirds have made great use of all the downed trees; in season you will see Carolina chickadees and hooded warblers darting in and out of the long branches smashed into the ground. If you don't see them, you will surely hear them. All of the tree fall has created quite a haven for red-bellied woodpeckers too.

Keep an eye open to the right at about 0.5 mile to see the remains of the Scales/Simms House, named for two African American families who lived and farmed here in the nineteenth century. Just beyond the house, to the left, are long views of the Chesapeake Bay in the distance.

Reach the junction with Parkers Creek Trail at 0.7 mile. Here, the Turkey Spur descends about 0.25 mile downhill to the marsh. This is a wonderful excursion on a steeply cut path known as a "sunken road" because many wagons and footsteps over the years carved this sunken channel in the soft earth. Enter the lowland, which hosts a variety of birds and a colony of muskrats recognizable only by the tops of their lodges rising through the tall grass in the marsh.

Beast and the beauty.

Returning to Parkers Creek Trail, turn left (southwest), and follow the path through mature poplar and oaks over a wide flat plain. Then walk a roller coaster of ups-and-downs circling a deep hollow. Just before dropping to Parkers Creek, reach a vista overlooking the creek at the 1-mile mark. Descend steeply into the hollow. The path flattens out as you reach the lowlands and begin your journey upstream. Cross boardwalks over the wet areas and see what wildlife appears. The bottomland is a real treat—a primordial swamp that holds many surprises.

At the end of the hollow, reach the tall marsh grasses of Parkers Creek's 0.5-mile-wide drainage. It is a classic Chesapeake view, and yet when you look behind you, you cannot help but be reminded of forest above the fall line. The trail follows the marsh, just inside or just outside the tree line, for 0.5 mile, wending in and out of hollows. Look for gnawed-on tree stubs, evidence of a beaver colony in the area.

Pass the junction with Double Oak Road Trail at 1.8 miles. The bench here offers a wonderful place to sit and watch the day go by on the shoreline of Parkers Creek.

Parkers Creek Trail continues straight ahead, along the marsh, for a spectacularly remote and wild stretch, as the water turns fresh and the beavers abound.

Arrive at the junction with Parkers Creek Road Trail at 2.1 miles. Before turning right to head up the path, follow the Bridge Spur about 50 yards to the raft, a favorite feature for hikers. Crossing Parkers Creek using the raft's chain-and-pulley system is well worth this quick detour. ACLT's North-South Trail, a hilly, 2.2-mile-long route that connects to ACLT's South Side trails, begins on the opposite bank.

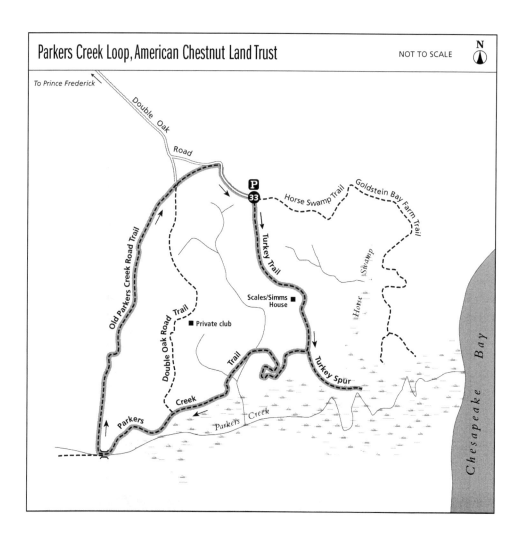

To Prince Frederick

Double Oak Road

Old Parkers Creek Road Trail

Horse Swamp Trail

Goldstein Bay Farm Trail

Turkey Trail

Double Oak Road Trail

Scales/Simms House

Private club

Horse Swamp

Trail

Turkey Spur

Parkers Creek

Parkers Creek

Chesapeake Bay

After returning from the raft, start the long ascent up Parkers Creek Road Trail. The beginning of this trail includes two tall staircases that lead up to a ridgetop with spectacular views. Off to the right, Parkers Creek winds through the marsh to the Chesapeake Bay. To the left, beavers have been hard at work building and repairing one of their dams. Soon the path widens, a remnant of the old dirt road that once carried traffic over the creek and gave this trail its name. As you continue the long, gradual climb, the many changes in forest type you encountered on the descent replay themselves in reverse.

Pass by the junction with the PF2Bay Trail, and continue to Double Oak Road at 3.3 miles. Cross the road and rejoin the trail straight ahead, following the path as it cuts through the woods and then runs parallel to the ACLT driveway. The end of the 3.8-mile loop is nearly in sight, but the trail has one last twist in store, curving downhill and climbing back up again before ending near the barn.

Miles and Directions

0.0 Start at the trailhead to the right of the barn on the Turkey Trail.

0.7 Reach the junction with Parkers Creek Trail and Turkey Spur, and go left.

1.0 Reach the Parkers Creek overlook.

1.8 Pass the junction with Double Oak Road Trail. Continue straight on Parkers Creek Trail. Turn right and head uphill on Parkers Creek Road Trail.

3.3 Reach Double Oak Road; go straight to continue on Parkers Creek Road Trail back to the barn.

3.8 Arrive back at the trailhead.

Options: It's hard to say which is more enjoyable, kayaking this creek or hiking it. Guided canoe trips are offered by reservation to the public by ACLT throughout the spring, summer, and fall; see www.acltweb.org.

For a longer outing, explore the 4.5-mile Prince Frederick to the Bay Overlook (PF2Bay) Trail, which connects Main Street in Prince Frederick to ACLT's existing North Side Trails. You can now hike 12.2 miles round-trip from Prince Frederick to the Bay Overlook and back.

34 Jug Bay Blue Loop, Patuxent River Park

Jug Bay is part of the Patuxent River Park system, with numerous options to hike, paddle, and fish. It also features the Patuxent Rural Life Museums, which tell the story of life in southern Maryland at the turn of the century. Additionally, the marshes along the Patuxent River are a critical stopover point for migrating soras and other birds.

Start: The trailhead is off the north side of the parking area just behind the restrooms.
Distance: 4.1-mile loop
Hiking time: About 2.5 hours
Difficulty: Easy
Elevation gain: About 80 feet
Trail surface: Natural packed dirt; rolling forested plateau above the river; boardwalks; lowlands/marsh
Best season: Year-round
Schedule: Daily 8 a.m. to dusk
Other trail users: None on this trail
Canine compatibility: Leashed dogs permitted
Land status: Part of the Maryland–National Capital Park and Planning Commission (M-NCPPC) system of parks and other venues
Nearest town: Bowie
Fees and permits: None

Camping: Primitive tent camping; no RVs or tent trailers; contact the park office for more information.
Trailhead facilities: Restroom and water
Maps: USGS Upper Marlboro quad; www .pgparks.com/wp-content/uploads/2023/06/ PRP-New-Trails-Map-3.30.2023.pdf
Trail contact: Patuxent River Park, 16000 Croom Airport Rd., Upper Marlboro, MD; (301) 627-6074; www.mncppc.org/4634/Jug-Bay-Natural -Area-Trail; patuxentriverpark@pgparks.com
Special considerations: The park offers guided trips as well as daily canoe and kayak rentals. Visitors can also enjoy the Chesa-peake Bay Critical Area Tour, a 4-mile roadway that connects the park with Merkle Wildlife Sanctuary and one of the nation's first African American airports.

Finding the trailhead: From Bowie, Maryland, take Route 301 south for 15 miles. Turn left onto Croom Station Road and continue for 1.6 miles. Turn left onto Croom Road (Route 382) and continue for 1.5 miles. Turn left onto Croom Airport Road and continue for 2 miles. At the entrance, either continue straight to Group Camp Area or turn left and proceed 1.7 miles to the park office. GPS: N38 46.356' / W76 42.705'

The Hike

The trailhead is just behind the restrooms, adjacent to the parking lot. Follow the sign to the Rural Life Museums, cross the campus, and follow the sign for the purple/brown trail to the Blue Loop. The trail descends to the marsh and a series of boardwalks within view of the Patuxent River. The marsh is partly due to the engineering of beavers and is loaded with wildlife, from turtles to birds to reptiles, muskrat, and maybe a beaver. The hillside above the marsh is peppered with red oak, beech, red maple, holly, and mountain laurel. Be careful here because stretches of the boardwalk are at water level and may be wet and slippery. You will pass stairs on the right to a viewing platform; a wonderful spot to stop and watch for redwing blackbirds, kingfishers, and great blue heron. Spatterdock, a kind of water lily, fill the marsh with bright yellow bulbs in the spring.

Farther along you will see the beaver dam ahead, and mud flats beyond where the soras feed on wild rice in the fall as they migrate north. Here also is a rare grove of bald cypress, a beautiful, water-loving tree in danger of extinction due to their limited ranges and their sensitivity to climate change. The trees produce "knees" that protrude from the water like miniature volcanoes. Their function is not clearly understood, but they may help anchor the tree or help to aerate the tree's roots.

At the junction, around 0.3 mile, turn right through the cypress on and off boardwalks. Follow the brown trail markers uphill into the forest until you reach the sign for the blue trail. This is the start of the Blue Loop; turn left. From here, the trail ascends to the plateau above the river, following it upstream. Add sweet gum, swamp oak,

Beautiful bright-orange "Chicken of the woods" fungi.

sassafras, and catalpa to the tree inventory as you exit the marsh. Ferns are also abundant, with Christmas fern and the large common wood fern most predominate, along with princess pine as ground cover. Continue straight for about a half mile to the Overlook Trail at 0.9 mile. The Overlook Trail offers a sweeping vista of the Patuxent in about 0.3 mile as the ridgeline narrows to a point with Swamp Point Creek on the left. The tall vegetation along the mud flat is the aptly named arrow arum. Returning to the Blue Loop, continue clockwise (left).

The trail, adjacent to Swan Point Creek, winds around the gullies that mark the plateau from here. As compared to many woodlands in the region, the lack of invasive species here is notable and welcomed. You will cross a bridge where by chance you may see the bright-orange chicken-of-the-woods fungus, which is reportedly edible ("tastes like chicken"), on a rotting tree stump. "Finding chicken of the woods (*Laetiporus* sp.) is known to inspire wild chicken dances in the middle of the forest" (www .mushroom-appreciation.com/chicken-of-the-woods.html), so beware!

Ascending again to the plateau through holly and the towering poplar trees, this is a particularly delightful section of the trail. At about 2.3 miles, you reach the green/

Jug Bay Blue Loop, Patuxent River Park

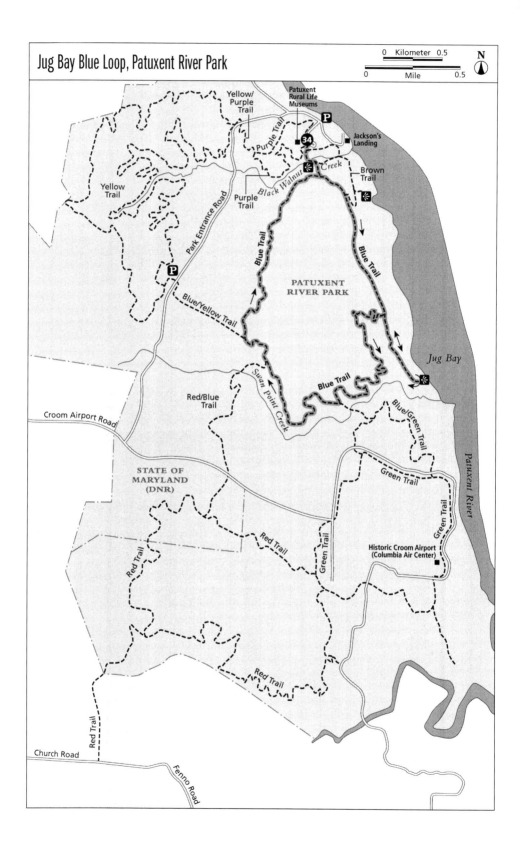

Yellow/Purple Trail

Patuxent Rural Life Museums

P

Jackson's Landing

34

Purple Trail

Black Walnut Creek

Brown Trail

Yellow Trail

Purple Trail

P

Blue Trail

Blue Trail

PATUXENT RIVER PARK

Blue/Yellow Trail

Jug Bay

Swan Point Creek

Red/Blue Trail

Blue Trail

Croom Airport Road

Blue/Green Trail

Green Trail

Patuxent River

STATE OF MARYLAND (DNR)

Green Trail

Green Trail

Red Trail

Green Trail

Historic Croom Airport (Columbia Air Center)

Red Trail

Red Trail

Red Trail

Red Trail

Church Road

Fenno Road

0 Kilometer 0.5

0 Mile 0.5

N

blue connector trail that leads to the site of the historic airport, one of the first African American owned and operated airports in the nation. Stay right and continue clockwise on the plateau past a huge beech that is perhaps 350 years old on the left.

At about 2.9 miles the red/blue trail intersects from the southwest. It too leads to the airport. Stay right on the blue trail and you shortly reach the yellow/blue service road going off left (northwest). (*Caution:* The blazes have faded with time and may no longer match the color of the park's map, but the map is accurate.) Notice the remnants of a rusted old cement mixer just off the trail. Now you turn away from the Swamp Point hollow and walk atop the plateau through beech, white oak, and groves of holly. At 3.6 miles there's an unmarked junction that's not on the park map (maybe another access road). Go left and north through a thicket of mountain laurel to the intersection with the brown trail at 3.7 miles. Go left following the brown/blue trail leading to steps going back down to the marsh with the viewing platform you passed near the beginning of the hike. Follow the sign right around the marsh to Jackson's Landing.

At the next fork, go left, past the beaver dam, watching for turtles sunning themselves on fallen logs in the marsh, to the access road to Jackson's Landing, where you can launch a kayak or canoe. Walking uphill, you reach the parking area and nature center where you started.

Miles and Directions

0.0 Start at the trailhead.

0.3 Cypress swamp and beginning of Blue Loop.

0.9 Junction with Overlook Trail.

2.3 Junction with green/blue connector to Croom Airport.

2.9 Junction with red/blue trail.

3.7 Brown/blue trail junction.

4.1 Reach parking area and nature center.

Options: There are a number of other inviting trails in the park, some through the woods, some to the airport as mentioned. Check the park map for these alternatives.

35 Calvert Cliffs State Park

A hike through forest and along a beaver-engineered bog down to the Chesapeake Bay, where fossils are abundant below the sandstone cliffs.

Start: From the trailhead kiosk, follow the Red Trail over the wooden bridge.
Distance: 3.6 miles out and back
Hiking time: About 2 hours
Difficulty: Moderate
Elevation gain: Minimal
Trail surface: Natural sand path
Best season: Spring through autumn
Schedule: Sunrise to sunset
Other trail users: Bikers; equestrians can use the service road
Canine compatibility: Leashed dogs permitted
Land status: Calvert Cliffs State Park on the Chesapeake Bay; at the southern end of Calvert County, Maryland, about 7 miles north of Solomon's Island
Nearest town: Lusby
Fees and permits: Fees are charged.
Camping: Youth group camping is available by registration.

Trailhead facilities: Restroom facility near parking lot; port-o-toilet available close to the beach
Maps: USGS Cove Point MD
Trail contact: Calvert Cliffs State Park, 9500 H.G. Trueman Rd., Lusby, MD; (443) 975-4360; https://dnr.maryland.gov/publiclands/pages/southern/calvertcliffs.aspx; park-smallwood @dnr.state.md.us. Correspondence only: Calvert Cliffs State Park, c/o Smallwood State Park, 2750 Sweden Point Rd., Marbury, MD 20658.
Special considerations: About half the park is open to hunting in various seasons, including spring turkey season. Check at the kiosk for the schedule. There is no hunting along the Red Trail to the beach. In addition, access below the cliffs is prohibited due to significant threat of landslides.

Finding the trailhead: From Baltimore or Washington, D.C., go south on US 301 to MD 4 south. Go 22 miles to Prince Frederick, then 14 more miles to MD 765. Turn left and follow signs to the park. GPS: N38 23.680' / W76 26.102'

The Hike

Calvert Cliffs State Park is unique among hiking opportunities in the region for its up-close views of the Calvert Cliffs from below, fossil-hunting opportunities, and hiker-only access to the Chesapeake Bay shoreline along half a mile of sandy beach. The cliffs and the shores below contain more than 600 species of fossils from the Miocene epoch, more than 10 million years ago. The cliffs were formed when southern Maryland was under a shallow sea. Adding to the pleasure? Foraging for fossils on the sandy beach is permitted—but no digging is allowed. Kids love it. In fact, in January of 2023 a 9-year-old girl discovered a megalodon shark's tooth that was bigger than her hand. Pair the trip to Calvert Cliffs with a visit to Battle Creek Cypress Swamp or Solomon's Island, with its maritime museum and waterside restaurants, and you have a great day of discovery.

Nature's engineers at work.

Calvert Cliffs is designated as a state wildland. While the Red Trail to the fossil beach is the most popular path, it is on the park's other trails that you will find solitude. Tuesday is the least crowded day, when you are sure to hear more birds than people on the beach.

From the trailhead kiosk, to the left of the restrooms as you enter the park, follow the Red Trail over the wooden bridge around a small trout-stocked pond, and enter the woods to the left. Hike along the unpaved service road. Although cliffs and fossils get top billing, the woods here are pleasing. There is surprising diversity in the trees in this transition zone from upland forest to swampy land below. As you descend toward the bay, you can watch the character of the woods and topography change.

Leave the dirt road about 0.25 mile in, turning right onto a narrow footpath, passing through an abundant thicket of mountain laurel, and dropping down the bank beside Grays Creek. The service road continues left to the beach; to make a loop of this hike, you can walk back via the road. Pass the yellow-blazed Grays Nature Trail at 0.3 mile, and enjoy the loblolly pines and black oaks along the stream.

The Blue Trail, at 0.6 mile, and the White Trail, at 0.7 mile, lead right and left, respectively, toward circuit options in the park. No trails lead up to the top of the cliffs. Public access to the cliffs was halted in 2001 because the cliffs are eroding—they are literally falling into the bay over time. The marsh overlook, at 1.3 miles, is a scenic place for a rest stop. A boardwalk leads 80 yards along a shallow pond formed by Grays Creek as it bottoms out in a broad, flat wetland just above the bay. All around

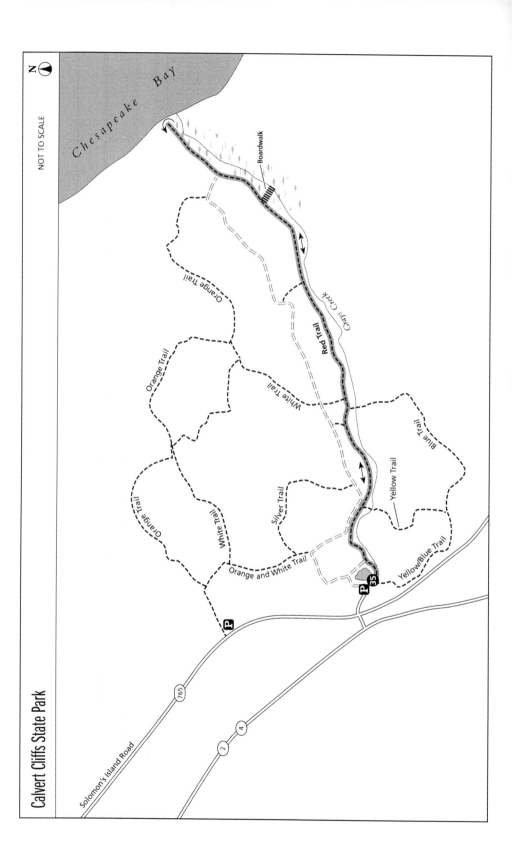

Calvert Cliffs State Park

Chesapeake Bay

NOT TO SCALE

Boardwalk

Orange Trail

Orange Trail

Orange Trail

White Trail

White Trail

Grays Creek

Red Trail

Silver Trail

Orange and White Trail

Yellow Trail

Blue Trail

Yellow/Blue Trail

P

P 35

Solomon's Island Road

765

2

4

Searching for sharks' teeth below the cliffs.

the pond, you see evidence of beavers, the originators of the pond long ago—it is now managed with the use of culverts as a kind of perpetual beaver pond. Critters to watch for include muskrats, mallards and wood ducks, red-winged blackbirds, herons, turtles, and water snakes.

Pass the service road leading back to the trailhead at 1.6 miles. This road makes for a slightly longer return and makes a nice quiet loop out of this hike. It also connects with other trails in the park. Reach the beach 300 yards farther. Just off shore is the LNG gas terminal, and just south you can see the Cove Point lighthouse. If possible, time your hike for low tide so that you can see what the sea has stirred up. Reverse your steps and follow the Red Trail back, or for a longer, less traveled route, try the Yellow Trail.

Miles and Directions

- **0.0** Start at the trailhead kiosk.
- **0.3** Pass the Grays Creek cutoff.
- **1.3** Reach the marsh overlook.
- **1.6** Pass the service road leading back to trailhead.
- **1.8** Arrive at the beach. This is your turnaround point.
- **3.6** Arrive back at the trailhead.

Options: Create a loop by returning on the dirt service road, or explore other trails in the park.

36 Greenwell State Park

Take a swim after a walk along the western shore of Maryland's Patuxent River. The trail travels through fields, meadows, and woods and offers dramatic views of the river, with visits to two historic barns.

Start: From the kiosk in the parking area, walk 100 feet down the drive toward the Manor House and go left at the paved path leading to the river.
Distance: 4.3-mile loop
Hiking time: About 2 hours
Difficulty: Easy
Elevation gain: Minimal
Trail surface: Wide mowed grass path; farm roads
Best season: Open year-round, but the best views are Sept through early June.
Schedule: May–Sept 7 a.m. to sunset, Oct–Apr 8 a.m. to sunset
Other trail users: Bikers, equestrians
Canine compatibility: Leashed dogs permitted
Land status: Greenwell State Park; St. Mary's County, Maryland

Nearest town: Hollywood
Fees and permits: As of this writing, $3 per car for Marylanders, $5 per car for out-of-state residents
Camping: None
Trailhead facilities: Portable privy
Maps: USGS Bristol MD and Upper Marlboro MD; state park map through the website
Trail contact: Greenwell State Park, 25420 Rosedale Manor Lane, Hollywood, MD; (301) 872-5688; https://dnr.maryland.gov/public lands/Pages/southern/greenwell.aspx; pointlookout.statepark@maryland.gov
Special considerations: Some trails are closed to hikers during hunting season; check with the park office.

Finding the trailhead: From the Baltimore Beltway, travel south on I-97/MD 3 to US 301. Go south on US 301 to the junction with MD 5. (From the Capital Beltway, travel south on MD 5.) Take MD 5 south to MD 235, toward Hollywood. Turn left onto MD 245 east (Sotterley Gate Road) and travel 2.5 miles. Make a right onto Steer Horn Neck Road. Turn left on Rosedale Manor Lane at the sign for the park. Follow the gravel road straight to the parking area just before the manor house. There is a kiosk at the parking area. The hike begins 100 feet to the left of the parking area toward the Manor House. GPS: N38 22.184' / W76 31.240'

The Hike

The Patuxent River is the star of this hike. Here the river is wide, and the views it offers are downright dramatic. The hike visits three coves and one sandy beach. Greenwell's trails take you through a variety of settings typical of traditional rural St. Mary's County. The area was originally farmland, and as you hike the old farm roads around the fields, you will witness the forest recovering the grounds it once inhabited. In a nod to local recreational preferences, the land is managed primarily for game wildlife and hunting. Open fields separated by hedgerows and stream valley woodlands predominate. These open fields offer hikers a welcome change of view, a

One of the bucolic coves on the Patuxent River.

chance to see many birds you'd miss on a forest hike. The delightful surprises include two historic tobacco barns, seemingly far from anywhere, for hikers to explore.

Because the trail system is designed in part to provide separation for hunters, there are a lot of trails and junctions. The route is not well marked and can be confusing. To help you stay on track, the description that follows is more detailed than is typical for a hike of this length. In addition, the park map and the trail signs don't match some in places; there is no Gray Trail on the map but you will see signs for it as you hike, for example.

From the kiosk, walk to the first path left off the driveway downhill to the paved path with the iron railing. When the trail meets the water, venture left along the bank a short distance to the beach. Just before the beach, as of this writing, there is a 20-foot section along the water's edge that requires some rock-hopping. *Caution:* Some of the rocks are ancient limestone embedded with fossil shells and maybe even sharks' teeth, but they are very irregular and craggy. Be very careful crossing these rocks. In warm weather you may want to wade around them in the shallow water. This is the only tricky element of the hike.

As soon as you reach the beach, look into the woods to see a small path through the English ivy. This is the start of the Orange Trail. Follow the path into the woods. Notice a huge beech tree on the left, along with American holly, sycamore, walnut, and willow oak. You walk up a slight slope to horse pastures, before dipping in and out of the woods until you reach a paved road at 0.6 mile. Go right on the road to

Read the story of these historic barns on the placards in the buildings.

the next cornfield and an intersection. Go left around the cornfield to the opposite corner, where there is another trail intersection with trails going in all directions at about 0.7 mile. You will see a trail marker there. Follow the signs to the Blue Trail to the left. The park map says it's the Brown Trail and the trail marker says it's the Gray Trail, but it will get you to the Blue Trail!

Pass by another cornfield uphill and presently you will see two old tobacco barns ahead of you. These are interesting structures built using traditional post-and-beam construction. You can go into the barns, where there are some interpretive postings explaining what you are seeing.

Pass to the right of the barns where the trail proceeds straight ahead to a junction with the Blue and Red Trails; follow the Blue Trail on a farm road. At the next fork, go right (counterclockwise) on the Blue Trail at 1.1 miles. This is the beginning of a loop that takes you to the Patuxent River and is undoubtedly the best stretch of the hike. Shortly you come to another intersection, where you go left. Here you will notice the trees on your left are very young, a sign of a once planted field that has been left to regenerate back to woodland, with sycamore, white pine, black locust, and goldenrod where there once were crops. Watch for groundhogs scampering in front of you along the path. Numerous invasive species are also angling for their share of the woodlands, which makes seeing through the understory difficult. But do listen for owls hooting in the treetops.

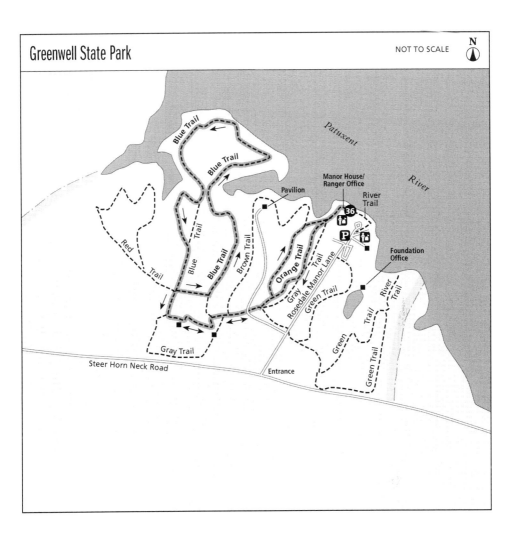

Greenwell State Park

NOT TO SCALE

N

Following a ravine on the right, past a stand of ghostly white sycamore, you come to a cove at about 1.5 miles. At 1.7 miles you arrive at another intersection, where you head right and east along the cove to the river. The trail now loops around this neck, along the Patuxent, and will return you to this spot.

You will make a long circle around another regenerating forested field, visiting the river for a long stretch. Unfortunately, there are no carved-out spots along the bluff to stop and enjoy the view, so the best time to enjoy this trail is when the leaves are off the trees.

At 2.5 miles as you begin heading southwest away from the river but are still walking along another cove, look through the trees and across the cove to an oyster aquaculture operation on the opposite shore. The Hollywood Oyster Company grows oysters in floating cages in this cove and the river to be sold to local markets and restaurants. Additionally, keep eyes peeled for osprey soaring above the water in the warmer months.

Continue around the loop to the four-way intersection at about 2.8 miles, where this loop started, and go left and then left again. You can also go straight at the second left if you want a shorter hike. Where the Blue Trail meets with the shortcut is a giant sycamore that was once three trees now grown together as one. There is also evidence of coyotes here as they mark the trail with their scat.

Continue until you reemerge at the tobacco barns and retrace the track you came in on to the road around the cornfield. At 3.7 miles you're back at the paved road. Across the road is a mowed path just to the left of a wooded section. This is the return leg of the Orange Trail. Follow it along the field through a small stand of pines. Look for the hairpin turn right down an embankment, under large white oaks, to the beach you visited earlier, at about 4 miles. Refresh your aching feet in the water and/or walk around the beach to the rock-hopping section where this adventure started. Again, be careful crossing the rocks, and then retrace your footsteps back to the parking area at 4.3 miles.

Miles and Directions

0.0 Start at the trailhead 100 feet to the left of the kiosk.

0.7 Intersection to Blue Trail.

0.9 Barns.

1.1 Junction with Red/Gray/Blue marked on signposts; turn right.

1.5 Reach the second cove.

3.7 Return leg of the Orange Trail.

4.0 Hairpin turn right to the beach.

4.3 Arrive back at the parking area.

Options: The park trail system offers a number of shorter options; check at park headquarters for ideas.

Great blue heron on White Clay Creek.

37 Chestnut Hill Trail, Judge Morris Estate, White Clay Creek State Park

A short but exquisite walk in the woods over varied terrain above Pike Creek, just minutes from Newark, Delaware.

Start: The trail begins at the trailhead kiosk. Follow the gravel path to the post marking the junction with the Middle Run (Tri Valley) Trail.
Distance: 3.6-mile loop
Hiking time: About 2 hours
Difficulty: Easy to moderate
Elevation gain: Minimal
Trail surface: Natural packed dirt; lowlands
Best season: Mar 1–Nov 30
Schedule: Sunrise to sunset
Other trail users: Bikers
Canine compatibility: Leashed dogs permitted
Land status: Judge Morris Estate area of White Clay Creek State Park; on Polly Drummond Road just north of Kirkwood Highway (DE 2), 3 miles northeast of Newark, Delaware

Nearest town: Newark
Fees and permits: An entrance fee is charged.
Camping: None
Trailhead facilities: Kiosk with map; composting privy
Maps: USGS Newark East DE; state park map through the website
Trail contact: White Clay Creek State Park, 76 Polly Drummond Hill Rd., Newark, DE; (302) 368-6900; https://destateparks.com/Trails; Nicholas.McFadden@state.de.us
Special considerations: Visitors should follow wet-weather rules for trail use. For hikers this means staying on the trail and walking through puddles; for bicyclists it means taking the day off and awaiting drier weather.

Finding the trailhead: From Newark, travel east on Kirkwood Highway (DE 2) approximately 3 miles to Polly Drummond Road. Turn left and travel 1 mile to the park entrance on the right (about 0.25 mile past the Judge Morris House entrance). GPS: N39 42.293' / W75 42.557'

The Hike

It would be easy to say there is little that's notable about this nice ramble on the Chestnut Hill Trail through woodlands east of Newark, but that would miss the mark. The quiet and solitude offered by this trail are remarkable because the park's southern edge is adjacent to busy Kirkwood Highway.

The Judge Morris Estate forms the southeastern corner of a nationally renowned conservation effort in the White Clay Creek watershed. Since the 1970s, as the population epicenter of New Castle County has shifted from Wilmington to Newark, the collaboration among Delaware, Pennsylvania, and local agencies and nonprofits has created a kind of "Central Park." White Clay Creek is designated as part of the nation's Wild and Scenic River system. Hikers interested in a real leg-stretcher can depart from the Judge Morris trailhead and walk the Tri-Valley Trail into Chester County, Pennsylvania, through woods, meadows, and farm fields—crossing only five roads en route.

Painted trilliums are a flowering beauty in midsummer.

This little ramble on the Judge Morris Estate begins at the trailhead kiosk. Follow the gravel path to the post marking the junction with the Middle Run (Tri-Valley) Trail and the beginning of the Chestnut Hill Trail loop. Go right, cutting across a field and entering the woods under 70-foot chestnut oaks and beech and sizable poplar trees, sidling around a small hill covered with invasive multiflora rose and honeysuckle in early summer. Although they are nonnatives, the aroma is heavenly. And incidentally, you may notice fenced-off areas where park management is attempting to remove some of the invasive species; a yeoman's task the managers and volunteers should be commended for. The forest opens above a small creek, where you turn right on Chestnut Hill Trail at 0.3 mile; cross the creek on a footbridge, then ascend steeply beneath towering trees.

As you continue through dense woods, there might be a faint sound of traffic, but even at rush hour, birdsong is more likely to get your attention, especially in spring when wood thrushes and chickadees are in full voice. At 0.8 mile pass Richard's Lane trail on the right and the cutoff trail to the left at 0.9 mile. Continue straight where the terrain is flat and the hiking's easy as you pass through a small clearing and through younger woods. The open meadow serves up wildflowers in spring and blackberries in summer. Pass an access trail to Upper Pike Creek Road on the right at about 1 mile. Stay left, then cross a footbridge over a small run. The understory is open, with scattered witch hazel and serviceberry. Christmas ferns festoon the forest along the hillside, named as such because they remain green through to Christmas. A

Chestnut Hill Trail, Judge Morris Estate, White Clay Creek State Park

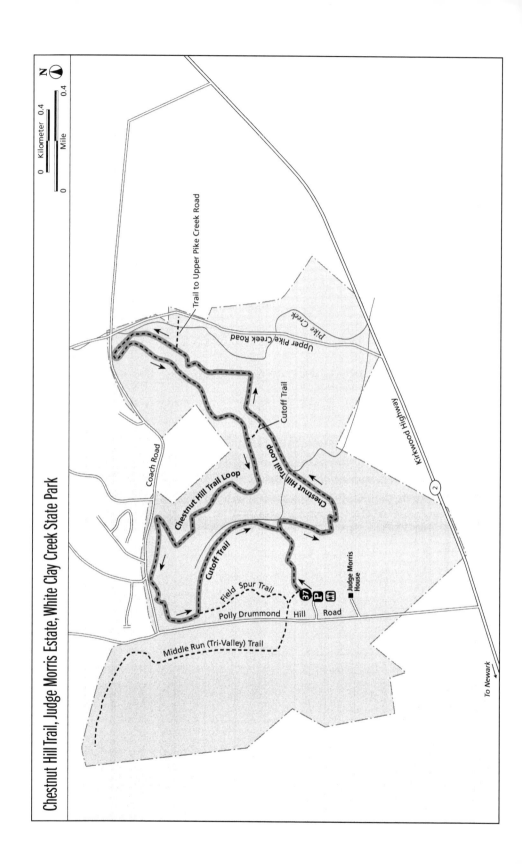

lush wetland along Pike Creek is just below to the right, filled with great bouquets of skunk cabbage in the early summer.

Soon the forest character changes yet again. Hollies line the hillside leading to Pike Creek's wide bottomland as you slab around the hill above the creek and the adjacent road. Descend for a closer look at the creek just as the trail makes a 180-degree turn left at 1.5 miles, near the junctions of Upper Pike Creek and Coach Roads, just outside the park's northeast boundary. While there is no parking or trailhead at Coach Road, an informal path makes it possible to make an emergency exit there.

Leaving the road behind, ascend Chestnut Hill again. You'll only gain 50 feet or so in altitude, but a breeze will greet you atop the hill. An abundance of huge oaks and poplars, along with walnut and cherry, populate this trail segment. In fact, the trail passes between two massive poplars, a sight itself worthy of the hike, into a pine grove, followed by a stand of great beech trees. Farther along, a mammoth poplar stands astride the trail that is perhaps 350 years old. It was a seedling almost 200 years before Judge Morris was born.

Just beyond, at 2.1 miles in an open forest, is the other end of the cutoff trail passed earlier. Shortly you come to a thicket of sassafras, with mitten-shaped leaves, and sweet cherry, with its smooth red-brown bark. The trail skirts a field to the right and goes down into deep woods of white oak, sensitive fern, and painted trillium, named for its three propeller-like leaves and petals.

As you exit the hollow, the trail parallels the road and crosses a bridge over a stormwater outfall off Polly Drummond Hill Road. At 2.9 miles you reach the junction with the Field Spur Trail. To wander through the farm field on your return, stay straight (right) at the junction and enter the field. If you have never walked through a field of hip high soybeans or waist-high corn, this is your chance. Or venture left, back into the forest, for the most rewarding section of the trail. Keep an eye out for vole and fox scat on the trail, and your ears open to the plethora of songbirds throughout this section.

The trail leaves the road noise and circumnavigates a knob around the field, along an ephemeral creek. Listen for the rat-tat-tat of the pileated woodpecker high in rotting oak boughs. The trail connects with the pathway you started on and ends at the parking lot at 3.6 miles.

Miles and Directions

- **0.0** Start at the trailhead kiosk.
- **0.9** Reach the first junction with the cutoff trail.
- **1.5** Turn left near the junction of Coach and Upper Pike Creek Roads.
- **2.1** Reach the other end of the cutoff passed earlier.
- **2.9** Reach junction with Field Spur Trail. Go left into the woods on the Chestnut Hill Trail.
- **3.6** Arrive back at the trailhead.

Option: You can shorten your hike by taking the cutoff trail.

38 Middle Run Valley Loop, Middle Run Valley Natural Area

This easy loop in a peaceful, wooded stream valley leads through beech, oak, maple, and poplar not far from Newark, Delaware. Wild raspberries are a treat in mid-July.

Start: The trail begins behind the kiosk on the east side of the parking area.
Distance: 4.4-mile loop
Difficulty: Moderate
Hiking time: About 2 hours
Elevation gain: Minimal
Trail surface: Gravel, packed dirt; upland forest
Best season: Year-round
Schedule: Dawn to dusk
Other trail users: Bikers
Canine compatibility: Leashed dogs permitted
Land status: Middle Run Valley Natural Area (county natural area); 2.5 miles north of Main Street, Newark, in northwestern New Castle County, Delaware

Nearest town: Newark
Fees and permits: None
Camping: None
Trailhead facilities: Information kiosk and map
Maps: USGS Newark West DE
Trail contact: New Castle County Department of Parks and Recreation, Department of Special Services, 187-A Old Churchman's Rd., New Castle, DE; (302) 395-5720 or (302) 239-2334; www.delawarenaturesociety.org/centers/middle-run-natural-area/
Special considerations: In midsummer, sweet wild raspberries encroach on the trail. They are sticky and delicious.

Finding the trailhead: From Newark travel north on Paper Mill Road 1.6 miles to Possum Park Road (DE 72). Turn right, then immediately left onto Possum Hollow Road (Road 299). Proceed 0.4 mile to Middle Run Valley Natural Area on the left. Follow the gravel entrance road around a big bend for 0.4 mile to the parking area. GPS: N39 42.946' / W75 43.406'

The Hike

Middle Run Valley Natural Area lies in the eastern reaches of the rambling White Clay Creek Preserve, a wonderful network of parks and open space that stretches from busy Kirkwood Highway, near Newark, Delaware, into Chester County, Pennsylvania.

You can get totally lost in Middle Run. In an area as densely populated as middle New Castle County, this is a real blessing. You will share the trail with mountain bikers, but they have done a great job maintaining the trails and they are courteous, letting you know when they are coming and how many are to follow.

The terrain is varied, the woods are deep, and the trail system is devised to make maximum use of the acreage. The path visits tall poplar stands and large red and white oaks, passes through two farms fields, hugs a high side of a steep, narrow gorge above Middle Run, crosses the run . . . and all this takes less than 2.5 hours.

From the kiosk at the trailhead, follow a paved path toward the woods about 50 feet to the Lenape Cutoff; turn right and follow the well-worn bike path skirting the field. Ducking quickly into the woods, you may be greeted by a wood thrush.

Historic stepping stones were used to cross the river when the water was high.

Traverse the hillside with the creek below to the left, and at the junction bear right on the Lenape Trail.

The trail tags along the Middle Run wetland to the intersection with the Lenape Trail/Tri-Valley Trail at 0.3 mile. Stay right/straight, continuing along the run. Walk through a young forest and along the banks of Middle Run to the next junction, with the Snow Goose Connector. Cross the bridge over Middle Run on the connector to a fork with the Tri-Valley Trail. Go right (uphill) and stay right on the Mill Race Trail. Follow the path along the edge of the creek, taking care on the wet rocks into the water. Walk along the berm of the millrace, a canal dug by hand that channeled water from the creek to power the mills below. Follow the well-worn path along the race into beech and poplar.

At the next junction with the Snow Goose Trail and connector, follow the Snow Goose Trail right, walking above and along the cascading creek to the bridge over Middle Run at 1 mile. This is a wonderful place to sit and enjoy the woods, with the stream bubbling below. The Snow Goose Trail goes straight and loops back to the junction you passed 0.25 mile back.

Crossing the bridge, notice the round cement pads north and south in Middle Run—these are man-made footstones created before the bridge was built. Fashioned to look like logs standing upright in the stream, they formed a series of stepping stones to help hikers cross the run.

Middle Run meandering through oak and poplar.

Over the bridge, follow the unmarked Possum Hollow Trail left and southeast along the other side of the run and back into the woods. Along this side of the hollow, a botanical garden of ferns covers the ground—the largest being wood fern and the greenest being Christmas fern, so named because it stays green through Christmastime.

The trail bears steadily right to a pond and stone shed. Go left around the pond, which is filled with painted turtles and bullfrogs, to a four-way junction, and proceed right, along the pond, to the old stone shed at 1.6 miles. This is the spot to indulge in the wild raspberries that line the trail for a few hundred yards when in season. Passing the shed, go left (uphill), past the houses on the left, into a farm field at 1.8 miles. Cross three fields, ducking through a piece of woods midway, and enter a mature forest of large oak, walnut, and beech.

Crossing a tributary marked by an ancient poplar leaning into the creek, reach the unmarked junction with the Double Horseshoe Trail at 2.5 miles, and turn left onto it. The trail wanders along a flat ridgeline, circling the highest point on the hike at 282 feet, with another stream below to the left. Enter and cross another field, then again duck into the woods leaving the field. This segment is remarkably similar to the earlier wooded section but with larger oak and beech and even some black walnut. Easily identified by their compound leaves, large walnuts have almost disappeared in some regions because the wood is in such high demand. Notice the very large beech with its smooth gray bark and initials carved into it a hundred feet before the bridge.

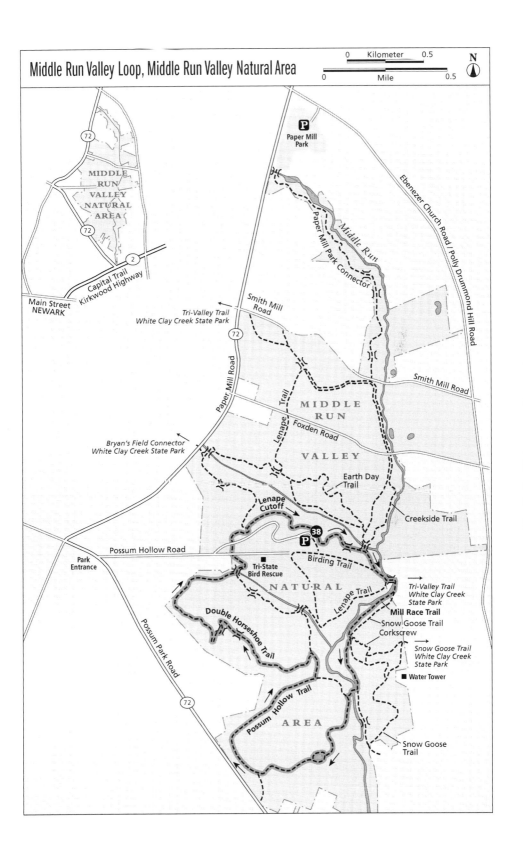

Middle Run Valley Loop, Middle Run Valley Natural Area

Kilometer 0 0.5

Mile 0 0.5

N

MIDDLE RUN VALLEY NATURAL AREA

72

72

2

Capital Trail
Kirkwood Highway

Main Street
NEWARK

Paper Mill Park

Ebenezer Church Road / Polly Drummond Hill Road

Paper Mill Park Connector

Middle Run

Smith Mill Road

Tri-Valley Trail
White Clay Creek State Park

72

Smith Mill Road

Paper Mill Road

Lenape Trail

MIDDLE RUN

Foxden Road

VALLEY

Bryan's Field Connector
White Clay Creek State Park

Earth Day Trail

Lenape Cutoff

Creekside Trail

Possum Hollow Road

38

Birding Trail

Park Entrance

Tri-State Bird Rescue

NATURAL

Lenape Trail

Tri-Valley Trail
White Clay Creek State Park

Mill Race Trail

Snow Goose Trail
Corkscrew

Double Horseshoe Trail

Snow Goose Trail
White Clay Creek State Park

Water Tower

Possum Park Road

72

Possum Hollow Trail

AREA

Snow Goose Trail

Rejoin the Lenape Trail at the bridge at 3.7 miles. Cross the bridge, ascend the rise, cross Possum Hollow Road, then follow the trail through the tree line—but don't get distracted by the numerous bike trails. Cross the park entrance road, continue to the junction with the Lenape Cutoff, and go right. Wander quietly through the woods to the parking area at 4.4 miles.

Miles and Directions

0.0 Start at the trailhead kiosk, go 50 feet, and turn right on Lenape Cutoff Trail.

0.3 At the junction of the Lenape and Tri-Valley Trails, go right/straight on the Lenape Trail.

1.0 Reach the bridge crossing of Middle Run and the start of the Possum Hollow Trail.

1.6 Reach the stone shed.

2.5 Reach the Double Horseshoe connector; stay left, over the creek, on the Double Horseshoe Trail.

3.7 Rejoin the Lenape Trail. Cross another bridge.

4.4 Arrive back at the trailhead.

39 White Clay Creek Preserve Loop, White Clay Creek State Park

A short but rewarding hike travels through the floodplain woodlands along White Clay Creek. This is a relatively unspoiled area close to Newark, Delaware, with brook trout in and wood duck on White Clay Creek. It also poses a good opportunity for fishing and wading in the creek.

Start: The trailhead is across the entrance road from the nature center.
Distance: 2.5-mile loop
Hiking time: About 2 hours
Difficulty: Easy
Elevation gain: 150 feet but hilly
Trail surface: Natural packed dirt; lowlands
Best season: Mar 1–Nov 30
Schedule: 8 a.m. to sunset
Other trail users: Bikers
Canine compatibility: Leashed dogs permitted
Land status: White Clay Creek State Park; northwestern New Castle County, Delaware, about 4 miles from Newark
Nearest town: Newark

Fees and permits: An entrance fee is charged.
Camping: None
Trailhead facilities: Restrooms, nature center
Maps: USGS Newark West DE, Newark East DE; state park map through the website
Trail contact: White Clay Creek State Park, 750 Thompson Station Rd., Newark, DE; (302) 368-6900; https://destateparks.com/White ClayCreek; ParkInfo@state.de.us
Special considerations: Pets are permitted in some areas of the park, but they must be leashed. Check the signs at the trailhead, or inquire at the contact station. Some trails are closed during hunting season.

Finding the trailhead: From Newark travel north on New London Road (DE 896) 2.9 miles to Hopkins Road. Turn right onto Hopkins Road and proceed 1 mile to the preserve entrance on the left. Follow the dirt road 0.3 mile to the nature center parking area on the left. The trailhead is across the entrance road. GPS: N39 43.605' / W75 46.041'

The Hike

White Clay Creek Preserve Loop is the only trail in the park that actually runs along White Clay Creek, following its banks to the Pennsylvania state line, where the preserve extends across the border. The area is popular with birders, botanists, and other naturalists who like "going afield." A public journal at the nature center notes sightings of the many local birds, including red-bellied, downy, and pileated woodpeckers, ospreys, great blue herons, kingfishers, wild turkeys, cedar waxwings, and blackburnian warblers. There are also wild geraniums, wood violets, trillium, and trout lilies in abundance, as well as mammals large and small. Reports say there is even a mountain lion roaming this neck of the woods.

Great blue heron flying low over White Clay Creek.

From the parking lot, cross the entrance road to the trail marker. Do not go down the bank to the creek—that trail has been rerouted. Proceed down the road through the gate and enter the woods to the right on the blue-blazed Nature Preserve Trail at 0.3 mile. The path travels along a farm field to the creek in the shade of maples, oaks, poplars, and sycamores, making even a midsummer walk a refreshing experience. Reach the creek, where the water is slow moving, splashing easily along, and birdsong rings from the branches of the big old trees. Duck under a huge sycamore that crosses the trail. You may scare up wood ducks and/or herons in the creek. The creek is loaded with bluegill, sunfish (sunnies), and brook trout in the pools.

Pass a field edge full of darting butterflies in summer, and continue along the stream's still, sunlit pools (good for swimming) and running torrents to Chambers Rock Road at 1 mile. As you approach the road in the heat of summer, the smell of hot tar mixes with the sweet and musty smell of the creek. Go straight across the road and into the parking area. Continue across the parking lot and onto a mown path left of the kiosk along the edge of a field, under the bowing branches of sycamores and to a chorus of birdsong. The trail follows the creek upstream from here, and it's fly fishing only, so bring a four-weight rod.

A fisherman below railroad trestle ruins on White Clay Creek.

Follow a woodland edge and the blue blazes, with a field and a border of young trees on the left. To the right are bigger, more mature trees and the now slow, still creek. Leaving the field, the path plunges into deep forest and continues along the stream. Follow the trail as it bends left, where rapids shoot over the rocks beneath the stone ruins of an old railroad bridge, and continue to the Pennsylvania state line at 1.2 miles.

Beyond the Pennsylvania state line, the Mason-Dixon Trail heads right; the Penndel Trail goes left. Turn left here, and proceed on a wide path marked by a blue blaze. You are now traveling on the western slope of the creek valley, on a trail that's open to mountain bikers.

At 2 miles leave the woods, cross Chambers Rock Road again, and continue on a wide path, with a wooded thicket on the right and open fields on the left. As you walk along in open country, watch for red-winged blackbirds, kingbirds, and barn swallows in the tall grasses, flickers in the trees, red-tailed hawks in the air, or for the blossoms of Queen Anne's lace and goldenrod in the late summer. The trail bends left into the woods at the edge of the field, passes through a gate, and continues back to the trailhead on the dirt road you walked on earlier. Reach the nature center and your car at 2.5 miles.

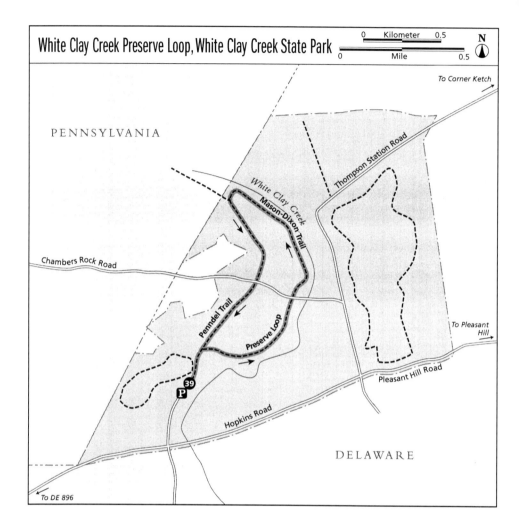

White Clay Creek Preserve Loop, White Clay Creek State Park

PENNSYLVANIA

Chambers Rock Road

White Clay Creek
Mason-Dixon Trail

Penndel Trail

Preserve Loop

Thompson Station Road

To Corner Ketch

To Pleasant Hill

Pleasant Hill Road

Hopkins Road

DELAWARE

To DE 896

Miles and Directions

0.0 Start at the trailhead at the dirt entrance road.

0.3 Go right on Nature Preserve Trail into woods bordering farm field.

1.0 Reach Chambers Rock Road. Go left before crossing.

1.2 Reach the Pennsylvania state line and go left.

2.0 Cross Chambers Rock Road again.

2.5 Arrive back at the trailhead.

Option: You can continue into the Pennsylvania section of the preserve on a 3-mile trail that follows the east branch of White Clay Creek to London Tract Road.

40 Twin Valley Trail, White Clay Creek State Park

Hike through the rolling hills of Delaware's piedmont through meadows, old fields, and impressive deep woodlands. The hike concludes with a wonderful view of the farm on the property.

Start: Find the trailhead in the northwest corner of the parking area, marked by a post with arrows on it.
Distance: 3.9-mile loop
Hiking time: About 2 hours
Difficulty: Easy
Elevation gain: 170 feet
Trail surface: Natural packed dirt; rolling hills
Best season: Apr–Nov
Schedule: 8 a.m. to sunset
Other trail users: Bikers
Canine compatibility: Leashed dogs permitted
Land status: Walter S. Carpenter State Park of White Clay Creek State Park; northwestern New Castle County, Delaware, 2.6 miles north of Newark

Nearest town: Newark
Fees and permits: An entrance fee is charged.
Camping: None
Trailhead facilities: Restrooms, water, picnic area, telephone
Maps: USGS Newark West DE, Newark East DE; state park map through the website
Trail contact: White Clay Creek State Park, 750 Thompson Station Rd., Newark, DE; (302) 368-6900; https://destateparks.com/WhiteClay Creek; ParkInfo@state.de.us
Special considerations: Observe signs regarding pets; they are permitted in some areas of the park but must be kept on a leash.

Finding the trailhead: From Newark travel north on New London Road (DE 896) 2.6 miles to the entrance of Walter S. Carpenter State Park. Turn right into the park, and proceed 0.2 mile, past the fee booth, to the picnic area parking lot. GPS: N39 42.769' / W75 46.602'

The Hike

One of several sections of White Clay Creek State Park, Walter S. Carpenter State Park lies to the west of White Clay Creek's floodplain, its gently rolling hills rising up from the valley. Like the other small parcels of the preserve, the landscape is a mixture of old fields, thickets of honeysuckle and blackberries, saplings, and stream-laced woodlands with wonderful groves of beech and tulip trees. When you are finished hiking in the woods here, the preserve's shady picnic area and disc golf course make it a great place for an all-day family outing.

Find the trailhead in the northwest corner of the parking area, marked by a yellow post with arrows on it. Follow Twin Valley Trail, which is marked with a yellow blaze. It is a wide grassy path passing hedgerows and open meadows. The trail bends right, up the hill, passing the Life Course fitness trail, and continues through a mowed disc golf course and then along the hilltop overlooking the fields and forests rolling down to White Clay Creek.

Playing Frisbee golf in White Clay Creek State Park.

At 0.4 mile the yellow trail, marked Twin Valley Connector on the signpost cuts abruptly left and downhill into the woods. Watch for a sharp right 400 feet into the woods on the Twin Valley Trail. The trail winds through the woods, past an unusual stand of red spruce, until arriving at a T intersection at 1 mile. Do not follow the yellow trail left; go right (uphill) to a picnic area at the top of the hill. There are a number of trails coming into the site. The trail cuts left before the picnic area back into the woods.

Thus begins a wonderful stretch through an impressive grove of tulip trees. As you follow the trail down to a stream crossing, stop and survey the stately tulip poplars, so called for the bright yellow-orange flowers that bloom on their high branches each spring. The tallest hardwood in North America, tulip trees grow up to 200 feet tall in the Southern Appalachians. This stand does not reach that height, but it is glorious nonetheless. In late spring the trail is covered with the poplar flowers falling from above you.

At 1.3 miles you come to the ruins of an old cabin, or perhaps a mill. Pass the obelisk, cross the bridge, and start a slow descent. Cross a second bridge (a nice place to stop and soak in the deep woods) and turn right where the Twin Valley Trail meets the Mason-Dixon Trail heading uphill.

From here, the trail climbs to an unmarked junction; go left and begin a long descent, passing another ruin, cross a bridge, and walk the rolling ridge above a

Scenic farm overlook at the end of the hike.

streambed. Watch for deer, and peer into the dense canopy below and through the boughs of immense old trees.

Follow the yellow trail to another junction with the Mason-Dixon Trail at 2 miles and make a right turn back uphill. Ascend the ridge to the next unmarked fork by a large poplar at 2.5 miles, and stay left on the yellow trail. Pass a bench overlooking the floodplain. It's a nice, quiet rest stop deep in the woods, but the multiflora rose is taking over in the wetlands below.

Reach Wells Lane at 3 miles; go left across the lane and cut back up into the woods on the blue-and-yellow-blazed trail just 100 feet down the road. Climb into a beautiful, older, wooded section, the hay-scented ferns covering the forest floor emblematic of the eastern deciduous forest.

The trail comes to a road at the top of the rise and the red-blazed Mason-Dixon Trail at 3.4 miles. Continue right on the blue-and-yellow trail. Parallel the road for a few hundred feet and then break hard right, heading downhill along an ephemeral creek through a small but very pretty hollow. Smell the hay-scented ferns and the dampness rising from the creek. Take a left across the creek and enter a farm field (uphill). Traverse the edge of the field, where groundhogs lumber into the tall grass

Twin Valley Trail, White Clay Creek State Park

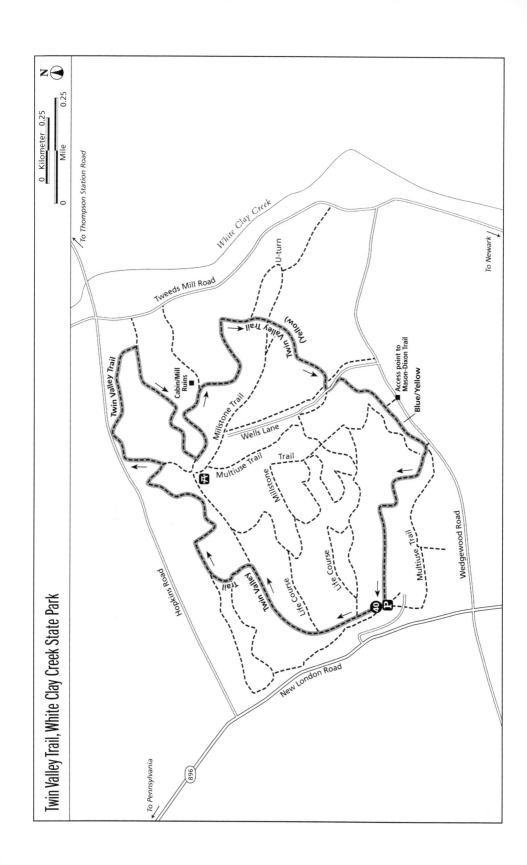

as you pass. Stop at the top and take in the view of the farm across the field, which is part of the park. Proceed on the wide, grassy path back to the picnic area and the trailhead at 3.9 miles.

Miles and Directions

0.0 Start at the trailhead in the northwest corner of the parking area.

0.4 Go left at the yellow trail post.

1.0 At the T junction, go right (uphill).

1.3 Past the cabin ruins.

2.0 Make a turn to the right (uphill), still on the Twin Valley Trail.

3.0 Reach Wells Lane. Turn left onto the road and pick up the blue-and-yellow trail on the right.

3.4 Reach the junction with Mason-Dixon Trail. Go right, following blue and yellow blazes.

3.9 Arrive back at the trailhead.

Options: Several footpaths wind through the park, from a 5-mile multiuse trail to a 1.5-mile fitness trail. Create long or short circuits from the 12 miles of trails.

41 Swamp Forest Trail, Lums Pond State Park

A long but easy family hike leads through woods and wetlands full of ferns around Delaware's largest freshwater pond, with the possibility of seeing beaver and other swamp-dwelling critters.

Start: The trail begins across the road from the parking area.
Distance: 7.5-mile loop
Hiking time: About 4 hours
Difficulty: Easy
Elevation gain: Minimal
Trail surface: Natural packed dirt; lowlands
Best season: Fall through early summer
Schedule: Daily 8 a.m. to sunset
Other trail users: Bikers, equestrians
Canine compatibility: Leashed dogs permitted
Land status: Lums Pond State Park; 8 miles south of Newark in central New Castle County, Delaware, just north of the Chesapeake & Delaware Canal

Nearest town: Glasgow
Fees and permits: Entrance fee required
Camping: A 68-site camping area is open Mar-Nov. For reservations, call (877) 987-2757.
Trailhead facilities: Restrooms, water, picnic area
Maps: USGS St. Georges DE; Delaware Trails guidebook; state park map
Trail contact: Lums Pond State Park, 3355 Red Lion Rd., Bear, DE; (302) 368-6989; https://destateparks.com/PondsRivers/LumsPond; Mike.Moyer@state.de.us
Special considerations: Hunting is permitted in the park; check with the park office for season information.

Finding the trailhead: From I-95 near Newark, follow DE 896 south 5.6 miles. Turn left onto Howell School Road, following Lums Pond State Park signs. Turn right into the park at 0.4 mile. Continue past the park office and fee booth to the Whale Wallow Nature Center on the left. Maps are available at the office. The trail begins across the road from the parking area, through the picnic area. GPS: N39 33.792' / W75 43.760'

The Hike

Before Delaware's largest freshwater pond existed, Saint Georges Creek flowed through the hardwood forest and was the site of several Native American hunting camps. Lums Pond was created in the early 1800s when Saint Georges Creek was impounded to supply water for the locks of the new Chesapeake & Delaware Canal.

This area was first used as a state park in 1963. Today the pond covers 200 acres and is surrounded by oak and poplar forests, wetlands, and beaches. Swamp Forest Trail circles the entire pond, following the shoreline and occasionally drifting from the water's edge into the forest and along the edges of a wooded swamp.

From the parking area, cross the park entrance road and proceed to the far-right corner of the grassy picnic area to pick up the trail. Cut through a hedgerow of trees on the right, and then turn left at the kiosk onto the Swamp Forest Trail. Cross the spillway and then turn left onto the footpath, which is well marked for its entire length.

Fishing platform on Lums Pond.

Follow the pond edge through a forest of red maples, poplars, and sweet gums. The presence of these trees, which tend to be adaptable colonizers of cleared land, shows that the shores of the pond were logged into the beginning of the twentieth century, probably supplying the mill powered by the dammed Saint Georges Creek. There are also big, old oaks in the pondside forest, and many of the fast-growing poplars have also reached impressive proportions. Also, the shoreline is crowded with at least five varieties of fern, the tallest of which is the cinnamon fern, named for the cinnamon-colored tufts along its stalk. Although this section is quite peaceful, road noise is very apparent.

Within the first 0.5 mile, the trail also crosses wetland areas on a series of board-walks, where you may see herons or ducks in the tall reeds. Reach a junction at 0.7 mile with the Little Jersey Trail. Stay left through the woods.

At 1 mile follow the trail left, where it briefly leaves the multiuse path and returns to the edge of the pond. Continue on the edge of the pond, with views across the green rippling water to the woods on the opposite side. It is a nice stretch of easy, pleasant walking. The path travels in the shade of oaks, a stray walnut, and giant poplars, with mayapple and trillium underfoot. Ducks are often visible on the pond. Another vocal resident, the kingfisher, which favors wooded areas along waterways, may be seen diving for a fresh catch. Anglers here have a lot of luck reeling in bluegill, largemouth bass, catfish, crappie, and pickerel. Shaded benches are placed along the route to rest and enjoy all the activity.

At 1.8 miles you again come to a junction with the Little Jersey Trail; go left across the boardwalk. The boardwalk bends hard away from the pond and traverses 300 feet of swamp that can be alive with turtle, snakes . . . even muskrats. This is also home to many species of ferns. See how many you can count. In this wooded swamp you may also see gnawed stumps and fallen trees—the work of several active beaver colonies in the park.

At the end of the boardwalk, a short trail leads right to the camping area, but continue on the Swamp Forest Trail. The trail cuts right just above the boat launch at 2.2 miles. In 150 feet the trail connects with a gravel path that leads back to the campsite; go left, following the path around a bend to a small sewage treatment plant. (You are on the Little Jersey Trail now for a short distance.) This sounds incongruous with a hike in the woods, but it is not terribly intrusive and has but a mild odor. Follow the gravel path across the access road, past a holding pond, and back into the woods. In an eighth of a mile, it rejoins the Swamp Forest Trail; go left, before a small stream, and back to the pond. The Little Jersey Trail continues straight. Stay on Swamp Forest.

For the next 3 miles, the trail follows the pond's doglegged shoreline. The views from the water's edge continue to be nice, and the trail begins to have a wilder feel as you pass the youth camping areas on the right and, at 4 miles, begin tracing a fishtail around the northeast edge of the pond. Perhaps it is the distance from the park's swimming and picnic areas that makes this stretch seem more remote than it actually is—whatever the cause, it is quiet here and feels far from the surrounding civilization.

Midway through the fishtail, from 4.6 to 5.6 miles, the well-marked trail makes several short breaks from the pond and travels along the edge of fields and thickets. At 5.6 miles the footpath traces the wooded edge of a park recreation area, popular with disc golf players. At the south edge of this area, turn right into the clearing; in 25 yards turn left, following the edge of the playing fields and passing the swimming area on the left at 6 miles. If you are walking on a summer day, this is a great place for a rest and a swim (the swimming area is open only when guards are on duty, during summer daylight hours).

Cut through the beach picnic area on the wide gravel path and cross a footbridge at 6.5 miles. The pond is picturesque here, especially to the right, where it has the look of a mountain lake. The trail bends left, then follows the shoreline and continues through the boat rental pavilion. After passing the Life Course fitness trail on the right at 7 miles, cross another footbridge, bend left at the parking area, and continue through the woods along the shore back to the trailhead.

Miles and Directions

0.0 Start at the trailhead at the far-right corner of the picnic area.

0.7 Follow the Swamp Forest Trail left.

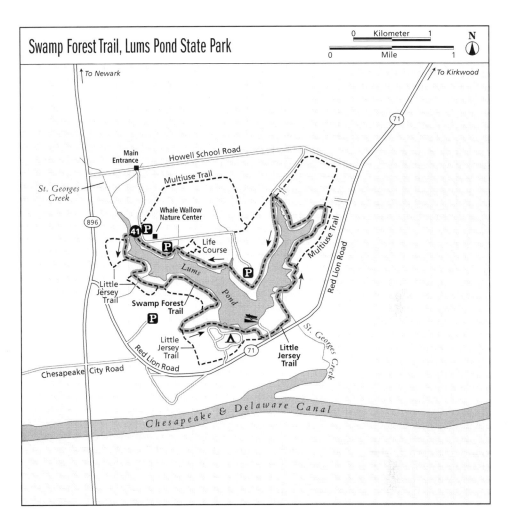

Swamp Forest Trail, Lums Pond State Park

1.8 Reach the wetlands, and follow the trail along the edge.

2.2 Cross the boat ramp access road. Continue through the woods.

4.0 Begin tracing the fishtail around the edge of the pond.

6.0 Reach the swimming area.

6.5 Cross the footbridge; the trail bears left.

7.0 Pass the fitness trail on your right, then cross another footbridge.

7.5 Arrive back at the trailhead.

Options: Make a day of your visit to Lums Pond—there are picnic areas, playing fields, a swimming beach, boat rentals, and a nature center.

42 Blackbird State Forest Loop, Tybout Tract

An easy walk through natural and managed coastal-plain woodlands in Blackbird State Forest, famous for its Delmarva bays—the small, upland ponds of mysterious origin that dot the forest's ten tracts. This is a good trail for joggers and birders.

Start: The trailhead is behind the headquarters building opposite the picnic pavilion. Look for the post marking the trail.
Distance: 4.3-mile loop
Hiking time: About 2 hours
Difficulty: Easy
Elevation gain: Minimal
Trail surface: Natural packed dirt and sand; wooded coastal plain
Best season: Sept–May; mosquitoes can be bad in the summer.
Schedule: Dawn to dusk
Other trail users: Bikers, equestrians
Canine compatibility: Leashed dogs permitted
Land status: Blackbird State Forest's Tybout Tract; southwestern New Castle County, Delaware, about 15 miles north of Dover

Nearest town: Smyrna
Fees and permits: None
Camping: Camping is available; a permit is required.
Trailhead facilities: Picnic area
Maps: USGS Clayton DE; map available at forest office
Trail contact: Blackbird State Forest, 502 Blackbird Forest Rd., Smyrna, DE; (302) 653-6505; www.visitdelaware.com/listings/blackbird-state-forest/5377; James.Dobson @state.de.us
Special considerations: Delaware state forests are open to hunting during fall and winter. Hiking during the state's deer-hunting season is not recommended.

Finding the trailhead: From US 13, 5 miles north of Smyrna, travel southwest on Blackbird Forest Road (DE 471) for 2.2 miles. Turn left into the forest's main office (where you can grab a map) and follow the winding entrance way to the picnic pavilion at its end. The trailhead is across the parking area from the pavilion marked with a post adjacent to the signboard. GPS: N39 20.716' / W75 40.544'

The Hike

Like many of Delaware's other managed woodlands, much of Blackbird State Forest has been a "forest" for less than fifty years. The trails on the Tybout Tract, for instance, pass through areas that were tilled fields until 1941, when the state acquired the land and began cultivating stands of loblolly and white pine. Along with the managed parcels, acres of natural hardwood forests border the Blackbird trails. These are lovely tracts of red and white oak, red maple, sweet gum, and poplar, with the lush understory of ferns, flowering trees, and shrubs common in wild coastal-plain woodlands.

The trail entrance is marked with a yellow-topped post across from the pavilion. It's a wide road-like trail through young sweet gums and poplars, the colonizers of fields and clearings. Throughout the hike, the path crisscrosses dirt roads created for hunters, but trail markers are regular and easy to follow. Don't be confused; follow the

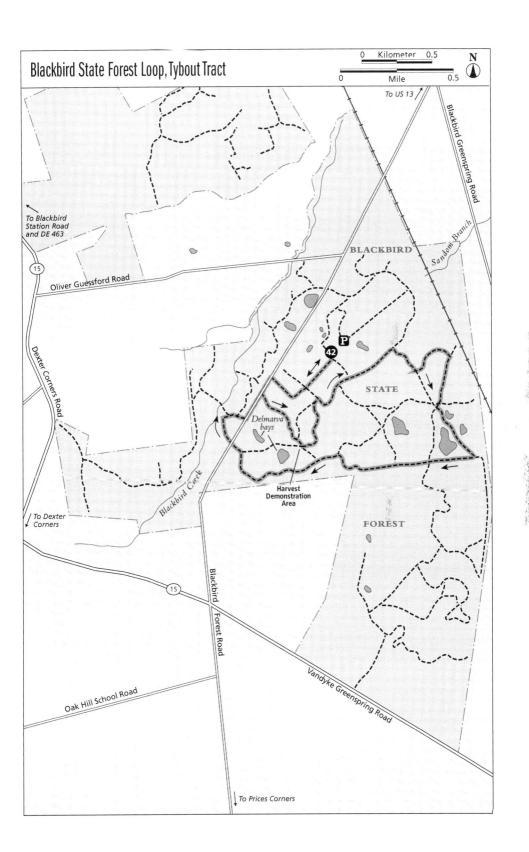

Blackbird State Forest Loop, Tybout Tract

0 Kilometer 0.5

0 Mile 0.5

N

To US 13

Blackbird Greenspring Road

To Blackbird
Station Road
and DE 463

BLACKBIRD

Sandom Branch

15

Oliver Guessford Road

Dexter Corners Road

P

42

STATE

Delmarva
bays

To Dexter
Corners

Blackbird Creek

Harvest
Demonstration
Area

FOREST

15

Blackbird Forest Road

Oak Hill School Road

Vandyke Greenspring Road

To Prices Corners

markers past another picnic area into the woods. The trail reaches the main road at 0.4 mile and makes a long loop left away from the road.

Follow the wide, sandy path through pine and oak into the woods. No sign marks the Harvest Demonstration Area at 0.5 mile, but you will know it by the scent of pine from the grove on the left. The area was planted with white, red, and loblolly pine more than sixty years ago. Pass the first swampy "Delmarva bay," just right off the path. Small upland ponds that harbor a variety of rare plants, Delmarva bays are also known as Carolina bays, loblollies, and whale wallows. The latter refers to just one of the many origin stories of these unique depressions. Whatever their origins, the bays are considered a natural treasure and are protected by the Delaware Natural Areas Preservation System.

Proceed on a sandy dirt road with pines on the left and hardwoods on the right until you reach another picnic area at 1.0 mile. Go right and travel along the road until you reach a junction with the blue trail at 1.4 miles. Turn right through two large maples to Sandom Branch, a wetland stream forded by two short bridges. Continue on the blue-blazed path into the fragrant, wild woods, traveling among scrambling squirrels and lively songbirds. Remain on the blue trail for the rest of the hike.

Leave the pines for red and white oak, and maple, until you reach an unusual woodland intersection, a kind of star with trails radiating in six directions, at 2.0 miles. Simply follow the blue-topped post straight ahead and ignore the rest. Here, still in the wild forest, dogwoods and pink azaleas blossom abundantly in spring.

At 2.3 miles reach an unmarked intersection with a trail going sharply right. Here you have a choice to follow the blue trail south for a one-mile loop or take the shortcut right, which rejoins the blue trail in about a quarter mile. Going right, follow the wide path to the junction with the blue trail at the corner of a large farm field. Proceed through huge tulip poplars, oaks, and maples to a yellow gate at 3.2 miles marked by a pair oaks in the center of the triangle of pathways.

Following the blue trail on the crushed-rock road through shady groves of mixed hardwoods, watch for weasels along the road edge and small dark piles of vole scat. Pass through two red gates to Blackbird Forest Road at 3.6 miles. Crossing the road, the trail bends right along the road to another picnic area. Cross the picnic area back to the road and walk along the road for a few hundred yards to a parking area on the left. Cross the road and duck back into the woods directly across from the parking area and pick up the trail you traversed earlier and head back to your starting point at 4.3 miles.

Miles and Directions

0.0 Start at the trailhead, across from the pavilion, following yellow-topped trail posts.

0.5 Reach the Harvest Demonstration Area.

1.4 Reach the junction with the blue trail. Cross Sandom Branch; turn right onto this trail.

2.0 Reach "star junction"; go straight, following the blue-topped posts.

2.3 Go left on unmarked trail.

3.6 Cross Blackbird Forest Road, following the blue-blazed trail into the woods.

4.3 Arrive back at the trailhead.

43 Bombay Hook National Wildlife Refuge Loop

A circuit hike travels round the dirt roads of a Delaware Bay wildlife refuge. This is an especially rewarding hike for those interested in watching migrating shorebirds and waterfowl, nesting bald eagles, and resident woodland mammals such as deer, foxes, woodchucks, and raccoons.

Start: Pick up the trail, a gravel road, in front of the visitor center.
Distance: 8.3-mile double loop
Hiking time: About 4 hours
Difficulty: Easy
Elevation gain: None
Trail surface: Gravel/dirt road; wooded marshes, upland fields and forests
Best season: Sept–May
Schedule: Sunrise to sunset
Other trail users: Bikers
Canine compatibility: Leashed dogs permitted
Land status: Bombay Hook National Wildlife Refuge; eastern Kent County, Delaware, about 15 miles northeast of Dover
Nearest town: Dover
Fees and permits: A use fee is charged.

Camping: None
Trailhead facilities: Restrooms, water, nature center, gift shop
Maps: USGS Bombay Hook DE; refuge auto tour map
Trail contact: Refuge Manager, Bombay Hook National Wildlife Refuge, 2591 Whitehall Neck Rd., Smyrna, DE; (302) 653-9345; www.fws.gov/refuge/bombay-hook; tina_watson@fws.gov
Special considerations: Wildlife is abundant on the refuge year-round. Pets must be kept on a leash. Some areas may be closed due to hunting; check with the refuge manager. During the summer months, visitors should bring insect repellent and wear long-sleeve shirts and long pants.

Finding the trailhead: From US 13 halfway between Smyrna and Dover, travel 3.8 miles east on DE 42 to DE 9. Turn left onto DE 9; proceed north 1.5 miles, and turn right onto Whitehall Neck Road. Go 2.3 miles to Bombay Hook National Wildlife Refuge. Continue through the entrance 0.2 mile to parking at the visitor center on the left. GPS: N39 15.555' / W75 28.366'

The Hike

Bombay Hook National Wildlife Refuge, on the shores of the Delaware Bay, is one of the best birding sites in the region, rivaling New Jersey's Cape May and Brigantine National Wildlife Refuge. Its extensive salt marsh—at 13,000 acres one of the largest undisturbed tracts on the East Coast—along with its 3,000 acres of freshwater pools, wooded marshes, upland fields, and forests, provides diverse habitat for more than 260 species of nesting and migrating birds. And the birds are not alone: Thirty-four species of mammals and a wide variety of reptiles, amphibians, and fish also make the refuge their home. The dikes, dirt roads, and short walking trails that circle and cross the refuge pass through all the area's landscapes and provide great opportunities for watching wildlife.

The cool seasons are a magical time to hike oceanside trails. PHOTO COURTESY OF DELAWARE DIVISION OF PARKS AND RECREATION/DNREC

Please note before embarking on a trip to Bombay Hook that you may share some of your walk with cars. The dirt roads you will travel are designed for slow-moving automobiles, most driven by avid birders cruising and stopping, cruising and stopping, with binoculars in hand. But serious birding does not really draw a crowd. Hiking here, especially on weekdays, is a lot like walking on an old country road. If that sounds appealing, you should enjoy a day of exploring Bombay Hook.

Pick up the trail—here a gravel road—in front of the visitor center, and turn left into the refuge. At 0.2 mile turn right and begin a partial loop around Raymond Pool, one of the refuge's freshwater impoundments. Before drawing close to the edge of the pool at 1.1 miles, you will pass through marshland grasses, meadows, open fields, and stands of sweet gum and red maple, a sampling of refuge habitats clearly favorable to the local birds. Their songs and wild flights here seem to be expressions of pure delight.

Proceed around the edge of Raymond Pool, with marshland stretching far into the distance on the right. On the flats near Raymond Pool, look for long-legged waders, such as black-necked stilt, ibis, and great blue heron. At 1.7 miles go right, following signs to Shearness Pool, and continue along the edge of the vast salt marsh. This stretch is prime birding territory. During fall Shearness Pool is alive with some thirty species of ducks that pass through the refuge. In spring look for migrating shorebirds—black-bellied plovers, yellowlegs, and sandpipers—resting and feeding on the mud flats of the marsh. And soaring over the whole scene are the bald eagles that use the refuge for feeding.

At 3 miles the trail bends to the left, away from the salt marsh, traveling through forest as it passes Parson Point Trail, a 0.5-mile spur into the woodland to the edge of Shearness Pool. If you are up to adding a mile to your hike, Parson Point Trail is a nice walk through the woods, where you may see black-crowned night herons, wild turkeys, and spring wildflowers such as jack-in-the-pulpit.

After Parson Point the road travels briefly through woods and grassland and then splits at 3.3 miles. Go right and begin a loop around Bear Swamp Pool. At 3.6 miles another short spur, the 0.3-mile Bear Swamp Pool Loop, takes you to an observation tower on the edge of the pool. It is worth the detour. From the tower, which feels like a tree house set in the branches of the surrounding oaks and maples, there are great views across the mud flats of Bear Swamp and the salt marsh to the east. In the flats, look for the meandering, crisscrossing tracks of many creatures, from herons and egrets to the peculiar trails of tail-dragging turtles.

Back on the road, continue around Bear Swamp Pool, with marsh on either side. At 4.7 miles the road bends away from the marsh and travels through the woods. Look for deer on the flats to the left, or for one of the refuge's resident foxes retreating lazily from a sunny spot in the road into the surrounding forest.

Continue through woods and upland fields. At 5.8 miles, at Dutch Neck Road (the road to Allee House, where you may see an eagle's nest), turn left and follow the road to the junction, at 6.1 miles, that completes the loop around Bear Swamp Pool. From the junction, retrace the route past Parson Point and Shearness Pool to the loop around Raymond Pool at 7.7 miles. Go straight at the junction with the Raymond Pool loop. Pass the Shearness Observation Tower on the right and then turn right, at 8.1 miles, to return to the trailhead at the visitor center.

Miles and Directions

0.0 Start at the trailhead in front of the visitor center.

0.2 Turn right and begin the loop around Raymond Pool.

1.1 Draw close to the edge of the pool.

1.7 Go right, following signs to Shearness Pool.

3.0 Pass the Parson Point Trail junction.

3.3 Come to a split in the road. Go right and begin the loop around Bear Swamp Pool.

3.6 Reach the junction with Bear Swamp Pool Loop. Follow the spur to the observation tower if you wish before continuing on the loop road.

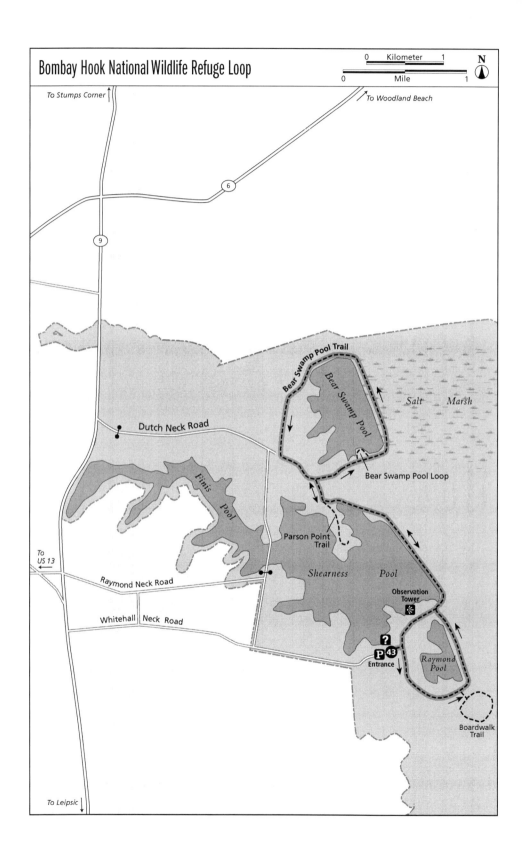

Bombay Hook National Wildlife Refuge Loop

0 Kilometer 1

0 Mile 1

N

To Stumps Corner

To Woodland Beach

6

9

Bear Swamp Pool Trail

Bear Swamp Pool

Salt   Marsh

Dutch Neck Road

Bear Swamp Pool Loop

Finis Pool

Parson Point Trail

To US 13

Shearness   Pool

Raymond Neck Road

Observation Tower

Whitehall Neck Road

?

P 43

Entrance

Raymond Pool

Boardwalk Trail

To Leipsic

4.7   The road bends away from the marsh to travel through woods.

5.8   Reach Dutch Neck Road (to Allee House). Turn left and follow the road back toward the start of the loop.

6.1   Reach the junction, completing Bear Swamp Pool Loop. Retrace your steps to Shearness Pool.

7.7   Go straight at the junction with the Raymond Pool loop.

8.1   Reach the spur to the visitor center and turn right.

8.3   Arrive back at the trailhead.

Options: There are short but interesting detours on the Parson Point, Bear Swamp Pool, and Boardwalk Trails. You also can create an 11.6-mile round-trip by including other roads and trails; see the auto tour map at the visitor center for additional routes.

44 Norman G. Wilder Wildlife Area Loop

A long, easy walk on dirt fire roads passes through mature forests and upland swamps in an area managed for wildlife.

Start: The trail begins on the dirt road at the parking lot.
Distance: 8.5-mile loop
Hiking time: About 4 hours
Difficulty: Easy
Elevation gain: Minimal
Trail surface: Natural packed dirt and sand; flat upland swamps
Best season: Feb–Aug
Schedule: Dawn to dusk Feb–Aug; open Sun only the rest of the year
Other trail users: Bikers, equestrians
Canine compatibility: Leashed dogs permitted
Land status: Norman G. Wilder Wildlife Area; Kent County, Delaware, about 10 miles southwest of Dover

Nearest town: Viola
Fees and permits: None
Camping: None
Trailhead facilities: None
Maps: USGS Marydel DE and Wyoming DE
Trail contact: Delaware Division of Fish and Wildlife, 89 Kings Hwy., Dover, DE; (302) 284-1077 or (302) 284- 4795; https://dnrec .maps.arcgis.com/apps/MapSeries/index.htm l?appid=0ef028ff152047ed811e0a162f6 15e47 or https://documents.dnrec.delaware .gov/fw/Wildlife-Areas/Norman-G-Wilder -Overview.pdf; dylan.nicholson@delaware.gov
Special considerations: Use insect repellent during summer.

Finding the trailhead: From Dover travel 8.5 miles south on US 13 to Canterbury Road. Turn right, and proceed 0.7 mile to the intersection with Evens Road. Go straight on Evens Road. In 1.1 miles, at the stop sign, turn right on Firetower Road and go 0.5 mile to the parking lot on the right. The trail begins on the dirt road at the parking lot. GPS: N39 02.475' / W75 35.952'

The Hike

Named for a notable Delaware conservationist and wildlife biologist, Norman G. Wilder Wildlife Area is a preserve managed primarily for hunting. The trails are well-maintained fire roads (closed to vehicles) that pass through fields, forests, and swamps protected to provide habitat for game. During the hunting seasons, September through January, a trip here would be ill-advised. But during the rest of the year, the lengthy trail and the flat, wooded terrain make this a good hike for those who like to walk far and fast.

The trail begins on the dirt road at the parking lot. Walk between a thicket on the left and a wooded hedgerow on the right, where young red maples, sweet gums, and willows shade the path. Pass fields and meadows on the left, and then enter the woods. The trail here is wide, soft, and shady; the forest is young but lush, with holly and bayberry tangling beneath a canopy of loblolly pine, sweet gum, and tulip poplar.

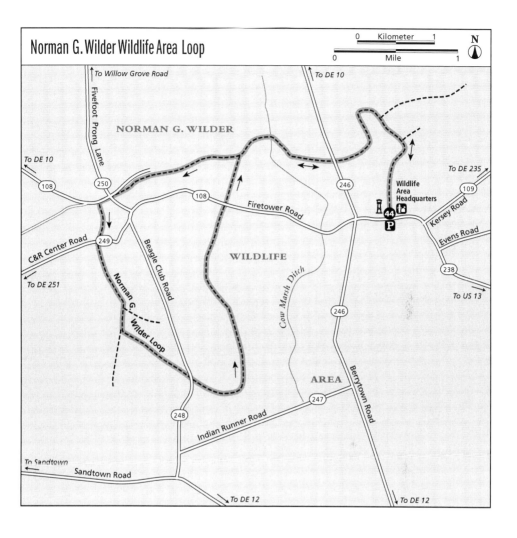

Stay to the left as the trail passes two spurs and a wildlife clearing on the right. Continue through the woods as the fire road makes a horseshoe bend and crosses Berrytown Road at 1.5 miles. Metal gates block automobile access to the fire road on both sides—duck under the gates or step around them.

Beyond the road the trail is sandy, and the trees beside the lane provide little shade. A hat, sunglasses, and some extra water will help get you through this sunny stretch. And it is worth the exposure. Soon the trail passes through an impressive stand of mature oaks, some as tall as 100 feet. Also look for honeysuckle and wild azalea.

At 1.8 miles, after passing a clearing on the right, cross Cow Marsh Ditch, which is aptly named. It is a drainage channel that looks every bit like a ditch. The water is a dark, muddy shade of brown that appears rather toxic but is actually colored by the organic content of the soil.

Leaving Cow Marsh Ditch behind, continue on the sunny trail past a side trail on the left at 2.1 miles, and on to the junction of Fivefoot Prong Lane and Firetower Road at 3.3 miles. Cross Fivefoot Prong Lane, which enters the intersection from the right, and then cross Firetower Road. Turn right and follow Firetower Road for about 150 yards on a rutted horse trail, then turn left into the woods on a narrow, shady footpath.

Go straight into the woods, passing a fire road on the right. The trail winds through a holly grove and crosses C&R Center Road at 3.7 miles. Again a sandy fire road, the trail continues through the woods. At 4.3 miles a spur shoots off the trail to the left. Soon after, follow the narrow hiking trail that cuts off the road to the left. Be careful here—the trail is not marked, and it is easy to miss. If you come to an area of wide-open croplands, you have gone too far.

Once on the shady foot trail, pass through a young pine forest and then cross Beagle Club Road at 5.1 miles. Passing a field on the left, the fire road then makes a long bend to the left and continues through the woods. This is a nice stretch. The trail does not cross a road for nearly 2 miles, and it passes through shady groves of old oaks with honeysuckle and wild azalea winding through the understory.

At 7 miles the fire road meets Firetower Road. Cross over the Firetower Road and locate the wooden bridge that leads to a trail through the forest and to the main trail, where you should make a right turn, which will lead back to the trailhead. Arrive back at the trailhead at 8.5 miles.

Miles and Directions

0.0 Start at the trailhead on the dirt road leading out of the parking lot.

0.5 Cross Berrytown Road.

1.8 Cross Cow Marsh Ditch.

3.3 Cross Fivefoot Prong Lane and Firetower Road.

3.7 Cross C&R Center Road.

5.1 Cross Beagle Club Road.

7.0 The fire road meets Firetower Road; cross the road.

8.5 Arrive back at the trailhead.

Options: There are 16 miles of fire road trails in the wildlife area. It would be hard to create a longer loop, but you could add some spurs to your walk or plan a shuttle hike.

45 Killens Pondside Nature Trail, Killens Pond State Park

Take a walk around an eighteenth-century millpond, passing through diverse wetland and upland forests.

Start: The loop begins at the wooden sign marked Pondside Nature Trail just off the parking area.
Distance: 3.2-mile loop
Hiking time: 1 to 1.5 hours
Difficulty: Easy
Elevation gain: Minimal
Trail surface: Dirt, mulch, crushed gravel
Best season: Year-round
Schedule: 8 a.m. to sunset
Other trail users: None
Canine compatibility: Leashed dogs permitted
Land status: Killens Pond State Park; Kent County, Delaware, 13 miles south of Dover

Nearest town: Felton
Fees and permits: An entrance fee is charged.
Camping: Primitive and improved sites are available, in addition to cabins.
Trailhead facilities: Restrooms, water, picnic areas, telephone
Maps: USGS Harrington DE
Trail contact: Killens Pond State Park, 5025 Killens Pond Rd., Felton, DE; office (302) 284-4526, nature center (302) 284-4299; https://destateparks.com/PondsRivers/KillensPond
Special considerations: Bring insect repellent in summer.

Finding the trailhead: From US 113, travel west on DE 12 through Frederica and continue 5 miles to Chimney Hill Road. Turn left onto Chimney Hill Road and go 1.2 miles to Killens Pond Road. Turn right and in 0.1 mile turn left into the park. Continue 0.7 mile on the park entrance road to the parking lot.

Alternative: From US 13, about 13 miles south of Dover, travel east on Killens Pond Road 1.3 miles and turn right into the park. Continue 0.7 mile on the park entrance road to the parking lot. GPS: N38 59.112' / W75 32.225'

The Hike

Set in the farm country of central Delaware, Killens Pond State Park straddles the boundary between southern and northern forests. Here you will see the loblolly pine and American holly forests typical of the wet, sandy plain to the south, as well as stands of mature hardwoods common in the rolling hills to the north. In places on the Killens Pondside Nature Trail, the trail itself seems to be the boundary between the two habitats, with the tall pines and dense undergrowth of coastal lowlands on one side and groves of giant poplars and oaks on the other—both, in rather different ways, quite beautiful. Add several nice views of the pond, and you have all the ingredients for an interesting, scenic, and refreshing walk.

The well-marked loop begins at the wooden sign marked Pondside Nature Trail. The pine duff path enters the woods and meets the trail's return loop at 0.1 mile. Go right, and continue counterclockwise with the pond to the left. For the next 0.5 mile, the trail passes through the pine and hardwood forest. Here flowering dogwoods

Boardwalk through the lowlands surrounding Killens Pond.

and several species of oaks mingle between the sweet bay, ferns, climbing vines of the marsh, and the upland stands of poplar. There may not be a better place to experience the diversity of Delaware's woodlands.

At 0.3 mile, at a fork in the trail, you may go left 50 yards for a view of the 66-acre pond. It is worth the detour. You pass two very large loblolly pines on the right and, in the spring, the pinxter flower, sometimes called pink azalea, blooms abundantly. Wild blueberries also border the trail. From the edge of the pond, you can gaze over the still water, listen to birdsong, and watch for ducks and cormorants.

Back at the fork, bear to the left and continue through a lovely grove of tall, stately poplars. The trunk of one giant, just to the left of the trail, takes two people to reach around!

At 0.8 mile the trail bends left around the edge of the pond and then intersects a sandy road. Turn left and, at 0.9 mile, cross a bridge over the narrow Murderkill River. Before it was made a millpond in the late 1700s, the Killens Pond area was the floodplain of the Murderkill and the site of the Lenape peoples' settlements and hunting camps. The river's peculiar name, legend has it, commemorates the massacre of a group of Dutch traders by the local tribe. And the name is not redundant: The

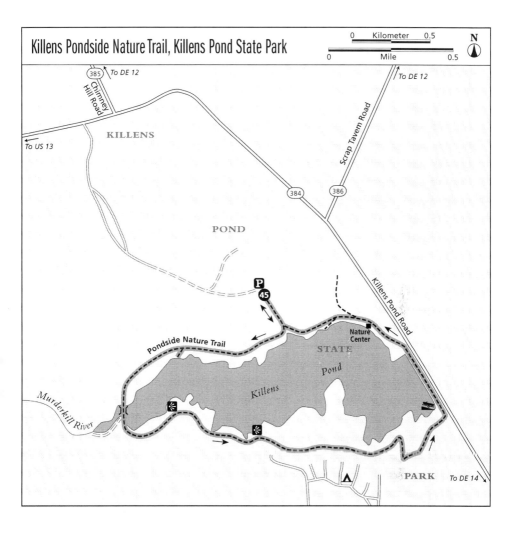

Killens Pondside Nature Trail, Killens Pond State Park

KILLENS

POND

Pondside Nature Trail

Murderkill River

STATE

Killens Pond

Nature Center

PARK

To DE 12

To DE 12

To US 13

To DE 14

Chimney Hill Road

Scrap Tavern Road

Killens Pond Road

385

384

386

45

Kilometer

Mile

N

Dutch *kill* is a stream, creek, or channel. From the bridge the view of the pond and the surrounding marsh forest is quite nice.

You may ask yourself why the river is so green, as is the pond. The pond is surrounded by fertilized agricultural lands that drain into the river and pond's watershed. Excess fertilizer runs off the fields and into the local waterway, generating green algae growth that discolors the water. It may be dangerous to swim in or allow dogs to swim in or drink water where there are harmful algae blooms. Check with a park ranger if there's a concern.

Beyond the bridge, turn left into the woods in about 500 feet. The trail bends along the pond through holly and up a rise to a bench and a view at 1.1 miles. From a little clearing surrounded by oak and poplar, dogwood, and pink azalea, the view and the setting here invite a rest.

Bear left at the fork, following trail markers down the rise and close to the pond. Watch the snags for sunning turtles and perching ducks, and note the dead bald cypress, well drilled by woodpeckers. Continue in the lowlands over a long boardwalk at 1.3 miles, and then up a slight rise at 1.5 miles to another nice view of the pond.

At 1.6 miles the trail enters Killens Pond Campground, with cabins on the right. Continue straight, across an unpaved access road, and head back into the woods on a slope above the marsh following the trail signs. The trail runs through the woodlands behind the campground and, at the T junction, turns right following the shoreline.

Proceed, winding through beech, chestnut oak, holly, and maples to the boat launch at Killens Pond Road at 2.3 miles. Turn left and cross the new bridge above the spillway at the edge of the pond; another good place to fish, sit, and enjoy the view. Follow the wide path past a large walnut tree, around the canoe-rental center at 2.5 miles, and enter the woods on a sandy trail in the shade of loblolly pines. This is a good opportunity to visit the Nature Center. The trail goes around the Nature Center to the right.

Continue to the fork at 2.8 miles, and bear to the left, following the Pondside Nature Trail sign. After 50 yards another spur breaks left from the trail to the edge of the pond. Proceed to the right through mixed pines and hardwoods to the entrance spur at 3.1 miles. Turn right, and return to trailhead.

Miles and Directions

0.0 Start at the trailhead marked by a wooden sign.

0.1 At the Pondside Nature Trail junction, go right.

0.3 Reach a fork. Go left on the spur for a view of the pond. Back at the fork, bear left.

0.9 Cross the bridge over the Murderkill River, and turn left 500 feet after the bridge.

1.1 Reach a bench with a view, then bear left at a fork.

1.6 Enter the Killens Pond Campground. Continue straight.

2.1 The trail turns right.

2.3 Reach the boat launch at Killens Pond Road. Turn left.

2.6 Visit the nature center.

2.8 Bear left at the fork, following the Pondside Nature Trail.

3.1 At the entrance spur junction, turn right.

3.2 Arrive back at the trailhead.

Options: Bring a fishing rod or rent a canoe and visit the Murderkill River. Visit the nature center to view native reptiles and amphibians from Delaware.

46 Prime Hook National Wildlife Refuge Loop

This short walk passes through coastal forest and wetlands on the western shore of Delaware Bay. Year-round, this is a terrific indulgence for birders and waterfowl. Bring your binoculars and bird book.

Start: The route begins on the Boardwalk Trail, across the parking lot from the visitor center.
Distance: 1.6-mile lollipop
Hiking time: About 90 minutes
Difficulty: Easy and partly accessible
Elevation gain: None
Trail surface: Dirt, wooden walkway, packed sandy path; coastal marsh
Best season: Year-round, but waterfowl are abundant in the winter.
Schedule: Dawn to dusk
Other trail users: Occasional fishermen
Canine compatibility: Dogs on short leashes permitted
Land status: Prime Hook National Wildlife Refuge; Sussex County, Delaware, 22 miles

southeast of Dover and 13 miles northwest of Rehoboth Beach
Nearest town: Milton
Fees and permits: None
Camping: None
Trailhead facilities: Visitor center, restrooms, picnic tables
Maps: USGS Lewes DE and Milton DE
Trail contact: Prime Hook National Wildlife Refuge, 11978 Turkle Pond Rd., Milton, DE; (302) 684-8419; www.fws.gov/refuge/prime-hook; fw5rw_phnwr@fws.gov
Special considerations: Biting flies and mosquitoes in late spring and summer make the Refuge Loop a true Oct-to-Apr trail. In any season, bring binoculars for bird-watching.

Finding the trailhead: From the Delaware seashore resorts, travel north on DE 1 for 1.5 miles north of the Broadkill River to DE 16. Go right on DE 16 (Broadkill Road) and, after 1.2 miles, turn left onto Road 236 (Turkle Pond Road) into Prime Hook National Wildlife Refuge. Trailhead parking is 1.5 miles ahead at the visitor center. GPS: N38 49.836' / W75 14.915'

The Hike

Prime Hook National Wildlife Refuge—10,144 acres of fresh and tidal marsh, upland forest, and croplands on the shores of the Delaware Bay—is home to a wonderful array of birds, mammals, and reptiles and is an important stopover for migrating waterfowl. On an easy 1.5-mile stroll on the Refuge Loop, you can see fine examples of each of the coastal habitats, as well as of the area's abundant wildlife. The Dike Trail from the parking area to the viewing platform is hard sand but accessible to wheelchairs, strollers, and scooters.

The Refuge Loop begins on Boardwalk Trail, across the parking lot from the visitor center. For the first 0.25 mile, the trail is like a garden path: a wide, grass walkway bordered on both sides by multiflora rose teeming with songbirds, rabbits, and groundhogs.

A short detour to the left at 0.1 mile leads to the site of the Jonathan J. Morris Homestead, thought to have been established around 1750. The bright white stones

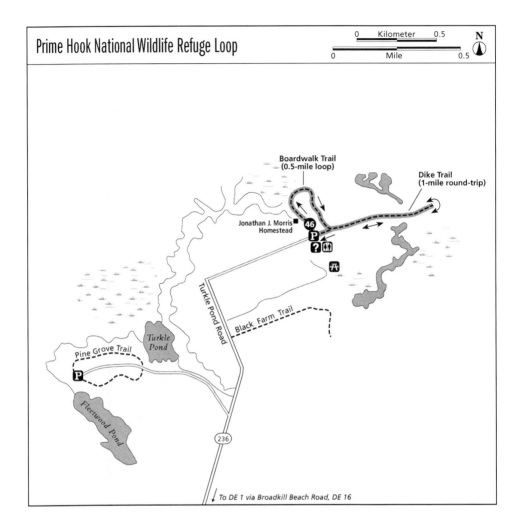

0   Kilometer   0.5

N

0   Mile   0.5

Boardwalk Trail
(0.5-mile loop)

Dike Trail
(1-mile round-trip)

Jonathan J. Morris
Homestead

46

P

Turkle Pond Road

Black Farm Trail

Turkle
Pond

Pine Grove Trail

Fleetwood Pond

P

236

To DE 1 via Broadkill Beach Road, DE 16

of the family cemetery are all that remains, but in this peaceful setting it is easy to imagine life on the Morris farm.

Continue on the trail under sweet gum trees to the marsh boardwalk at 0.2 mile, and proceed into wetlands about 50 yards. On the boardwalk pause to observe the teeming life of a marsh community. Close to the boardwalk you may see turtles and green frogs sunning, or ducks and muskrats swimming by in the shallow water. In the marsh grass, red-winged blackbirds roost, and hunting hawks glide just above. In the winter ducks and geese abound. Look for green-winged teals, northern shovelers, common pintails, and tundra swans. In all seasons, across the vast wetlands, forested islands are bright with color. The boardwalk continues through white pine and holly; the woods rustle with warblers and thrashers hopping in the brush, blue jays flitting in the branches, and woodpeckers hammering away at rotten trunks.

At the end of the boardwalk, the trail splits. Go left along the water. The trail will exit the woods in sight of the parking area. Go left on the sandy Dike Trail at 0.5 mile. Dike Trail is accessible and runs a straight 0.5 mile along the edge of another great expanse of marsh. The woods dissipate to the left and the marsh opens to the right; the birding is excellent. Summer will bring ospreys, great blue herons, egrets, hawks, and vultures, as well as ducks and shorebirds. In fall the legions of migrating geese are an annual Atlantic-shore spectacle. In the winter migrating ducks and swans are the scene-stealers.

At 1 mile the trail dead-ends at the viewing platform. Bring your binoculars. Turn around here and return to the trailhead.

Miles and Directions

0.0 Start at the trailhead across the parking lot from the visitor center on the Boardwalk Trail.

0.1 A short detour leads to the Jonathan J. Morris cemetery.

0.2 Reach the marsh boardwalk.

0.3 Wind through upland forest.

0.5 Reach the junction with Dike Trail and turn left onto the trail.

1.0 Reach the end of Dike Trail, your turnaround point. Stay straight past the boardwalk turnoff to return to the trailhead.

1.6 Arrive back at the trailhead.

Options: Pine Grove Trail, an 0.8-mile loop, Blue Goose Trail, a 1.7-mile walk, and Black Farm Trail, a 2-mile walk, are three more hikes in the Prime Hook woodlands.

47 Gordons Pond Trail, Cape Henlopen State Park

This walk weaves along a tranquil mile-long tidal pond, then past a salt marsh, and ends at Herring Point in the main portion of Cape Henlopen State Park. This scenic trail offers an arm's-length view of more than a dozen species of shorebirds and waterfowl. Will Penn established Cape Henlopen as one of the first "public lands" in what was to become the United States.

Start: The trailhead is in the left Pavilion parking lot. Look for the kiosk.
Distance: 2.6 miles one-way or make a loop by walking along the shore to the parking area at 5.2 miles
Hiking time: About 2.5 hours
Difficulty: Easy
Elevation gain: None
Trail surface: Crushed stone and elevated boardwalk
Best season: Fall through spring
Schedule: 8 a.m. to sunset
Other trail users: Bikers
Canine compatibility: Leashed dogs permitted
Land status: Cape Henlopen State Park; Sussex County, Delaware. The park stretches along the Atlantic coast from Rehoboth Beach to Lewes; the Gordon Pond loop is 1 mile north of Rehoboth.

Nearest town: Rehoboth Beach
Camping: Camping is permitted in the park's north end; a fee is required.
Trailhead facilities: portable toilets
Fees and permits: Entrance fees are collected daily Mar 1–Nov 30. There is no fee for bicycle or pedestrian entry.
Maps: USGS Cape Henlopen DE
Trail contact: Cape Henlopen State Park, 15099 Cape Henlopen Dr., Lewes, DE; (302) 645-8983; https://destateparks.com/ Beaches/CapeHenlopen; https://destate parks.com/Contact
Special considerations: Some areas of the preserve are subject to closure during nesting season. Check the trailhead kiosk. For much of the hike, there is no shade—a hat is advisable.

Finding the trailhead: From Rehoboth Beach, at the intersection of Rehoboth Avenue and First Street, go north on Rehoboth (if you're facing the beach, go left). Go 5 blocks to Lake Avenue and turn right. Turn left onto Surf Avenue and follow it to Henlopen Avenue/Ocean Drive. Turn right and follow Ocean Drive to the park entrance. The trailhead is in the left parking lot. GPS: N38 44.527' / W75 04.912'

The Hike

Many books and articles have been published about the fascinating history of Cape Henlopen, but one of the most significant milestones occurred after 1682, when the current lands of the state of Delaware were granted to William Penn. Penn proclaimed that Cape Henlopen and its natural resources were to be for the common usage of the citizens of Lewes and Sussex County, thus establishing some of the nation's first "public lands."

Crouching near the great tidal pool known as Gordons Pond, watch from behind the rushes as a great blue heron prepares to strike a fish at its feet. When it does, the commotion sets a dozen shorebirds into flight. As you follow them, you notice a small plane in the distance. It flies beyond the sand dunes, out over the ocean. This is your only clue that you're just a couple of beach miles from busy Rehoboth Beach. Otherwise, it's you and the shorebirds—and other wildlife.

The first 0.7 mile of this easy stroll follows a crushed-limestone path, open to bicycles, along the southern shore of Gordons Pond to an observation deck. From the deck the trail continues close to the shore amid the reeds and bayberry bushes for another 1.9 miles, ending at Herring Point, overlooking the ocean. The return is a walk either retracing your steps back on the trail or along the ocean beach back to the Gordons Pond parking area.

Begin at the trailhead kiosk. Your first ten steps from the parking area are like stepping behind a curtain into the wild. Look for Carolina wrens darting among the grasses. Little more than 0.25 mile in, a bench welcomes you to dawdle in the hope of seeing a willet in flight, flashing its distinctive black-and-white wing pattern.

Circling the pond's lower reaches, at about 0.5 mile there is a long view of a World War II watchtower a mile away. Except to Delawareans, the towers seem a bit out of place. They were built to triangulate targets at sea, working in tandem with guns placed up the coast as part of Fort Miles Coastal Defense system. An interpretive display tells the story.

Reach the observation deck at 0.7 mile. From the platform in winter you might be treated to the sight of snow geese, northern pintails, green-winged teals, northern shovelers, and scaup. In summer great egrets, with their white plumage and black legs, ply the shallow waters. A splendid spot any time of year, the deck is downright dramatic during migration.

Leaving the deck, the trail passes along the pond. Listening to the reeds rustle, lulled by the breezes, you might be startled by a sudden splash nearby as a bird dives for its supper. Along the way, a bench sits several feet from the pond. It's a fine place to sit and listen.

At 1.1 mile pass between the pond to your right and a vast, wild salt marsh to your left, again full of ducks and other birds. Enter a pine grove, which offers up the first shade of the hike, at about 2.2 miles.

The trail changes to an elevated boardwalk, protecting rare plants and historic shell middens. The ocean is 0.25 mile away, over the sand. Along the way are two more observation platforms: one to view the salt marsh and another the dunes and ocean beyond. At 2.6 miles the trail ends at the Herring Point parking area. Walk up toward the upper parking area and overlook. Here you get a great view of the Atlantic Ocean and the World War II battery foundations at Herring Point. You can easily visualize how American soldiers used the towers to the north and south to direct guns at targets in the Atlantic Ocean. Fortunately, no shots were ever fired.

After a visit to Herring Point, walk south along the beach past an observation tower. You might share the beach with a few trucks, as there is vehicle access for fishing.

At 5.4 miles reach Cape Henlopen State Park's south beach at a rock jetty, closing the loop. If you haven't stopped along the way for a swim yet, now is your chance. From the beach it is 175 yards up the path to the trailhead.

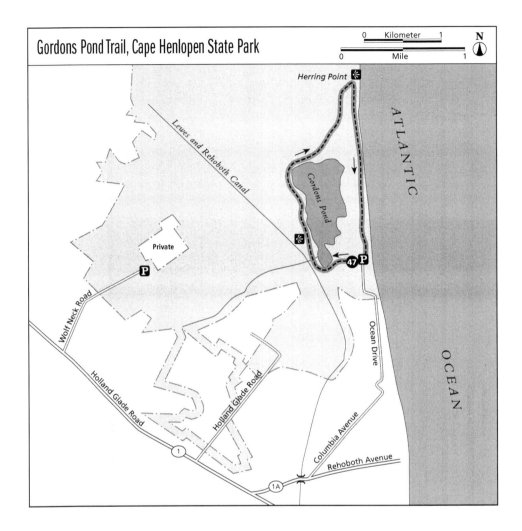

Gordons Pond Trail, Cape Henlopen State Park

Miles and Directions

0.0 Start at the trailhead kiosk.

0.7 Reach the observation deck.

1.8 The trail enters a pine grove.

2.2 Start of elevated boardwalk.

2.7 Reach the Herring Point scenic overlook. Walk south along the beach.

4.5 Reach the state park's south beach and dune crossing.

5.2 Arrive back at the trailhead at the Gordons Pond parking area.

Options: Hike to the overlook (0.7 mile) or the dunes (2.5 miles) and return by the same route.

48 Burton Island Loop, Delaware Seashore State Park

An easy hike on boardwalks, sand, and soft upland soil leads through salt marsh and coastal forest with open views of the Indian River Bay, the Rehoboth Bay, and the salt marsh. With restrooms and dining facilities near the trailhead, a walk on the nature trail at Burton Island makes a great family outing.

Start: The trail begins at the causeway leading across the channel from the parking area.
Distance: 1.3-mile loop
Hiking time: About 1 hour
Difficulty: Easy
Elevation gain: None
Trail surface: Sandy with walkways over the marsh; forested island lowlands
Best season: Oct–early Apr
Schedule: 8 a.m. to sunset
Other trail users: None
Canine compatibility: Leashed dogs permitted
Land status: Burton Island is just north of the Indian River Inlet in Delaware Seashore State Park, 50 miles southeast of Dover and 7.5 miles south of Rehoboth Beach.
Nearest town: Bethany Beach
Fees and permits: There is a daily entrance fee from Mar 1–Nov 30.

Camping: Camping is available at the Delaware Seashore State Park Campground; a fee is required.
Trailhead facilities: At the marina, about 150 yards before the trailhead, there are restrooms, a restaurant, picnic tables, and an observation deck.
Maps: USGS Bethany Beach DE; state park map through the website
Trail contact: Delaware Seashore State Park, 39415 Inlet Rd., Rehoboth Beach, DE; (302) 227-2800; https://destateparks.com/Trails; https://destateparks.com/Beaches/DelawareSeashore
Special considerations: Bring insect repellent during summer and binoculars for birding year-round.

Finding the trailhead: From Rehoboth Beach, travel 7.5 miles south on DE 1, and exit to the right into Delaware Seashore State Park and Indian River Marina, just north of Indian River Inlet Bridge. Turn right at the park office and proceed on Inlet Road 0.5 mile, past the marina and public boat storage area, to the trailhead parking area. GPS: N38 36.969' / W75 04.364'

The Hike

Burton Island is the largest island in an archipelago of small islands that separates Rehoboth Bay from Indian River Bay, just behind the barrier beach of Delaware Seashore State Park. This easy 1.5-mile walk around the island affords great views of inland bays and close-up observations of the creatures of the salt marsh and upland forest. From boardwalks over tidal marshes, you will see wading shorebirds, muskrat tracks, and skittering fiddler crabs, as well as ospreys, great blue herons, and egrets gliding over the wetland grasses. In addition, the island provides important nesting grounds for the diamondback terrapin. Stay on the trail at all times.

Burton Island Loop, Delaware Seashore State Park

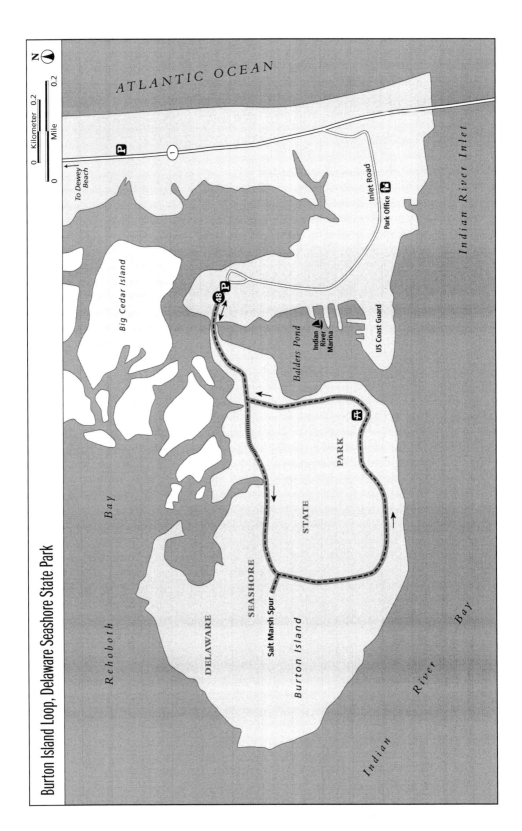

From the trailhead, cross the causeway to Burton Island and proceed on hard and soft sand through short cedars and marsh grass. To the right, out across the marsh, look for ospreys on a nesting platform. Nearly extinct thirty years ago, ospreys—or fish hawks—have made a strong comeback and may now be seen nesting and fishing all along the Delaware coast. In the winter months, the red-breasted merganser also calls these inlets home.

At 0.3 mile the return loop intersects from the left. Continue right to a board-walk at 0.4 mile, one of several that cross the tidal marshlands. At low tide look for muskrat paths in the grasses, or watch a retreating fiddler crab disappear into a hole in the mud, waving his oversize claw. Be careful not to step in the muskrat scat on the boardwalks. Gaze across the marshland flats, where sandpipers, herons, and egrets feed in the spawning grounds of crab, bluefish, and flounder. Horseshoe crab shells are abundant in the grasses, as the area is a prime breeding ground for the crabs in the spring, their eggs providing essential sustenance for migrating shorebirds. Unfortunately, the horseshoe crab numbers are dwindling due to over-harvesting, resulting in changes in the bird population, especially the red knot.

Beyond the boardwalk at 0.5 mile, the trail enters a shady grove of cedar, loblolly and white pine, and holly. Here the path changes from sandy to a soft upland soil that supports a more varied community of trees, vines, and shrubs. At 0.6 mile the trail bends left at a short spur. A 10-yard detour takes you into the marsh for wide-open views. This is another great spot for heron watching.

Back on the trail, wind through woods and wetlands to a sandy rise at 0.8 mile. Refreshing breezes and a lovely view of the inland bay make this an ideal spot to rest, eat, or daydream.

The trail continues along the beach for 30 yards before entering the woods and then crossing a boardwalk with the marina to the right. At 1 mile the trail completes the island loop. Turn right and proceed on the sandy trail back to the causeway and the trailhead.

Miles and Directions

0.0 Start at the trailhead 0.5 mile past the marina.

0.3 The return loop intersects from the left; continue right.

0.4 Reach a boardwalk and Rehoboth Bay salt marsh.

0.5 Enter a cedar, pine, and holly grove.

0.6 The trail bends left at a short spur.

0.8 Reach a rise above Indian River Bay.

1.0 Close the loop at the junction; turn right and proceed back to the trailhead.

1.3 Arrive back at the trailhead.

Option: Swim in the Atlantic or walk along the shore at a guarded swimming beach on the south side of Indian River Inlet.

49 Sea Hawk/Seahorse Trail, Holts Landing State Park

On the shore of Indian River Bay, this quiet walk passes through a diverse and historic landscape of marsh, pond, forest, meadow, and bay shore perfect for a spring day with children.

Start: The trailhead is on the north side of the parking area.
Distance: 2.1-mile loop
Hiking time: About 1.5 hours
Difficulty: Easy
Elevation gain: None
Trail surface: Natural packed dirt (can be wet in places), elevated walkway; lowland forest
Best season: Year-round
Schedule: 8 a.m. to sunset
Other trail users: Bikers, equestrians on Seahorse Trail
Canine compatibility: Leashed dogs permitted
Land status: Holts Landing State Park; Sussex County, Delaware, on Indian River Bay, about 6 miles northwest of Bethany Beach

Nearest town: Millville
Fees and permits: Entrance fees are in effect Mar 1–Nov 30.
Camping: Primitive campsites are available for organized youth groups.
Trailhead facilities: Restrooms, picnic pavilion, shady picnic areas
Maps: USGS Bethany Beach DE; state park map through the website
Trail contact: Holts Landing State Park, 9415 Inlet Rd., Rehoboth Beach, DE; (302) 227-2800; https://destateparks.com/holtslanding; https://destateparks.com/Contact
Special considerations: None

Finding the trailhead: From DE 1 in Bethany Beach, travel west for 3.5 miles on DE 26 to White's Neck Road (Road 347). Turn right onto White's Neck Road, go 2 miles, and turn right onto Road 346; look for the park sign. Go 0.9 mile to the Holts Landing State Park entrance. The trailhead is on the northwest side of the parking area. GPS: N38 35.448' / W75 07.753'

The Hike

Not to be overlooked, Holts Landing State Park offers an outdoor escape full of history and diversity. The quiet 203-acre area contains a variety of beautiful landscapes, from shoreline to grassy fields and hardwood forests. Historically, the shores of the inland bays were home to the Lenape and Nanticoke peoples, who harvested seafood and hunted in the surrounding marshes and forests. After the arrival of European settlers in the 1600s, Western-style agriculture gradually developed in the area.

From salt marsh to freshwater ponds and poplar groves, the Sea Hawk Trail winds through different worlds created by various activities over the years, from farming to several old borrow pits dug by the state highway department. Short and easy, with a rebounding forest and lots of wildlife, this is a great trail for introducing children to the outdoors.

From the parking lot, you will see the trailhead sign on the northwest corner of the lot; this is the start of the Sea Hawk Trail. The path begins by crossing the marsh on an elevated walkway. Just 0.1 mile into the hike, you have already reached a nice view of the bay, its far shore to the north, and Burton Island to the east.

Songbirds dart in and out of the woods, a squawking blue heron may sail above the trees and perch on a pine branch over the pond, and egrets wade carefully in the dark, shallow water while jabbing for minnows and frogs.

Continuing along the path, you begin to see signs of human activity and the tangled webs of blown-down pines created by storms. In the 1940s the Holt family operated a poultry farm here, but twenty years later, the property was sold to the highway department. Along a row of phragmites, the invasive and pervasive marsh reed crowded with red-winged blackbirds, the trail bends right into the woods and continues through skinny pines, maples, and sweet gums.

A pond on the left at 0.9 mile is partially hidden by a hedgerow of pine and oak. To the right you pass long, wide, open areas in the forest labeled camping areas on the park map. You can indeed camp here, but it's far from pristine, looking to be the remnants of past clearing activities. The freshwater pond is teeming with life in the spring; no doubt you will hear spring peepers in early April. At the end of the ponds are a series of "borrow pits" created by the highway department. These pits are where material has been dug for use at another location. The concrete pipes jutting conspicuously from the ground mark the pits.

At 1 mile the trail begins a rectangular "loop"—or box—through the woods. From the junction with the Sea Hawk and Seahorse Trails, go left for a shortcut back to the parking area, or continue straight on the Seahorse Trail to Marlin Drive at 1.3 miles.

When you reach Marlin Drive, turn left (east) to the intersection with the park entrance road and go left again. At 1.6 miles, after passing more ponds on the left, reach the place where the Sea Hawk Trail comes through the woods. Duck back into the woods, looking carefully through the undergrowth for the Sea Hawk Trail, which is about 100 feet off the road to the left.

Proceed north on the Sea Hawk Trail, passing between two ponds dotted with birdhouses mounted on posts. The houses provide nesting sites for wood ducks and other cavity nesters, birds that typically nest in now-rare climax forests. The metal collars on the posts protect the ducks' eggs from raccoons and snakes. In the light of day, it is unlikely that you will see those predators lurking around the ponds, but the sunning turtles will wait a long time before they slide off their logs into the dark green water.

The trail bends around the pond on the left and then breaks into the woods to the right, emerging in a clearing near the fee booth at 2 miles. The path then bends left at the edge of the clearing, cuts back into the trees, and winds through the forest to the trailhead.

Miles and Directions

0.0 Start at the trailhead at the ball field.

0.1 Reach the view of Indian River Bay, then continue along the beach.

0.5 At the junction with Seahorse Trail, go left.

0.8 Reach a woodland pond; at the end of the pond, trail begins a rectangular loop.

1.3 Reach Marlin Drive and go left.

1.6 Return to the Sea Hawk Trail in the woods, just off the road to the left.

2.0 Emerge into the clearing near the fee booth.

2.1 Arrive back at the trailhead.

Options: Holts Landing is home to the only pier on Delaware's Inland Bay that was built specifically for crabbing, but fishing is permitted as well. The sturdy pier, opened in 2001, overhangs the shallow bay waters, allowing crabbers and anglers alike to fish for blue crabs and other mid–Atlantic delicacies. The pier is open 24 hours if actively crabbing or fishing.

To take the shortcut from the junction of the Sea Hawk Trail and the Seahorse Trail at 1 mile, take the Sea Hawk Trail to the left, traveling briefly through a young stand of poplars growing in the shade of oaks and pines. The trail crosses primitive camping clearings to the wood's edge just before the entrance road, turns left at 1.1 miles, and follows the other side of the ponds back to the parking area.

50 Paul Leifer Nature Trail, Furnace Town Historic Site

A short, easy walk through bald cypress swamps and upland forests in the Nature Conservancy's beautiful 3,000-acre Nassawango Creek Preserve explores acreage where a thriving town once stood. Many historic structures have been reconstructed.

Start: The trail begins in the historic village at the old Nassawango Iron Furnace.
Distance: 1-mile loop
Hiking time: About 1 hour
Difficulty: Easy
Elevation gain: Minimal
Trail surface: Natural packed dirt; lowlands
Best season: Apr 1–Oct 31
Schedule: Dawn to dusk
Other trail users: None
Canine compatibility: Leashed dogs permitted
Land status: Furnace Town Historic Site is a private nonprofit operated by Furnace Town Foundation in Worcester County, Maryland, 135 miles southeast of Washington, D.C., and 15 miles southeast of Salisbury, Maryland.
Nearest town: Snow Hill
Fees and permits: An admission fee is charged.
Camping: None
Trailhead facilities: Restrooms and a nature shop at the visitor center, open Apr 1–Oct 31
Maps: USGS Snow Hill MD
Trail contact: Furnace Town Foundation, Box 207, Snow Hill, MD 21863; (410) 632-2032; www.furnacetown.com; info@furnacetown.org
Special considerations: Bring insect repellent in summer. Check for ticks after your hike.

Finding the trailhead: From the Salisbury, Maryland, bypass, travel 13.5 miles southeast on MD 12 and turn right onto Old Furnace Road. Proceed 0.5 mile to Furnace Town parking on the left. GPS: N38 12.559' / W75 27.566'

The Hike

Before European settlement, much of the farm country of the Delmarva Peninsula was a vast forest. Along the creeks of southeastern Maryland, the woodlands were lush groves of giant bald cypress, Atlantic white cedar, and loblolly pine. There were lady's slippers and other orchids, butterflies and salamanders, hawks and warblers, otters, and snakes. While much of the original forest has been cleared, a sliver much like the original survives on Nassawango Creek. Here, on the Paul Leifer Nature Trail, you can walk among the old groves, through the swamp on a boardwalk, and see an especially rich community of wild creatures. Bring the kids. The trail is short and easy, and the forest is wonderfully diverse, active, and mysterious, making this a great introduction to the outdoors.

The short loop trail begins near the old brick furnace, used by settlers between 1828 and 1850 to make pig iron from bog iron ore dug from Nassawango Creek, oyster shells from the bay, and charcoal produced from the surrounding woodlands. From a tended lawn at the base of the furnace, the path enters a forest that was clear-cut from 1825 to

Furnace Town Historic Site connects natural and human history. Photo courtesy of Furnace Town Foundation, Inc.

1850. In just a few steps, you truly are in the woods. The loblolly pines are giants, the birdsong is sweet, and the forest floor is dense with groves and tangles. Beneath the old, thick-trunked pines are maples and oaks, sweet gums and sassafras. Holly, highbush blueberry, and sweet pepperbush form a lush understory. And springing up at trailside are jack-in-the-pulpits, cranefly orchids, and the elegant flower of the pink lady's slipper orchid.

At the preserve boundary at 0.2 mile, the trail bends and winds through holly groves, soon crossing a series of boardwalks through a bald cypress swamp. An aquatic tree, the bald cypress sends many of its roots up for air rather than down into the soaked, oxygen-poor soil. From the boardwalks at 0.3 mile, look to the left where the knobby roots—or "knees"—rise up out of the shallows. Along with swamps in southern Delaware, the Nassawango swamps are home to the northernmost stands of bald cypress in North America.

Beyond the boardwalks, at 0.4 mile the trail leaves the wetlands and enters the drier upland forest. Here the path is covered in holly leaves and spiny sweet gum balls, and the woods are thick with ferns and muscadine grapevines. The birds are lively in the deep shade and dappled sunlight. Proceed through the woods to Furnace Town Canal, and turn right onto the canal towpath at 0.6 mile.

Dug in 1825, the mile-long canal carried barges from the creek to the furnace; the barges were loaded with oyster and clam shells for smelting or with pig iron on its way up the Chesapeake to the port of Baltimore. Following the canal towpath, with the forest on your right, look to the left for an interpretive sign pointing out an iron seep. Here, iron-rich water sinks into the sandy streambed, forming the "bog iron"

Paul Leifer Nature Trail, Furnace Town Historic Site

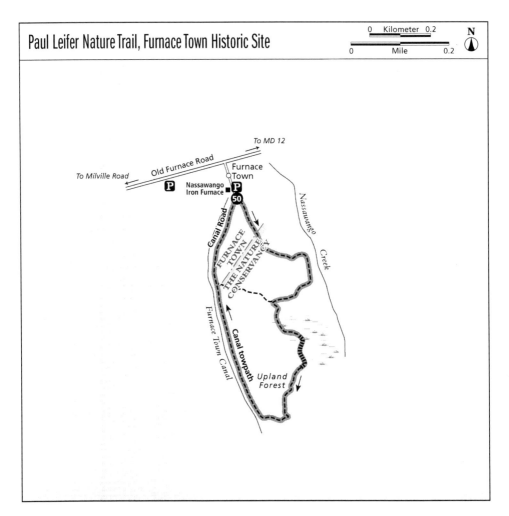

that drove the Furnace Town boom in the mid-1800s. Walking the towpath back to the furnace beneath the tall loblolly pines, be thankful that Nassawango Creek's iron was too impure to compete in the marketplace, ending a local industry that may very well have left little of the forest we enjoy today.

Follow the towpath back to the trailhead.

Miles and Directions

0.0 Start at the trailhead at the iron furnace.
0.2 Reach the preserve boundary; continue on the nature trail.
0.3 Cross a series of swamp boardwalks.
0.4 The trail enters upland forest.
0.6 Turn right onto the canal towpath.
1.0 Arrive back at the trailhead.

51 Pocomoke State Forest Trail

An easy loop hike leads through the woodlands and along the swamps of the Pocomoke State Forest on Maryland's Eastern Shore.

Start: The trailhead is 0.6 mile up Camp Road on the right.
Distance: 4.5-mile lollipop
Hiking time: About 2 hours
Difficulty: Easy
Elevation gain: Minimal
Trail surface: Natural bare soil, pine needles, gravel; wooded, flat in upland areas, moderate slopes close to the Pocomoke River
Best season: Oct-Apr
Schedule: Sunrise to sunset
Other trail users: Equestrians, bikers; hunters Sept 1-May 30
Canine compatibility: Dogs permitted
Land status: Pocomoke State Forest and Pocomoke River State Park; Worcester County, Maryland, about 140 miles southeast of Washington, D.C., and 22 miles southeast of Salisbury, Maryland
Nearest town: Snow Hill

Fees and permits: None
Camping: Camping is available at nearby Milburn Landing State Park. Reservations are needed for Pocomoke River State Park camping.
Trailhead facilities: None
Maps: USGS Snow Hill MD; state forest map through the website
Trail contact: Pocomoke River State Park (Milburn Landing), 3461 Worcester Hwy., Snow Hill, MD; (410) 632-2566; customerservice@dnr.state.md.us. Pocomoke State Forest, 6572 Snow Hill Rd., Snow Hill, MD; (410) 632-3732; https://dnr.maryland.gov/forests/Pages/publiclands/Pocomoke/Trails.aspx; https://dnr.maryland.gov/forests/Documents/milburn_landing_trail.pdf; mschofield@dnr.state.md.us
Special considerations: Where the trail is grassy, ticks are plentiful.

Finding the trailhead: Travel 16 miles south on MD 12 from the Salisbury Bypass. Turn right onto Nassawango Road (also called River Road) and proceed 5 miles to Camp Road, a dirt road on the right just after the Nassawango Country Club. Turn right onto Camp Road, and go 0.6 mile to trailhead parking on the left. GPS: N38 08.735' / W75 28.851'

The Hike

The Pocomoke River runs through southeastern Maryland, from southern Delaware down to the northern border of Virginia. Before emptying into the Chesapeake Bay at Pocomoke Sound, the river drains the fertile farmlands west of Ocean City and the deep, shady woods of southern Worcester County. In Pocomoke State Forest, you can experience the river's wilder side as you walk among the pine, poplar, magnolia, and mountain laurel that flourish on its banks.

From the parking lot, turn right on Camp Road and proceed 0.3 mile to the Milburn Landing Trail on the right. Cross a shallow gully, and walk into the woods following white blazes. The forest along the dirt road and the footpath is a classic example of the diverse mix of trees in Maryland's coastal-plain woodlands.

Loblolly pines, common in the South, are growing with hardwoods, common in the piedmont to the north. There are sweet gum, sassafras, and oak, as well as a lush evergreen understory of holly and sweet bay magnolia. In spring the blossoming mountain laurel is particularly showy.

Walking the footpath, you are soon traveling through holly groves in the shade of the oaks and pines. At 0.6 mile the trail bends left and can be a bit wet for a stretch. With the branches of young sweet gums and oaks offering shade, you may have to step over ruts in the trail that often hold enough water to harbor bugs, frogs, and tadpoles in the spring. But the path levels and grows grassy before long, and soon the going is easy again.

At 0.9 mile the trail crosses Nassawango Road. Duck under the gates on either side and proceed on the white-blazed footpath, with young, skinny pines on the left and a mixed forest on the right. Pass a bench where the pines begin to give way to hardwoods, and follow the trail as it bends left through mountain laurel and descends slightly into a grove of big tulip trees on the edge of the Pocomoke River wetlands at 1.2 miles.

Turn right, and travel along the edge of the forested wetlands. This is a very nice stretch. The tulip trees are tall and stately, and where they dominate, the ground is carpeted in ferns. In some places loblolly pines mix in, and at others the groves of holly and laurel are dense. At 1.7 miles the trail bends left, descending slightly to cross a streambed on an old, mossy culvert, and then ascends, bending right, into a more spacious wood where you can see far down the trail and into the trees.

At 2.1 miles the trail dips into a grassy meadow and forks. Turn left, following white blazes (if you go straight here, the two trails do rejoin, but the shortcut misses a nice stretch of forest and an old graveyard hidden in the woods). Proceed through another lovely grove of tulip trees and fern meadows. At 2.4 miles the trail turns right and then, shortly, right again at a log bench in a small clearing. Proceed into the woods, staying right and following white blazes.

On the left at 2.8 miles is an old, overgrown cemetery, where the mostly illegible gravestones collect moss or lay toppled against trees. For all its eeriness, the graveyard is a surprisingly lively place. There are white-tailed deer about, birds flitting in the sapling branches, and a busy hive of bees buzzing around a long crack in the trunk of an old loblolly pine.

Just beyond the cemetery, the trail travels through tall grasses, turns left into the woods, and then turns right, heading back to Nassawango Road. The trail is grassy here and infested with ticks. You may want to stop and pick them off as you go.

At 3.2 miles cross Nassawango Road, turn left, and pick up the trail on the right, where it continues through the woods to the forest boundary at 3.7 miles. At the boundary are a bench and a field visible through a thicket. The trail turns sharply right here, following white blazes and continuing through the forest. At 3.9 miles the trail bends to the right and then splits sharply left. Although this section of the trail is narrow, it is well marked. Follow it through the woods to the beginning of the loop

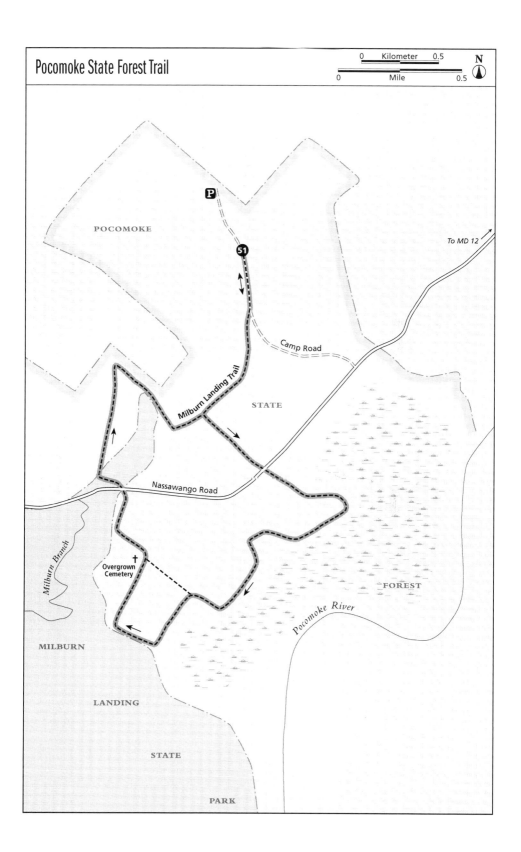

Pocomoke State Forest Trail

0   Kilometer   0.5

0   Mile   0.5

N

POCOMOKE

P

51

To MD 12

Camp Road

STATE

Milburn Landing Trail

Nassawango Road

Overgrown Cemetery

Milburn Branch

FOREST

Pocomoke River

MILBURN

LANDING

STATE

PARK

trail; turn left and proceed to Camp Road at 4.2 miles. Turn left onto Camp Road and return to the parking area.

Miles and Directions

0.0 Start at the trailhead parking area on Camp Road. Turn right onto the road.

0.3 Reach the trailhead on the right.

0.6 Trail bends left/southeast.

0.9 Cross Nassawango Road and proceed on the white-blazed footpath.

1.2 Enter the Pocomoke River wetlands, fringed by a grove of tulip trees.

1.7 The trail bends left; descend slightly to cross a streambed on a culvert.

2.1 Turn left at the fork, following the white blazes.

2.8 Reach the overgrown cemetery. Just after the cemetery, turn left into the woods, then turn right, heading back to Nassawango Road.

3.2 Cross Nassawango Road. Turn left and pick up the trail on the right.

3.7 Reach the forest boundary and bench.

3.9 Reach the forest trail turnoff. The trail bends to the right and then splits sharply right.

4.0 Reach the beginning of the loop.

4.2 Reach Camp Road and turn left.

4.5 Arrive back at the parking area.

52 Bald Cypress Nature Trail, Milburn Landing State Park

This short but enchanting walk leads through one of the northernmost stands of bald cypress in the United States. You may not think to drive all the way from Baltimore or Washington, D.C., for this quick stroll—but it just might be worth it. This hike is ideal for a short detour en route to the beach.

Start: The trailhead is at the opposite end of the parking area from the river; look for a big sign.
Distance: 1-mile lollipop loop
Hiking time: About 1 hour
Difficulty: Easy
Elevation gain: Minimal
Trail surface: Natural bare soil, pine needles, gravel; wooded, flat in upland areas, moderate slopes close to the Pocomoke River
Best season: Sept–May
Schedule: Sunrise to sunset
Other trail users: Bikers
Canine compatibility: Dogs permitted
Land status: Pocomoke River State Park; Worcester County, Maryland, about 145 miles southeast of Washington, D.C.

Nearest town: Snow Hill
Fees and permits: None
Camping: Developed campsites and small cabins are available; registration and a fee are required.
Trailhead facilities: Comfort station
Maps: USGS Pocomoke City MD; state park map available through the website
Trail contact: Pocomoke River State Park (Milburn Landing), 3461 Worcester Hwy., Snow Hill, MD; (410) 632-2566; https://dnr.maryland .gov/publiclands/Pages/eastern/pocomokeriver .aspx. Pocomoke State Forest, 6572 Snow Hill Rd., Snow Hill, MD; (410) 632-3732; mschofield@dnr.state.md.us.
Special considerations: The environment is extremely fragile; stay on the trail.

Finding the trailhead: From Salisbury, Maryland, travel south on MD 12 for about 13 miles from the Salisbury Bypass. Turn right onto Nassawango Road and go 6 miles, then turn left into Milburn Landing State Park. Turn right onto the boat launch access road, following signs to the launch. GPS: N38 07.350' / W75 29.723'

The Hike

This hike is very short and is out of the way for most hikers, except for local residents and visitors to the family campground. Although your leg muscles will forget the walk before you have left the park, the magic of the swampland is, without exaggeration, unforgettable.

From the Nature Trail sign, enter the pine forest and bear right at the fork. Giant loblolly pines grow straight to a towering height of 80 feet, forming the upper story above some of the tallest holly trees you will ever see.

Cross the park road at 0.3 mile and, 175 yards farther, reach the cypress swamp. The bald cypress grow in shallow, brackish swamps. To keep from drowning, the root systems develop knobby, knee-like outcrops that protrude from the water. These "bald" knees are the tree's breathing mechanism.

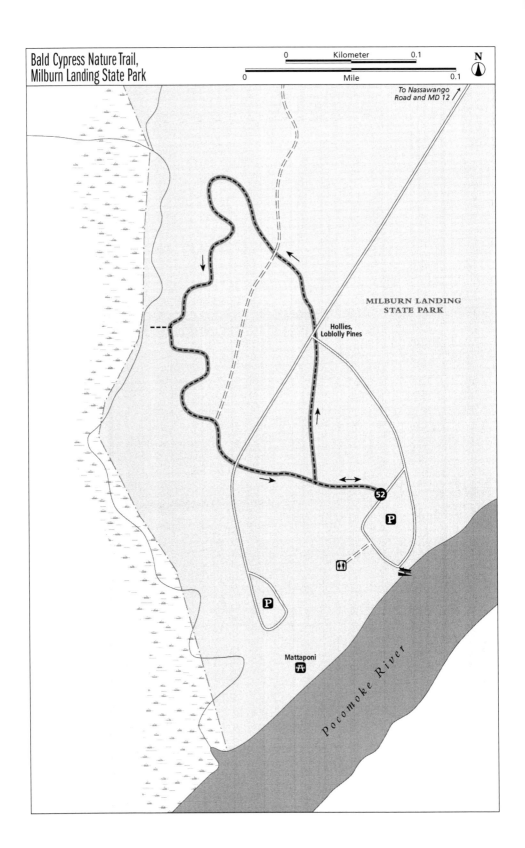

Bald Cypress Nature Trail,
Milburn Landing State Park

0   Kilometer   0.1

0   Mile   0.1

N

To Nassawango
Road and MD 12

MILBURN LANDING
STATE PARK

Hollies,
Loblolly Pines

52

P

P

Mattaponi

Pocomoke River

Maryland's wide tidal creeks are a distinctive feature of the Chesapeake Bay region. PHOTO COURTESY OF MARYLAND DNR

The trail is easy to follow; it would be difficult to get lost. Just plan to take longer to walk a mile than you usually do, because you will continually stop in wonder. Follow the signs and blazes. Cross the park road again at 0.7 mile, passing beneath the white pines and more loblolly. At the fork turn right to return to the parking lot.

Miles and Directions

0.0 Start at the Nature Trail sign. Bear right at the fork.

0.2 Stroll through hollies and loblolly pines.

0.3 Cross the park road.

0.4 Reach the cypress swamp.

0.7 Cross the park road again.

1.0 Arrive back at the trailhead.

53 Bob Trail, Trap Pond State Park

An easy circuit hike travels through a forest of stately conifers and hardwoods. Circle a pond and bald cypress swamp, the northernmost stand of bald cypress trees in the United States.

Start: The Baldcypress Nature Center is at the end of the trailhead parking lot; the Bob Trail starts at the nature center.
Distance: 4.6-mile loop
Hiking time: About 2.5 hours
Difficulty: Easy and accessible
Elevation gain: Minimal
Trail surface: Crushed stone; forested
Best season: Year-round
Schedule: 8 a.m. to sunset
Other trail users: Bikers
Canine compatibility: Leashed dogs permitted
Land status: Trap Pond State Park; southwestern Sussex County, about 55 miles south of Dover, Delaware, and 5 miles east of Laurel, off DE 24

Nearest town: Laurel
Fees and permits: Entrance fees are charged daily from Mar 1–Nov 30.
Camping: There are 142 campsites on the pond's northern shore, as well as 8 cabins, 2 yurts, and youth camping areas.
Trailhead facilities: Restrooms, picnic pavilion, nature center
Maps: USGS Trap Pond DE; state park map
Trail contact: Trap Pond State Park, 33587 Baldcypress Lane, Laurel, DE; (302) 875-5153; https://destateparks.com/TrapPond; William.koth@state.de.us
Special considerations: Wear a cap, and thoroughly check your scalp and skin for ticks after your hike. Bring a bottle of water.

Finding the trailhead: From the Delaware Seashore resorts, take DE 1 north to DE 24 and travel west 29.5 miles to Trap Pond Road. Turn left onto Trap Pond Road, and drive 1.2 miles to the main entrance of Trap Pond State Park. Turn left into the park, pass the entrance station, and make an immediate left turn. Arrive in the parking lot and turn right. GPS: N38 31.509' / W75 28.795'

The Hike

Tucked in the southwest corner of rural Sussex County, Trap Pond State Park is a jewel of a state park. Amid broad, flat fields of wheat and soybeans, the park protects a wonderful 3,900-acre parcel of wetlands, forest, and bald cypress swamp. In an afternoon on the park's trails, you can stroll through towering stands of loblolly pine and shady groves of oak, holly, dogwood, and sweet bay. Within the trees and swamps, birdlife is abundant. Walk quietly and you are likely to see kingfishers, ducks, great blue herons, ospreys, hawks, kestrels, and a great variety of songbirds. Where the trail hugs the shoreline of Trap Pond, there are great views of tall, thin-trunked bald cypress with their knobby roots bulging out of the shallows.

From the nature center, walk toward the pond and turn right onto the Bob Trail. The first mileage marker will be in front of the nature center. The trail goes through the picnic area, giving great views of the pond. During the fall and early winter, be

Walking through the falling leaves on the Bob Trail. PHOTO COURTESY OF DNREC/DELAWARE STATE PARKS

sure to watch for migratory waterfowl such as snow geese, ring-necked ducks, ruddy ducks, Canada geese, and hooded mergansers. Spring and summer birdlife includes pileated woodpeckers, warblers, summer and scarlet tanagers, eastern kingbirds, and myriad other bird species. Ask for a comprehensive bird list at the nature center.

Follow the trail past the screened pavilion and ball field on the right. The route enters the woodlands on a wide dirt and crushed-stone trail.

Walk on the Bob Trail through a mixed forest of maple, oak, hickory, Virginia pine, and loblolly pine. Pass the junction of the Island and American Holly Trails in about 0.25 mile. Shortly beyond, pass a small youth camping area on the left. When unoccupied this makes a great resting area, with a small pavilion and docks overlooking both ends of the pond. The docks are a favorite with local birders for spotting the bald eagles that frequent the park. During the fall, winter, and early spring, this is also an excellent area to spot river otters and beavers.

The Bob Trail continues for another mile until it meets with Wooten Road. Turn left onto Wooten Road and cross the Raccoon Pond Bridge (called Davis Pond by the locals; be sure to find the plaque located on the bridge). After crossing the bridge, the trail will duck back into the woods on the left-hand side of the road and wind through a grove of new-growth pines. The trail surface changes from half crushed stone/half dirt to a 5-foot-wide crushed-stone path. Follow this path for about 0.4 mile to a T. The Bob Trail continues to the left. The recently restored Bethesda

Church can be found by following the grassy area to the right for approximately 50 yards. Built in 1878, the renovated and restored church is an example of the small community churches that once stood throughout the county and rural Delaware. Read the wayside exhibit boards to find out about the church's history and how it was restored.

After turning left onto the Bob Trail, walk about 400 yards and approach a 150-foot bridge across a swampy area with a small stream. This stream is Thompson Branch and is one of the main tributaries of Trap Pond. Benches along the bridge make it a great resting area to take in the sights and sounds of the swamp. After crossing the bridge you will encounter a junction with a dirt road. Continue straight on the Bob Trail, crossing the dirt road.

This section of the Bob Trail gently meanders through woods and cleared areas. Many of these cleared areas are remnants of old fields and farmsteads. In a little more than 0.5 mile, cross a small bridge and the trail widens. There are several small ponds to the right of the trail; keep an eye out for turtles basking on logs and colorful male wood ducks on these small bodies of water. The wood ducks are wary, but if they fly off before you see them, they can be identified by their whistling as they take flight.

After passing the ponds, keep an eye out for the trail turning sharply to the left. If you come upon a paved road (Goose Nest Road), you have gone about 50 yards past the trail.

The trail narrows again after making this left-hand turn. This section winds through mixed forests with plenty of American holly groves. Holly is Delaware's state tree. It received this designation as Delaware citizens earned extra money during the Great Depression by making holly wreaths during the holidays. Continue for about 0.7 mile to a paved park road. Looking to the left, you will see the Trap Pond Camp Store. Continue straight across the campground road.

The Bob Trail skirts the outer edge of the campground for 0.25 mile and leads to the boat ramp. The boat ramp is an excellent place to see some of Trap Pond's famous bald cypress trees. Continue to the entrance of the boat ramp; there will be a narrow paved path to your left, paralleling Trap Pond Road. An elevated walkway juts out over the pond, with some large bald cypress trees behind it. Inset benches make this a great location to take a little rest and enjoy the pond view. It has also become a popular area for fishing, and you may see some families fishing here.

In another 100 yards the paved pathway bears to the left and crosses a rustic foot-bridge across the spillway. The spillway and dam were rebuilt during the 1930s by the Civilian Conservation Corps. More information on the Civilian Conservation Corps and the history of Trap Pond can be found at the nature center or by asking one of the park employees.

Once you have crossed the bridge, turn right on the wide crushed-stone path. Pass the boathouse on your left. Continue walking past the playground, on your right, to the nature center and trailhead.

Bob Trail, Trap Pond State Park

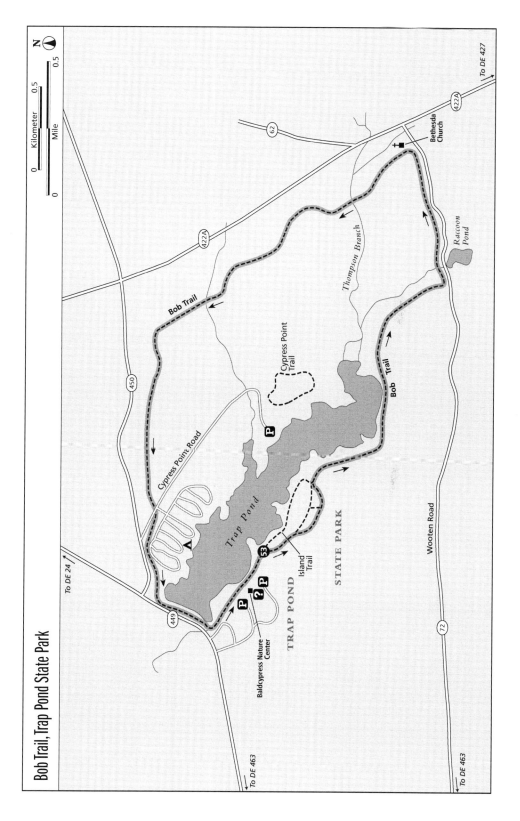

Miles and Directions

0.0 Start at the nature center and turn left onto the Bob Trail.

1.5 Reach Wooten Road. Turn left and cross the bridge. Turn left on the Bob Trail, back into woods.

2.0 At the T junction, turn left. Bethesda Church is to the right.

2.3 Cross a long bridge over a swamp.

2.4 Cross a dirt road, and continue straight on the Bob Trail.

3.0 Pass small ponds on the right.

3.1 Turn left on the Bob Trail.

3.8 Cross the campground road.

4.1 Walk past the boat ramp. Turn left onto the paved path.

4.4 Cross the spillway on the pedestrian bridge. Turn left beyond the bridge.

4.6 Arrive back at the nature center and trailhead.

Option: The Baldcypress Nature Center is open seven days a week during the summer and Wednesday through Sunday during the off-season. Be sure to stop in and check out the exhibits and live animals. The nature center highlights the area's connection to the Chesapeake Bay, natural history, and the park's past. Restroom facilities and brochures, including trail maps, are available even when the nature center is closed.

54 Nanticoke Wildlife Area Loop

An easy stroll through mixed hardwood and pine forest travels along the edges of fields and hedgerows through a nice blend of rural and woodland landscapes.

Start: This hike begins in the parking area for deer stands 1 and 2.
Distance: 2.5-mile loop
Hiking time: About 1.5 hours
Difficulty: Easy
Elevation gain: Minimal
Trail surface: Natural sand
Best season: Year-round, except during deer-hunting season
Schedule: Dawn to dusk
Other trail users: Bikers, equestrians
Canine compatibility: Leashed dogs permitted
Land status: Robert L. Graham Nanticoke Wildlife Area; in the southwest corner of Sussex County, Delaware, about 45 miles south of Dover and 5 miles west of Laurel
Nearest town: Laurel
Fees and permits: None
Camping: None
Trailhead facilities: None
Maps: USGS Sharptown DE; hunting maps suitable for hikers at the wildlife area
Trail contact: Nanticoke Wildlife Area, 4871 Old Sharptown Rd., Laurel, DE; (302) 875-2157; https://dnr.maryland.gov/wildlife/pages/publiclands/eastern/nanticoke.aspx; Robert.Gano@state.de.us
Special considerations: Do not hike during deer-hunting season.

Finding the trailhead: From US 13, travel west on DE 24 through Laurel and continue 1.2 miles to Road 494 (Old Sharptown Road). Turn right on Road 494, and at 2.2 miles bear left, staying on Road 494. Travel another 1.6 miles to the Nanticoke Wildlife Area entrance sign, and turn right on the access road. Proceed 0.2 mile to the parking area for deer stands 1 and 2, on the right. GPS: N38 33.002' / W75 39.378'

The Hike

The Nanticoke Wildlife Area is primarily managed as a hunting area, and the trails are mostly travel routes to deer stands tucked into the wooded corners of small clearings. Hiking here during deer-hunting season is not advised, but during the rest of the year, walking the area's paths is thoroughly enjoyable. Passing through dense forest and along the edges of cultivated fields, the trails provide an opportunity to stroll in both bright, open spaces and shady groves.

From the parking area, continue up the access road on foot beneath the branches of big oaks. On the left, at 0.1 mile, is a nineteenth-century graveyard—the burial plot for the Adams family, presumably a clan of Sussex County farmers. The old white stones, some listing and propped up, sit among wildflowers beneath a cedar tree bearing birthdates as early as 1806 and inscriptions such as that on the stone of Hyram M. Collins, who died in 1852: In Full Hope of Immortality.

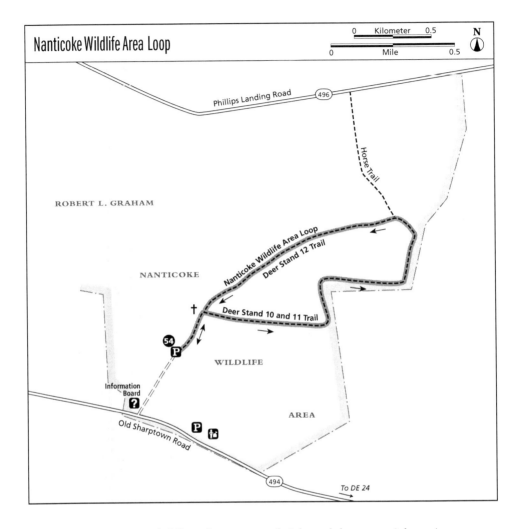

Nanticoke Wildlife Area Loop

Just past the graveyard, follow the access road right and then turn right again onto the trail leading to deer stands 10 and 11. There is a barrier here that defines a small parking area for hunters. Proceed on the trail with the forest on the left and a wooded hedgerow backed by a small field on the right. For the next 0.6 mile, walk along the edge of a typical coastal-plain forest of loblolly pines mixed with red maples, oaks, and sweet gums. Although this woodland community may be commonplace in Sussex County and the southern coastal region, it is hardly without charm. The tall loblollies are wonderfully fragrant and musical in the wind; the oaks stand strong and majestic. The sweet gums, with their star-shaped leaves, medicinal sap, and prickly fruit, are distinctive and beautiful.

On the right, the trail passes wood-bordered fields lined with wildflowers in the spring. These open areas are prime habitat for birds and other wildlife that favor browsing in the fields and perching on their edges. It is no accident that most of the hunting stands sit just inside the woods on the margins of clearings; at dusk you are likely to see deer gather here. Areas such as these are also good places to watch and listen to birds.

At the end of the field, the trail crosses a concrete barrier at the wildlife area boundary at 0.8 mile. Turn left here and follow the trail along the edge of a large cornfield on the right. Keeping to the field edge, the trail turns right, bends left at 1.3 miles, and soon breaks into the woods to an intersection with a marked horse path at 1.5 miles. Turn left onto the horse path, continue 100 yards, and then go left again on the trail to deer stand 12, where a gate blocks the path to stands 13 and 14.

The sun-dappled path winds through the woods and then passes a small clearing where you will see deer stand 12 in the back left corner. Beyond the clearing the path is soft and grassy and passes through nice stands of oak and pine with spacious groves of holly growing beneath their sheltering branches. At 2.2 miles the trail crosses a barrier and joins the sandy access road leading back to the trailhead.

Miles and Directions

0.0 Start at the trailhead at the parking area.

0.1 Reach the Adams family graveyard. Just beyond the graveyard, turn right onto an access road and then right again onto the trail.

0.8 Come to the wild area boundary and turn left.

1.5 Reach the horse trail and turn left.

1.6 At the deer stand 12 trail junction, turn left.

2.2 Cross the barrier and join the access road back to trailhead.

2.5 Arrive back at the trailhead.

Options: If you like walking on rural roads, you could extend your circuit hike, continuing past deer stands 13 and 14 to Road 496. Travel west (left) on Road 496, then south (left) on the unpaved access road for deer stands 15 and 16, and then back to the trailhead.

55 Old Schoolhouse-Holly Tree Loop, Wye Island

The Old Schoolhouse–Holly Tree Loop is an outstanding hike that showcases historic woods of towering old-growth oaks, loblolly pine, beech, hickory, and even sweet gum and holly. Visit a pair of tidal coves on the Wye River and then a 285-year-old holly tree.

Start: The Schoolhouse Woods trailhead is on the right, 1 mile past the office road.

Distance: 1.8-mile loop

Hiking time: About 1 hour

Difficulty: Easy

Elevation gain: Minimal

Trail surface: Packed dirt, coastal lowlands

Best season: Year-round

Schedule: Sunrise to sunset

Other trail users: Hikers only

Canine Compatibility: Leashed dogs permitted

Land status: Wye Island Natural Resources Management Area (wildlife management area); Queen Anne's County, Maryland, 20 miles east of the Chesapeake Bay Bridge and 5 miles off US 50

Nearest town: Wye Mills

Fees and permits: None

Camping: None

Trailhead facilities: Kiosk with trail map; trail maps for sale at the office

Maps: USGS Queenstown MD

Trail contact: Wye Island Natural Resources Management Area, 632 Wye Island Rd., Queenstown, MD; (410) 827-7577; https://dnr.maryland.gov/publiclands/Pages/eastern/Wyelsland/Trails.aspx; nrma.wyeisland@maryland.gov

Special considerations: Wye Island Natural Resource Area is open to hunting; check the kiosks or at the office for schedules.

Finding the trailhead: From the junction of US 50 and US 301 east of the Chesapeake Bay Bridge, go east on US 50 for 5 miles. Turn right onto Carmichael Road and travel about 5 miles. Bear right onto Wye Island Road and cross the bridge onto the island. Stay straight on the main road and then on the dirt road into the NRMA proper. Watch for the School House Trail parking area on the right 1 mile past the office road. Signs at each trailhead identify the trails reached from the lot. GPS: N38 53.621' / W76 09.391'

The Hike

Wye Island Natural Resources Management Area is a wonderful spot for kids. Every trail offers a scenic reward for very little effort—most also include a visit to a cove or bay. This loop, which incorporates the Schoolhouse Woods and Holly Tree Trails, travels through the largest remnant old-growth woodland on Maryland's Eastern Shore. On the way to Grapevine Cove on the Wye River, the trail passes a small wetland pond where wood ducks can be seen in summer. The hike is topped with a stop at a huge holly tree that began its growth thirty years before the American Revolution.

The trail enters the woods to the right just behind the kiosk. Immediately you get the sense that you have entered the land of the giants. Red and white oak, and poplar, some 3 to 5 feet in diameter, hickory and loblolly pine, dominate. Blue trail markers

Ancient Wye Island holly.

tell of these giants. This is the blue trail and it is magisterial. The remnant forest, left untouched when the land was cleared for pasture, is 0.75 mile long but only a couple hundred yards wide. Because it is so narrow, you don't get the feeling of utter darkness and isolation that you might expect in such an old woodland. Still, even on a bright day, the sunlight does not penetrate to the ground. And unless you have been lucky enough to live in an area of old growth, you rarely see this many trees of this size. These are perhaps the largest and oldest trees in Maryland.

Pass a wetland pond just outside the woods line at 0.2 mile. The pond is a low spot that drains the spongy forest floor. You might see a wood duck or perhaps a hawk hunting the fields just beyond the pond.

Reach a four-way intersection at 0.4 mile. Grapevine Cove on the Wye River is straight ahead. It's a loop that returns to the blue trail. Follow it to the cove, visible when the leaves are on the ground. Follow the loop back to the blue trail, more of an old farm road, to the left at 0.6 mile.

At 0.7 mile, at the farm field, go right on the Holly Tree Trail, following the field perimeter and the green post markers. At the end of the long field, Big Woods Cove is visible beyond the trees at 1.2 miles. The cove, a scenic location for a picnic lunch, is accessible via the Osage Trail.

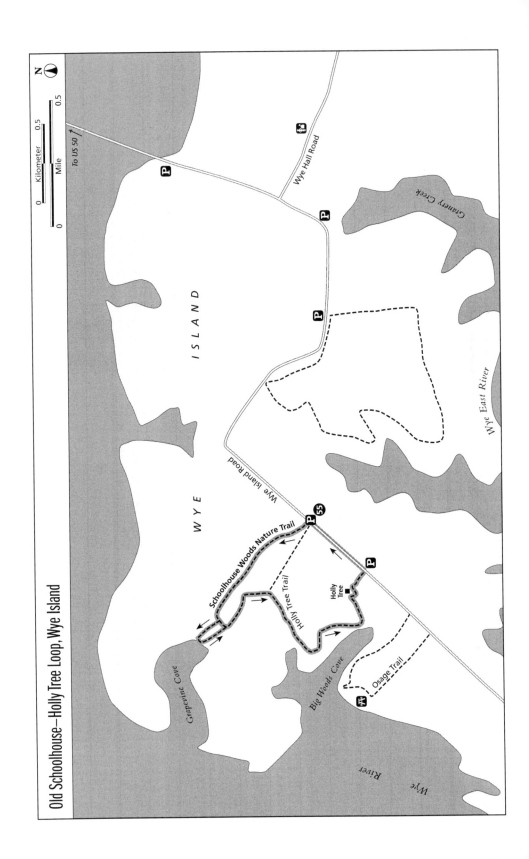

Old Schoolhouse—Holly Tree Loop, Wye Island

The ancient Wye Island Holly Tree is at 1.3 miles. You can walk beneath it. Almost as noteworthy as the holly's age is its demeanor. The tree has lost much of its upper length and its trunk is seriously degraded, but it hangs on robust and stately, with a crown like an outsized bonnet.

Leaving the holly, continue right around the field, turning left on the unpaved, unhurried road back to the Schoolhouse Woods parking lot at 2 miles.

Miles and Directions

0.0 Start at Schoolhouse Woods trailhead, just right of the kiosk.

0.4 Four-way—go straight to Grapevine Cove.

0.7 Turn right onto the Holly Tree Trail.

1.3 Reach the Wye Island Holly Tree.

1.8 Arrive back at the trailhead.

Option: For a detour to Big Woods Cove, turn right on the road, walk 0.2 mile, and turn left onto Osage Trail. It's just over 0.25 mile to the cove.

56 Tuckahoe Creek Loop, Tuckahoe State Park

Tuckahoe Creek might be the quietest stream valley on the Eastern Shore, offering a rich diversity of trees, terrain, creeks, and bogs, and passage through the Adkins Arboretum, where the Eastern Shore forest Maryland once was covered with has been reestablished. It is also the place of barred owls, bald eagles, and spawning shad.

Start: The trail begins by following the path behind the white farmhouse that serves as the park office through the field and toward the woods.

Distance: 6.1-mile loop

Hiking time: About 3 hours

Difficulty: Easy

Elevation gain: Minimal

Trail surface: Sandy soil, packed dirt; some low-lying areas, forested lowlands; some road walking

Best season: Year-round

Schedule: 10 a.m. to sunset

Other trail users: Equestrians, bikers

Canine compatibility: Leashed dogs permitted

Land status: Tuckahoe State Park is in Caroline and Queen Anne's Counties, Maryland, 8 miles west of Denton.

Nearest town: Centreville

Fees and permits: None

Camping: The park campground is located approximately 3 miles from the park office and trailhead; call (888) 432-2267.

Trailhead facilities: The park office has restrooms and a variety of displays, including "Scales and Tales," focused on raptors and reptiles.

Maps: USGS Price MD, Ridgely MD; state park map through the website

Trail contact: Tuckahoe State Park, 13070 Crouse Mill Rd., Queen Anne, MD; (410) 820-1668; https://dnr.maryland.gov/publiclands/Pages/eastern/tuckahoe.aspx; park-tuckahoe@dnr.state.md.us

Special considerations: As in many other Maryland parks, there are managed hunting periods during deer season. Check with the park office for information on the local critters.

Finding the trailhead: From the US 50/301 split, 9.5 miles east of the Chesapeake Bay Bridge, take US 50 east. Turn left onto MD 404 toward Denton, and travel approximately 8 miles. Turn left onto MD 480 (Ridgely Road), then almost immediately turn left onto Eveland Road. The park entrance is 3 miles ahead on the left. Watch for signs to the white farmhouse that serves as the office. GPS: N38 56.749' / W75 56.108'

The Hike

Follow the path behind the park office, past the white cinderblock building, between the fields, and toward the woods in the distance. Bluebirds foraging in the fields and hiding in the bushes delight the eye. At the woods edge are two posts: one leading right to the Arboretum Spur Trail, and the other pointing left toward the Tuckahoe Office Spur. Turn right and enter a plantation of loblolly pines. It has been thinned to allow a variety of wildflowers and berry-bearing shrubs to create an understory. A spring runs alongside the trail here. If you take time to explore, you may see fox scat or owl pellets.

Soaking in the day at Tuckahoe State Park.

At 0.5 mile turn right at the junction with Tuckahoe Valley Trail. Follow the blue blazes into the arboretum and a stand of beech and tall tulip poplars.

The woodland through here is remarkable for its silence. Busy MD 404, 3 miles south, might be packed with cars heading toward the beaches, but the land surrounding the park is rural to its roots. This is quiet. In late March, skunk cabbages sprout in profusion in the lowlands, being the first burst of green. A good portion of the trail is through and along wetlands. GPS says the elevation is -36 feet. Cross two bridges and listen for the owls.

Entering Adkins Arboretum, a number of winding trails intersect Tuckahoe Valley Trail, creating several opportunities for diversions. The Creekside Trail departs from Tuckahoe Valley Trail at 1 mile; it follows the creek for a few hundred yards, then rejoins Tuckahoe Valley Trail. Adkins Arboretum is worthy of an extended detour. The well-marked paths lead through a variety of habitats native to the Delmarva Peninsula. In these low areas in early spring, you will witness the throaty entreaties of the wood frog, coupled with the higher-pitched voices of the spring peepers. Pink lady slippers, a type of orchid, begin blooming in April.

The arboretum, owned by the State of Maryland and managed by a nonprofit organization, is one of a very few dedicated to restoring and stewardship of the native forests and lowlands of the Eastern Shore. Signs identify sweet bay magnolia, green ash, white oak, sycamore, and ironwood, the bark of which resembles the sinewy muscles of a long-distance runner. Ask for a map at park office.

Cross a bridge and go left, following the blue blazes through a number of intersections with the arboretum trails. The distinct brown tint to the streams here is due to the tannins leaching into the water from the woods, particularly the bark of oaks.

It seems no hike is complete without crossing a stream called Piney Branch (or some other Piney name). In early spring look for spawning hickory shad and/or alewife herring in the creek next to the trail as you approach the bridge. From the bridge you can see schools of them splashing around below. These were hugely important fish to the native peoples and the colonists. Cross the stream on a foot-bridge, leaving arboretum lands at 1.7 miles.

Just beyond, at 1.8 miles, is a three-way junction. Turn left on the North Tuckahoe Valley Trail and follow the wide blue-blazed path through mature stands of hard-woods and river birch just above Tuckahoe Creek.

Emerge from the woods at Crouse Mill Road at 2.4 miles, turning left toward scenic Tuckahoe Lake. The boat rental concession is just across the road beside the lake if you want to take some time to paddle around the lake.

Back on the trail, continue past the lake, turning left on Crouse Mill Road. Follow the road 0.25 mile to the equestrian center. Just past the center, pick up the orange-blazed Pee Wee's Trail on the bend in the road, and follow it through an old field in succession to a new forest. For the next couple of miles, follow the orange blazes. Enjoy the headwaters of the meandering Tuckahoe Creek, its wetlands and amphibians (spring peepers), turtles and water snakes, the deciduous forest, the owls, and the quiet.

Look for a great fallen oak tree with a hollowed-out trunk just as the trail leaves the swamp to traverse a farm field above the creek. You can't miss it. Tiny spring beau-ties and white-flowered bloodroot carpet the forest floor. Bloodroot gets its name from a reddish secretion in the stem.

Above the creek the trail splits, with one leg going up along the top of the rise and one along the creek. You can go either way as they reconnect a bit farther along. Going left, the creek opens up below, offering a nice view up and down the creek. Farther along, listen for the spring peepers in the marsh below the trail. You must step around another huge oak with a hollowed-out cavity in the trunk. Peek inside and see if the gnome is still there.

At 4.3 miles reach Scotts Branch. The trail splits above the creek, with horse travel prohibited because of the narrow bridge reserved for hikers. Hikers should proceed across the bridge, and make a hard left to the southeast, following orange-blazed Pee Wee's Trail south. The trail winds along the creek through the deepest forests of the park. The shad run brings in the bald eagles, and here you may see a white fantail as, having been spooked by your presence, they fly away from you into the treetops. Additionally, late in the day, listen for the barred owl's call, *hoo-hoo ho-hooooo*, and watch for them above the creek.

The trail skirts above a small hallow to a farm field. Walk the border of the field and back into the woods.

Cross a steel bridge over Tuckahoe Creek at 5.2 miles and go left. At the next junc-tion follow the Office Spur Trail, and wander through tall loblolly pines to reach the clearing where you started, at the junction with the Arboretum Spur Trail. Retrace your steps through the field to the trailhead parking area at 6.1 miles.

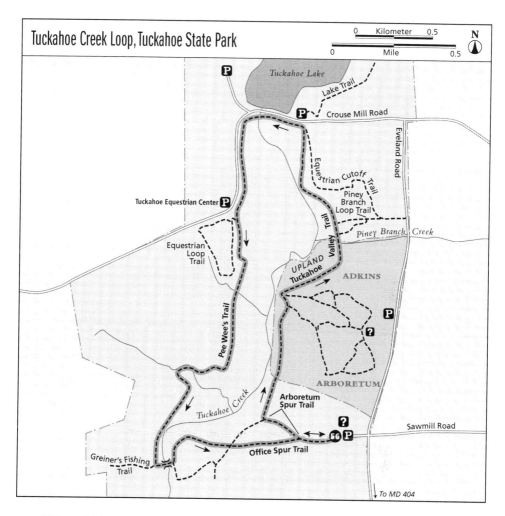

Tuckahoe Creek Loop, Tuckahoe State Park

Miles and Directions

0.0 Start at the trailhead behind the park office.

0.5 At the junction with the Tuckahoe Valley Trail, turn right.

1.0 Reach the Adkins Arboretum; the Creekside Trail separates from Tuckahoe Valley Trail.

1.7 Cross Piney Branch and turn left.

2.4 Emerge from the woods at Crouse Mill Road. Turn left toward Tuckahoe Lake.

2.6 Reach the equestrian center. Pick up orange-blazed Pee Wee's Trail.

4.3 Cross Scotts Branch.

5.2 Steel bridge over Tuckahoe Creek.

6.1 Arrive back at the trailhead.

Option: Hike through Atkins Arboretum to the Piney Branch junction, then retrace your steps, for a lovely 3-mile hike.

Honorable Mention

B Redden State Forest Loop, Delaware Seashore State Park

This trail takes an easy 5-mile meander through old woods and new on a tract of Delaware's largest state forest in the heart of loblolly pine country. It's an interesting hike for exploring the natural and cultural history of a relatively new wild and managed forest. The trail is unmarked but easy to follow.

Early in the 1900s, Redden State Forest was not a forest at all. Until the 1930s the 1,767 acres of woodlands here were primarily open fields and meadows separated by hedgerows—a quail-hunting retreat for the executives of the Pennsylvania Railroad Company. All the forest growth, both natural and managed, has occurred since then. A walk through the forest's natural groves of mixed hardwoods, and its planted and harvested stands of loblolly pine, reveals the young woodland's many layers of human and natural history.

The trail loops around Redden Lodge, built in the early 1900s to house the Pennsylvania Railroad's hunting retreats. The lodge was placed on the National Register of Historic Places in 1980. Renovated in 1995, it is wheelchair-accessible and available for meetings, celebrations, and educational programs.

The primary tree species in the forest is the loblolly pine, a southern species that occurs from east Texas to central Delaware. The tree—used for lumber, plywood, and paper—is the most valuable timber species in Delaware. It is also wonderfully fragrant, musical in the wind, and a provider of shady homes for many woodland creatures. Clear-cutting is the typical method of harvesting loblolly pines. This type of harvest yields a high financial return and, according to forestry officials, mimics natural fire by exposing loblolly seedlings to the direct sunlight they require to mature. As controversial and unsettling as the harvest may be, it does provide an edge habitat for birds and animals. As you walk along between woodlands and clearing, you may see hawks and songbirds, or a fox retreating into the forest. You will also pass through an area burned by a fire in April 1995. The fire was caused by a spark from a train on the nearby railroad and burned 209 acres of forest. You will see the charred bark of burned trees and a new generation of loblolly pines taking root in the clearing, as well as the tracks close by.

Finding the trailhead: Redden State Forest is in central Sussex County, 3.5 miles north of Georgetown and about 35 miles south of Dover. Travel 3.5 miles north from Georgetown on US 113 to East Redden Road. Traveling east on East Redden Road, go 0.4 mile and turn right at the entrance to the Headquarters Tract of Redden State Forest. Proceed 0.2 mile to parking at the office. GPS: N38 44.415' / W75 24.777'

Contact information: Redden State Forest, 18074 Redden Forest Dr., Georgetown, DE; (302) 856-2893; dda.delaware.gov/forestry/forest.shtml; erich.burkentine @state.de.us

Appendix A: Resources

Maryland

American Chestnut Land Trust
PO Box 2363
Prince Frederick, MD 20678
(410) 414-3400
www.acltweb.org
info@acltweb.org

Antietam National Battlefield
PO Box 158
Sharpsburg, MD 21782
(301) 432-5124
www.nps.gov/anti

Bear Branch Nature Center
300 John Owings Rd.
Westminster, MD 21158
(410) 386-3580
carrollcountymd.gov/government/
    directory
bearbranch@carrollcounty.gov

Calvert Cliffs State Park
9500 H.G. Trueman Rd.
Lusby, MD 20657
(443) 975-4360
https://dnr.maryland.gov/publiclands/
    pages/southern/calvertcliffs.aspx
customerservice@dnr.state.md.us

Catoctin Mountain Park
6602 Foxville Rd.
Thurmont, MD 21788
(301) 663-9388
Emergency: (301) 714-2235
www.nps.gov/cato/index.htm

Cedarville State Forest
10201 Bee Oak Rd.
Brandywine, MD 21613
(301) 888-1410
https://dnr.maryland.gov/publiclands/
    pages/southern/cedarville.aspx
Park-Cedarville@dnr.state.md.us

C&O Canal National Historical Park
11710 MacArthur Blvd.
Potomac, MD 20854
(301) 767-3714
Emergency: (866) 677-6677
www.nps.gov/choh/planyourvisit/
    greatfallstavernvisitorcenter.htm

Cunningham Falls State Park
14039 Catoctin Hollow Rd.
Thurmont, MD 21788
(301) 271-7574
Emergency: (800) 825-7275
https://dnr.maryland.gov/publiclands/
    pages/western/cunningham.aspx
customerservice@dnr.state.md.us

Deep Creek Lake State Park
898 State Park Rd.
Swanton, MD 21561
(301) 387-5563
www.dnr.maryland.gov/publiclands/
    pages/western/deepcreek.aspx
customerservice@dnr.state.md.us

Furnace Town Foundation
3816 Old Furnace Rd.
PO Box 207
Snow Hill, MD 21863
(410) 632-2032
www.furnacetown.com
info@furnacetown.gov

Green Ridge State Forest
28700 Headquarters Dr. NE
Flintstone, MD 21530
(301) 478-3124
https://dnr.maryland.gov/forests/pages/
    publiclands/western_greenridgeforest
    .aspx
customerservice@dnr.state.md.us

Greenwell State Park
25420 Rosedale Manor Lane
Hollywood, MD 20636
(301) 872-5688
https://dnr.maryland.gov/publiclands/
    pages/southern/greenwell.aspx
Pointlookout.statepark@maryland.gov

Gunpowder Falls State Park (North and
    South Loops)
1349 Wiseburg Rd.
White Hall, MD 21161
(410) 329-6809
https://dnr.maryland.gov/publiclands/
    Pages/central/GunpowderFalls/
    Hereford-Area.aspx
customerservice@dnr.state.md.us

Gunpowder Falls State Park (Wildlands
    Loop/Sweet Air)
2813 Jerusalem Rd.
PO Box 480
Kingsville, MD 21087
(410) 592-2897
https://dnr.maryland.gov/publiclands/
    pages/central/gunpowdercentral.aspx
customerservice@dnr.state.md.us

Herrington Manor State Park
222 Herrington Lane
Oakland, MD 21550
(301) 334-9180
https://dnr.maryland.gov/publiclands/
    pages/western/herrington.aspx

HerringtonManor.statepark@maryland
    .gov

Little Bennett Regional Park
Park Manager's Office
23701 Frederick Rd.
Clarksburg, MD 20871
(301) 495-2595
https://montgomeryparks.org/parks
    -and-trails/little-bennett-regional
    -park/
info@montgomeryparks.org

Morgan Run Natural Environment Area
Benrose Lane
Westminster, MD 21157
(410) 461-5005
https://dnr.maryland.gov/publiclands/
    pages/central/morganrun.aspx

New Germany State Park
349 Headquarters Lane
Grantsville, MD 21536
(301) 895-5453; cabin reservations (888)
    432-2267
https://dnr.maryland.gov/publiclands/
    pages/western/newgermany.aspx
NewGermany.statepark@maryland.gov

Oregon Ridge Park
13401 Beaver Dam Rd.
Cockeysville, MD 21030
(410) 887-1815
oregonridgenaturecenter.org
info@oregonridgenaturecenterr.org

Patapsco Valley State Park
8020 Baltimore National Pike
Ellicott City, MD 21043
(410) 461-5005
https://dnr.maryland.gov/publiclands/
    pages/central/patapsco.aspx
customerservice@dnr.maryland.gov

Patapsco Valley State Park, McKeldin
Area
11676 Marriottsville Rd.
Marriottsville, MD 21104
(410) 461-5005
https://dnr.maryland.gov/publiclands/
Pages/central/PatapscoValley/
McKeldin/McKeldin-Area.aspx
customerservice@dnr.state.md.us

Patuxent Research Refuge
National Wildlife Visitor Center
10901 Scarlet Tanager Loop
Laurel, MD 20708
(301) 497-5772
www.fws.gov/refuge/patuxent-research

Patuxent River Park
1600 Croom Rd.
Upper Marlboro, MD 20772
(301) 627-6074
https://dnr.maryland.gov/wildlife/
pages/naturalareas/southern/patuxent
-river-park.aspx
patuxentriverpark@pgparks.com

Pocomoke River State Park (Milburn
Landing)
3036 Nassawango Rd.
Pocomoke City, MD 21851
(410) 632-2566
https://dnr.maryland.gov/publiclands/
pages/eastern/pocomokeriver.aspx
pocomoke.statepark@maryland.gov

Pocomoke State Forest
6572 Snow Hill Rd.
Snow Hill, MD 21863
(410) 632-3732
https://dnr.maryland.gov/forests/pages/
publiclands/eastern_pocomokeforest
.aspx

Potomac State Forest
1431 Potomac Camp Rd.
Oakland, MD 21550
(301) 334-2038
https://dnr.maryland.gov/forests/pages/
publiclands/western_potomacgarrett
forest.aspx
pocomoke-garrett.stateforest@maryland
.gov

Rocky Gap State Park
12500 Pleasant Valley Rd.
Flintstone, MD 21530
(301) 722-1480
https://dnr.maryland.gov/publiclands/
pages/western/rockygap.aspx
rockygap.statepark@maryland.gov

Savage Park
Howard County Recreation and Parks
9299 Vollmerhausen Rd.
Jessup, MD 20794
(410) 313-4700
www.howardcountymd.gov/recreation
-parks/parks-playgrounds-trails

Savage River State Forest
127 Headquarters Lane
Grantsville, MD
(301) 895-5759
https://dnr.maryland.gov/forests/pages/
publiclands/western_savageriverforest
.aspx

Seneca Creek State Park
11950 Clopper Rd.
Gaithersburg, MD 20878
(301) 924-2127
Trail hotline: (301) 924-1998
https://dnr.maryland.gov/publiclands/
pages/central/seneca.aspx

Soldiers Delight Natural Environment
Area
5100 Deer Park Rd.
Owings Mills, MD 21117
(410) 461-5005
https://dnr.maryland.gov/publiclands/
pages/central/soldiersdelight.aspx

Stronghold Incorporated
7901 Comus Rd.
Dickerson, MD 20842
(301) 874-2024
www.sugarloafmd.com
sugarloaf46@aol.com

Susquehanna State Park
4122 Wilkinson Rd.
Havre de Grace, MD 21078
(410) 557-7994
https://dnr.maryland.gov/publiclands/
pages/central/susquehanna.aspx
Susquehanna.statepark@maryland.gov

Swallow Falls State Park
c/o Herrington Manor State Park
222 Herrington Lane
Oakland, MD 21550
(301) 387-6938 (summer); (301) 334-
9180 (other seasons); (410) 260-8835
(TDD)
https://dnr.maryland.gov/publiclands/
pages/western/swallowfalls.aspx

Torrey C. Brown Rail Trail, Gunpowder
Falls State Park
1349 Wiseburg Rd.
White Hall, MD 21161
(410) 592-2897
https://dnr.state.md.us/publiclands/
pages/central/tcb.aspx
customerservice@dnr.state.md.us

Towson Presbyterian Church
400 W. Chesapeake Ave.
Towson, MD 21204
(410) 823-6500
www.towsonpres.org
churchoffice@towsonpres.org

Tuckahoe State Park
13070 Crouse Mill Rd.
Queen Anne, MD 21657
(410) 820-1668
https://dnr.maryland.gov/publiclands/
pages/eastern/tuckahoe.aspx
tuckahoe.statepark@maryland.gov

Wye Island Natural Resources Management Area
632 Wye Island Rd.
Queenstown, MD 21658
(410) 827-7577
https://dnr.maryland.gov/publiclands/
pages/eastern/wyeisland.aspx
nrma.wyeisland@maryland.gov

Delaware

Blackbird State Forest
502 Blackbird Forest Rd.
Smyrna, DE 19977
(302) 653-6505
https://agriculture.delaware.gov/
    forest-service/state-forests
james.dobson@state.de.us

Bombay Hook National Wildlife Refuge
2591 Whitehall Neck Rd.
Smyrna, DE 19977
(302) 653-9345
www.fws.gov/refuge/bombay-hook/

Cape Henlopen State Park
15099 Cape Henlopen Dr.
Lewes, DE 19958
(302) 645-8983
www.destateparks.com/beaches/
    CapeHenlopen

Delaware Seashore State Park
39415 Inlet Rd.
Rehoboth Beach, DE 19971
(302) 227-2800
www.destateparks.com/beaches/
    delawareseashore

Holts Landing State Park
27046 Holts Landing Rd.
Dogsboro, DE 19939
(302) 227-2800
www.destateparks.com/beaches/
    holtslanding

Killens Pond State Park
5025 Killens Pond Rd.
Felton, DE 19943
(302) 284-4526
www.destateparks.com/PondsRivers/
    killenspond

Lums Pond State Park
1068 Howell School Rd.
Bear, DE 19701
(302) 368-6989
www.destateparks.com/PondsRivers/
    lumspond

Nanticoke Wildlife Area
4871 Old Sharptown Rd.
Laurel, DE 19956
(302) 875-2157
https://delmarvatrailsandwaterways.com
Robert.Gano@state.de.us

New Castle County Department of
    Parks and Recreation
187-A Old Churchman's Rd.
New Castle, DE 19720
(302) 395-5720
www.newcastlede.gov/2419/
    Parks-and-Recreation

Prime Hook National Wildlife Refuge
11978 Turkle Pond Rd.
Milton, DE 19968
(302) 684-8419
www.fws.gov/refuge/prime-hook

Trap Pond State Park
33587 Baldcypress Lane
Laurel, DE 19956
(302) 875-5163
www.destateparks.com/PondsRivers/
    trappond
William.koth@state.de.us

White Clay Creek State Park
750 Thompson Station Rd.
Newark, DE 19711
(302) 368-6900
https://destateparks.com/whiteclaycreek

Appendix B: Further Reading

Abercrombie, Jay. *Walks and Rambles on the Delmarva Peninsula*. Woodstock, VT: Backcountry Publications, 1985.

Delaware Trails Guidebook. Dover, DE: Department of Natural Resources and Environmental Control, 1994.

Fisher, Alan. *Country Walks Near Baltimore*. Baltimore, MD: Rambler Books, 1993.

Fisher, Alan. *Country Walks Near Washington*. Boston: Appalachian Mountain Club, 1994.

Gosner, Kenneth L. *A Field Guide to the Atlantic Seashore: Invertebrates and Seaweeds of the Atlantic Coast from the Bay of Fundy to Cape Hatteras*. Boston: Houghton Mifflin, 1979.

Harding, John J., and Justin J. Harding. *Birding the Delaware Valley Region*. Philadelphia, PA: Temple University Press, 1980.

Hikes in Western Maryland. Vienna, VA: Potomac Appalachian Trail Club, 1997.

MacKay, Bryan. *Hiking, Biking, and Canoeing in Maryland*. Baltimore, MD: Johns Hopkins University Press, 1995.

Maryland/Delaware Atlas and Gazetteer. Freeport, ME: DeLorme Mapping, 1993.

Peattie, Donald Culross. *A Natural History of Trees of Eastern and Central North America*. Boston: Houghton Mifflin, 1991.

Phillips, Claude E. *Wildflowers of Delaware and the Eastern Shore*. Hockessin: Delaware Nature Society, 1978.

Sutton, Allan. *Potomac Trails*. Golden, CO: Fulcrum Publishing, 1997.

Sutton, Ann, and Myron Sutton. *Eastern Forests*. New York: Alfred A. Knopf, 1985.

Taber, William S. *Delaware Trees: A Guide to the Identification of the Native Tree Species*. Dover: Delaware Department of Agriculture and Forest Services, 1995.

Trails of the Mid-Atlantic Region. Washington, D.C.: National Park Service, 1990.

Willis, Nancy Carol. *Delaware Bay Shorebirds*. Dover: Delaware Department of Natural Resources and Environmental Control, 1998.

Appendix C: Hiking Organizations for Maryland and Delaware

American Discovery Trail Society
PO Box 1514
Front Royal, VA 22630-0032
(800) 663-2387
info@discoverytrail.org

American Hiking Society
8403 Colesville Rd., Suite 1100
Silver Spring, MD 20910
(301) 565-6704 (Main)
(800) 972-8608 (toll-free)
www.americanhiking.org
info@AmericanHiking.org

Annapolis Amblers
824 Buckingham Dr.
Severna Park, MD 21146
(410) 960-6226
www.annapolisamblers.org
littlewalker1@comcast.net

Appalachian Trail Conservancy
799 Washington St.
PO Box 807
Harpers Ferry, WV 25425-0807
(304) 535-6331
www.appalachiantrail.org
info@appalachiantrail.org

Audubon Mid-Atlantic
3401 Reservoir Dr.
Philadelphia, PA 19121
(610) 990.3431
midatlantic@audubon.org

Baltimore Walking Club
250 Cinder Rd.
Lutherville, MD 21093
(410) 252-3165
www.baltimorewalkingclub.org

Capital Hiking Club
Washington, DC
capitalhiking@gmail.com
www.capitalhikingclub.org

Chesapeake & Ohio Canal Association
PO Box 366
Glen Echo, MD 20812-0366
(301) 983-0825
www.candocanal.org
inquiries@candocanal.org

Delaware Greenways
1910 Rockland Rd.
Wilmington, DE 19803
(302) 655-7275
www.delawaregreenways.org
greenways@delawaregreenways.org

Delaware Wild Lands Inc.
315 Main St.
PO Box 505
Odessa, DE 19730
(302) 378-2736
www.dewildlands.org
info@dewildlands.org

First State Webfooters
55 Gristmill Dr.
Dover, DE 19904-1955
(302) 697-1191
https://sites.google.com/firststate
    webfooters.org/firststatewebfooters/
    home
1ststatewebfooters@gmail.com

Maryland Outdoor Club
mdoutdoorclub@gmail.com
Mountain Club of Maryland
13740 Oster Farm Rd.
West Friendship, MD 21794
www.mcomd.org
contact@mcomd.org

The National Recreation Trails Program
American Trails
PO Box 491797
Redding, CA 96049-1797
(530) 605-4395
www.americantrails.org
trailhead@americantrails.org

The Nature Conservancy
425 Barlow Place, Suite 100
Bethesda, MD 20814
(301) 897-8570
www.nature.org
contactMDDC@tnc.org

Potomac Appalachian Trail Club
118 Park St. SE
Vienna, VA 22180-4609
(703) 242-0315
www.patc.net
administration@patc.net

Seneca Valley Sugarloafers
PO Box 3716
Gaithersburg, MD 20885-3716
(301) 926-6425
www.sugarloafers.org
president@sugarloafers.org

Sierra Club, Delaware Chapter
PO Box 2005
Wilmington, DE 19899
(302) 468-4550
sierraclub.org/delaware

Sierra Club, Maryland Chapter
PO Box 278
Riverdale, MD 20738
(301) 277-7111
sierraclub.org/maryland

Wanderbirds Hiking Club
www.wanderbirds.org

Washington Women Outdoors
4315 50th St. NW, Suite 100 PMB 7151
Washington, DC 20016
(240) 720-7819
www.washingtonwomenoutdoors.org
info@washingtonwomenoutdoors.org

Wilmington Trail Club
PO Box 526
Hockessin, DE 19707-0526
(302) 307-4017
www.wilmingtontrailclub.org
hiking@wilmingtontrailclub.org

Hike Index

About the Author

Terry Cummings began hiking in Maine on the Appalachian Trail at 10 years old. Since those early days in the forests of New England, and more recently in California, Colorado, and Ecuador, Terry has never stopped hiking. He spent three years as national program manager at the American Hiking Society, chaired the membership and public relations committees for the Potomac Appalachian Trail Club, and spent seventeen years working for the Chesapeake Bay Foundation in Annapolis as the Maryland grassroots director. He now builds furniture and raises bees in Annapolis with his cat, Lois.

THE TEN ESSENTIALS OF HIKING

American Hiking Society

American Hiking Society recommends you pack the "Ten Essentials" every time you head out for a hike. Whether you plan to be gone for a couple of hours or several months, make sure to pack these items. Become familiar with these items and know how to use them. Learn more at **AmericanHiking.org/hiking-resources**

 1. **Appropriate Footwear**

 6. **Safety Items** (light, fire, and a whistle)

 2. **Navigation**

 7. **First Aid Kit**

 3. **Water** (and a way to purify it)

 8. **Knife or Multi-Tool**

 4. **Food**

 9. **Sun Protection**

 5. **Rain Gear & Dry-Fast Layers**

 10. **Shelter**